Taking control
of IT costs

FINANCIAL TIMES
Prentice Hall

In an increasingly competitive world, it is quality of
thinking that gives an edge. An idea that opens new doors,
a technique that solves a problem, or an insight that
simply helps make sense of it all.

We work with leading authors in the fields of management
and finance to bring cutting-edge thinking and best
learning practice to a global market.

Under a range of leading imprints, including *Financial
Times Prentice Hall*, we create world-class print
publications and electronic products giving readers
knowledge and understanding which can then be applied,
whether studying or at work.

To find out more about our business and professional
products, you can visit us at **www.business-minds.com**

For other Pearson Education publications,
visit **www.pearsoned-ema.com**

Pearson
Education

Taking control of IT costs

Sebastian Nokes

FINANCIAL TIMES
Prentice Hall

An imprint of **Pearson Education**

Harlow, England · London · New York · Reading, Massachusetts · San Francisco · Toronto · Don Mills, Ontario · Sydney
Tokyo · Singapore · Hong Kong · Seoul · Taipei · Cape Town · Madrid · Mexico City · Amsterdam · Munich · Paris · Milan

PEARSON EDUCATION LIMITED

Head Office:
Edinburgh Gate
Harlow CM20 2JE
Tel: +44 (0)1279 623623
Fax: +44 (0)1279 431059

London Office:
128 Long Acre
London WC2E 9AN
Tel: +44 (0)207 447 2000
Fax: +44(0)207 240 5771

Website www.business-minds.com

First published in Great Britain 2000 © Sebastian Nokes 2000
Email: Nokes@IEEE.org   URL: http://www.ITVA.net
ITVA is a trademark of Sebastian Nokes.

ISBN 0-273-64943-4

Many of the designations used by manufacturers and sellers to distinguish their products are claimed as trademarks. Pearson Education Limited has made every attempt to supply trademark information about manufacturers and their products mentioned in this book. A list of trademarks and their owners appears on this page.

British Library Cataloguing in Publication Data
A catalogue record for this book is available from the British Library.

Library of Congress Cataloging in Publication Data
Applied for.

Trademark Notice
IBM Desktop and IBM Thinkpad are trademarks of International Business Machines Corporation. Intel is a trademark of Intel Corporation. Microsoft Office is a trademark of the Microsoft Corporation.

10 9 8 7 6 5 4 3 2 1

Typeset by M Rules.
Printed and bound by Biddles of Guildford Ltd.

The publishers' policy is to use paper manufactured from sustainable forests.

Contents

Acknowledgements

A habit of mine after reading a couple of chapters of a book is to go back and read the acknowledgements. I cannot explain my interest, but I do know that until it came to actually writing a book I did not fully appreciate the strength and sincerity of the acknowledgements pages. It is certainly true that this book could not have been written without ideas, encouragement and other input from very many people over a number of years, and I am heartily thankful to everyone who has helped me in this endeavour, wittingly or otherwise. It is customary in the acknowledgement not only to thank others but to remind the world that the faults and idiosyncrasies of the work are those of the author alone; again, it was not until I wrote a book that I appreciated the full meaning of this. I am painfully aware that what I have written does not do justice to the quality of advice given to me and the time that other individuals have given up along the way to help me in this endeavour. I know that the techniques I have tried to describe here do work in the real world, and I hope that I have described them in such a way that anyone using this book to try to control their IT costs will find it effective.

I would like to thank Ronnie Barnes, Andrew Capon, Catherine Griffiths, Colin Harris, Mark Kuntze, Andrew Sentance, and Pierre van der Spuy for their tremendous help and encouragement from right at the start of this project, and to thank them especially for their time. A very special thanks must go to Dave Hatter. It has been through working with management consulting clients and also colleagues in the IT and banking industries that I have learnt most about the practical aspects of controlling IT costs and exploiting IT for maximum advantage. There has been no client from whom I have learnt nothing, and I would like to thank all my consulting clients, and also all my colleagues. At the risk of presuming upon the reputations of some by mentioning them here and of offending others by not mentioning them, I would like to thank Clare Chalmers, Jodi Cohen, Stephen Dee, Frank Fanzilli, Clare Hantrais, Leslie Jones, Steve Long, David O'Leary, Jospeh Luciano, Elaine Miller, Graham Pimlott, Trevor Price, Philip Remnant, David Stobbs Stobart, Richard Stroud, and Deborah Threadgold. I have always felt that more than my fair share of colleagues have been helpful and supportive towards me, and I thank them all, especially Peter Robin, Ian Major, John Owen, Geoff Bamford, Paul Clutterbuck, Alec Nacamuli, Roy Varughese, Andy Ward, Jim Lodge, Duncan Wilson, Mike Matthias, Genevieve

Findlay, Geoff Henderson, Gill Stewart, Barry Jerome, David Walker, Giles Keating and Jeremy Marshall. In the 'almost colleagues' category I cannot omit to mention Andrew Milligan and Katarina Rosen. In the 'nearly employers' category Nicholas Haag and Neil Pidgeon also helped clarify vital aspects of some key issues. Other individuals who have helped me in many ways to complete this project are Humphrey Nokes, Nicola Nokes, Nigel Shakespear, Harvey Gates, Roger Scruton, Guy Treweek, Gordon Taylor, Ashley Burnell, Dorothy Edgington, David Wiggins, Chris Clayton, Andrew Mortimer, Peter Berendt, Chris Oldfield, Michael Ravell, Jeremy Johnson and Peter Burditt. Diana Burton has also contributed with morale-sustaining Greek quotations, if only I could understand them.

Steve Temblett, Katherin Ekstrom and everyone else at Pearson Education have been wonderful to work with in producing this book, and I will try to be more familiar with publishing protocol next time. I must also thank Leon Morgan and Stephen Digby at Davenport Lyons for taking the risk of working with a new author.

Finally, many institutions have provided facilities and training that have caused this book to be better than it would otherwise have been, and I thank them – London University, and in particular London Business School, Imperial College, SOAS and Birkbeck; London House; and the London Library.

Introduction

There is a well-known quip that the incredible productivity increase brought about by IT shows up everywhere except the figures. For 15 years as a manager and a management consultant there was a nagging question in my mind: how does a manager ensure that the right amount of a department's or a corporation's budget is spent on IT? The danger of spending too little is almost as great as the danger of spending too much. IT systems themselves are so complex and interconnected that often it seems there isn't enough time for a manager to understand the issues without giving up all other work. I ignored this question – there just weren't enough hours in the day. However, when an opportunity arose to join an advanced IT programme at one of the world's leading universities, I thought that a year or so spent among the experts learning how to program might answer this question. It didn't, although the year spent there was interesting and instructive in other ways. That was in 1994, and my class and indeed the whole computer science department used the Internet every day. In 1994 the Internet was hardly known about outside such places, and when it was discussed in business, senior executives scoffed at it and categorically stated that the Internet was a very minor passing fad. One of the most senior professors said more or less the same thing, but in a more technical way. So the technical experts, it turned out, don't know any more about what to invest in than the rest of us. Back in the commercial world I became a management consultant, and worked on a variety of problems – strategy projects, IT strategy projects, market definition or business process re-engineering projects, and some turnaround projects.

Despite the variety of the projects, the senior executives in the client organizations all had the same common worries: why were they spending as much as they were on IT? Why did the IT spend always go up and never down? Were they spending on the right areas within IT, or was a huge amount of money being wasted? Stated in this way the questions are obvious, but the senior executives were only ever so candid with the questions after I had got to know them, and usually such questions were only ever discussed late at night in bars. (Management consultants have a dull social life.)

However, one day a client asked directly for my team to undertake a short engagement to determine why her IT costs were so high, and what she should do about it. Like all consultants, I immediately searched the libraries for a book or conference proceeding with a title along the lines of *Why IT costs are so high and what to do about it*. A few titles addressed the first half of the question, but none had any guidance on what to do about it. On the other hand, many people have developed working solutions to the entire question, but they are very busy putting out fires all over the organizations where they work.

I have been lucky to work with a few of these people over the past few years, and here I have tried to present some answers to the question, concentrating more on the 'what to do about it.' This work is a first attempt, and I welcome feedback, ideas and criticism. I believe that improving the efficiency with which business selects IT investment opportunities is one of the most important tasks there is in business today, and one that besides having business benefits has much wider social and even moral benefits also.

One of the ways to control IT costs is to spend less on IT, to simply cut the IT budget. This idea has some appeal to managers who resent their IT departments. It seems that many non-IT managers resent their IT departments for a combination of three reasons. First, IT staff are well-paid by average standards; secondly, the helpdesk is often unable to help in the ways that the caller ('helpee' is how one helpdesk refers to callers) expects; and thirdly, IT is incomprehensible to outsiders.

Leaving the merits of these reasons aside, it seems odd that they should produce such resentment in many managers. The same features are found in the medical profession: doctors are well-paid by average standards, doctors are often unable to cure us (especially of heart disease and cancer), and medicine is unintelligible to most non-medics. Yet IT is now as important to business managers as doctors are to individuals in everyday life. In discussing this comparison between IT and medicine with many people, a common response is that it will just take time for IT to become as acceptable to ordinary managers as modern medicine is to society at large, time during which much understanding of how to manage IT, how to invest in it, and how to think about it will have to be developed. I hope that this book is some contribution to that process.

1 A problem for business management?

Study after study shows that there is simply no correlation between
IT spend and business success.

(Grindley, 1995)

Introduction

If spending more money on IT is an answer to business problems, then one would
expect there to be hardly any problems left at all in business by now. If more technical knowledge was certain to improve a manager's chances of being successful, then
all senior managers by now would be technologists, with no lawyers, scientists,
accountants, historians, artists, philosophers, or practical people at the top of anything. However, as we know the world is not quite like this. Organizations are run by
all sorts of people trained in all kinds of disciplines, and sometimes without any
formal training at all. Some of the best organizations are run by technically trained
people, and some are not. Sometimes a business opportunity or a business problem
is best addressed by investing money in IT, and sometimes it is not. The problem is
to identify those occasions where money should be invested, and to determine how
much to invest, and to know when not to invest in IT.

One of the biggest problems facing managers today at all levels is the problem of
investing in and using technology efficiently, especially IT. Too often IT costs appear
uncontrollable, or if the costs are controllable, the benefits appear uncertain. This is
the problem: whereas the average manager can usually grasp the fundamentals of an
ordinary business problem and determine what needs to be done to solve the problem efficiently, when it comes to IT-related problems even a very good manager with
reasonable experience of technology can work through the problem several times and
still be unable to determine a solution that is efficient when implemented. The problem is not any deficiency in the manager. The problem is that managing IT for
maximum efficiency is a very difficult task.

In later chapters we examine proven techniques for helping managers make the
best possible job of this difficult task. In this chapter our aim is to examine the
kinds of problems managers face when trying to make efficient IT investments or to

run existing IT efficiently. If you think your organization or your part of the organization has nothing to do with IT, think again. Years ago publishing had little to do with IT: now IT is in everything from the word processors authors use and the graphics packages designers and artists employ to the digital filmsetting equipment to the computer-controlled printing presses. In hospitals, operating theatres and wards depend on IT in a way they simply didn't 20 years ago when the current generation of hospital managers and senior housemen trained. In the military, a hacker with a computer virus can be worth several infantry soldiers with bayonets. In banking, there is a rush to dispose of branch buildings and clerical staff in favour of call centres and Internet-capable staff. In agriculture and primary industries the efficient use of IT makes the difference between competing profitably in the marketplace or suffering poor performance. Even in religion, technology is more important than 20 years ago as websites and electronic publishing become increasingly important tools of ministry. Now that IT is behind more of every business and organization, the managers in these businesses and organizations face the new challenge of managing IT investment efficiently.

All managers who have experience of IT effectiveness issues are familiar with the problems in maximizing the efficiency of IT investments. The first part of this chapter will set out the four interlinked kinds of problems in IT efficiency:

1. Projects go over budget or over time.

2. New systems fail to meet user expectations.

3. New systems have poor reliability.

4. New systems degrade core strengths of the organization which acquires them.

Each of these problems can manifest itself at a different level in an organization, at the strategic or corporate level, secondly at the divisional level, or thirdly at the subdivisional level. One of these problems operating at the strategic level will have a great impact on the organization, but at the same time a remedy is more likely because the problem will also be more obvious to senior management. A more subtle mechanism can take effect when one of these problems operates at the subdivisional level. These sorts of problems are usually well-hidden from senior management, but over time they can affect the organization just as much as problems that originated at higher levels in an organization.

A software firm operating primarily in the US and Europe – let us call it BlackSystems – faced two major problems in 1995. Most of BlackSystems' products were designed for DEC VAX machines, but in 1995 the main growth in the market was coming from UNIX and Microsoft NT machines, which had such a different architecture from the VAX machines that BlackSystems' products could not be adapted. Senior management rightly viewed this as a strategic problem and set about finding a solution. At the same time, however, a new sales management system had been installed. The idea behind this was that whereas previously individual salesmen had each kept their own paper-based records, so records of relationships with potential customers tended to get lost when salespeople moved on internally or left the firm for other employment, the new system would capture all the relevant information despite staff moves and changes, thereby increasing the rate of sales – or so management hoped. This was a very good idea, but in practice the new software had two problems. First, it did not allow enough space to write down all key aspects of the relationship with the prospective client, which forced salespeople to go on keeping their own records, and secondly it was very slow, which made salesmen who used it much less productive than before. Management used to photocopy the paper records of sales prospects, but after the new system was introduced management ceased this practice because they thought the new system would keep backups instead. Within a year BlackSystems had filed for bankruptcy. A competitor bought the business, and soon diagnosed that the major cause of bankruptcy had been the inefficiency of the new sales management software. This was a problem that had not even featured in the previous management's awareness.

Let us consider the example of BlackSystems in terms of the four interlinked kinds of problem set out above. The first kind of problem is not relevant to this case, because it wasn't the case that projects went over budget or over time. The second kind of problem, user expectations, is interesting. Did the new sales management system fail to meet user expectations? What actually happened at BlackSystems was better described by the question 'What expectations?' The sales management system was bought and implemented with so little thought that there was no detailed expectation anywhere. There was a very high-level and abstract expectation, if it can be called that, from the sales director and the CEO that this kind of system was the future. But no one had sat down and formed an opinion, and certainly not on any evidence, that the new systems would reduce sales cycles by $x\%$, increase the accounts one salesman could handle by $y\%$, or reduce the time taken for a newly appointed sales executive by z weeks.

The third kind of problem, reliability, certainly was an issue. The new sales management systems did have poor reliability, with availability to salespeople at just under 90%, which means that on average the system was unavailable for about an hour each day. However, the consequence of both the lack of any clear expectations and the unreliability was that the fourth kind of problem was created. In time the cumulative effect of the new system was that the deep knowledge of its customers and their businesses, the core strength of BlackSystems, was degraded. The paper-based system may have been messy, but it had worked, and in particular senior management had understood its customers' needs very well, through frequent reading of the photocopied administrative documents. They still read the summary reports generated by the new sales management systems, but for whatever reason these just didn't convey nearly such an accurate picture of what was happening in their market.

One of the first things done by the new owners was to throw out the new sales management system. Under new ownership and without the sales management system, the business prospered once more. This example shows how awareness of the four kinds of problems can help managers improve the efficiency of IT. First, by identifying which kind of problems may threaten the efficiency of your IT, existing or proposed. Secondly, by asking yourself whether the problem will be visible at your level of management or if you should check at another level. And finally by looking for linkages between the different kinds of problem – will this kind of problem now lead to another kind of problem later? However, this tool is only a starter, and in later chapters much more detailed tools will be introduced to help ensure your organization's IT efficiency is maximized.

The rest of the chapter will explore these four kinds of IT efficiency problem in more detail. The chapter concludes with a case study of Amazon, the Internet bookstore and one of its more conventional competitors. The case reiterates the huge difference in value created by an organization that really understands IT and how to use it efficiently, and value created by an organization less adept at using IT.

Projects go over budget and over time

IT-intensive projects which run significantly over budgeted costs or time are numerous. How often have you as a manager experienced any of the following?

- IT costs in your organization exceed the budget.
- No budget exists for individual IT projects and IT services.
- There is an IT budget but it seems to be uncontrollable compared to the budgets for other parts of the organization.
- It is not clear what projects, systems and data are supported under the remit of the IT budget, and which of these are supported by users or third parties.
- On paper the IT budget appears to be clearly broken down and properly matched to business needs, but in practice most managers in the organization know that it's not really like that.
- Deadlines and timescales for IT projects don't seem to be taken as seriously as deadlines and timescales for other business critical projects in the organization.
- Sometimes individual IT items or whole IT projects are cost-justified more on the basis of 'that's just the way things are – this kind of IT project always costs this much' rather than on a more rigorous basis.

These are some of the symptoms of IT projects going over time and over budget. These symptoms will be present to some degree in almost all organizations of any size. You have probably come across some of these symptoms in your own career, but to illustrate how widespread the problems of out of control IT costs and timescales are, here are a few of the larger examples.

Most major corporations in the US and elsewhere have experience of IT-intensive projects which have run significantly over time and budget. In some cases firms have been forced into a merger or even bankruptcy by these problems. The US Defense Department's Year 2000 project missed the March 1999 deadline set by the Office of Management and Budget. This project increased in cost by over 5% in the four months between November 1998 and March 1999.[1] In Europe the situation is no better, with large projects such as Concorde and the Channel Tunnel running late and over budget almost routinely. The UK government cancelled the Nimrod AWACS programme after £1bn ($1.7bn) of costs had been incurred.[2] Indeed in one survey of 1449 projects, only 12 were found that had delivered within their budgets,[3] in other words a success rate of less than 1%. The UK government even launched an inquiry to find out 'why so many of the big information technology projects . . . have gone so badly wrong. . . . "we don't have a good record in the UK in managing IT projects to fruition. . . ."'[4] If you have the feeling that most IT-related projects in your organization fail to deliver, you may well be right, but your organization is certainly not alone.

In business, management should be concerned about any projects which overrun their budgets or which look like they will run much beyond their deadlines. The management issues arising from these general problems will be particularly acute when the projects concerned are IT-related. This is because IT-related projects often have consequences that affect the overall organization far more than non-IT projects, and this happens through three mechanisms: costs, relationships and options for future action. Consider costs first. IT is expensive. Ten years ago clerical workers, designers, copywriters, draughtsmen, mathematicians and most people who worked in offices needed a desk and perhaps a telephone. Now the same people need a PC or workstation, networking, Internet access, a shared printer, regular software upgrades and an IT helpdesk. The point is that IT is expensive, and for many organizations IT-related costs are one of the greatest support costs in the organization, often second only to property-related costs after salaries in the corporate overhead. This means that for most organizations the potential downside in terms of dollar costs from overruns in IT projects is likely to be greater than from overruns in non-IT projects.

Secondly, IT-related projects tend to have long-term implications which are not easily reversed compared to many non-IT-related projects. A US department store replaced its old customer loyalty IT system with a new one in the late 1990s as part of a business process re-engineering initiative. On paper it appeared that massive benefits would result. However, the new system alienated many of the store's best customers. The project had taken seven months to implement, and it was not feasible to go back to the old system, because the old IT hardware had been thrown away and was no longer made, the programmers who had maintained the old systems had been told they were no longer needed and had all moved to new jobs, and all the secondary systems on which the main account management system depended had been modified and in some cases scrapped.

Any one of these changes may have been reversible, but in aggregate they weren't. It is almost a rule of IT that once an established system has been scrapped by an organization, it's not possible to get it back. The store lost many of its best customers forever and the store today is a lacklustre version of its former self. In contrast, when Coca-Cola alienated its customers on 23 April 1985 by switching to a new recipe for Coke, it was able to go back and recreate the original and run it alongside the new flavour Coke for a while until reverting almost entirely to the original.[5] But surely there's a big difference between an IT-intensive project and something like a new brand launch? Exactly so: one of the extra risks in IT projects is that it is much harder to undo them when they go wrong.

In this book we are less concerned with examining the reasons behind the problems in managing IT for maximum efficiency than in sharing the approaches taken by the most successful companies and the most profitable IT projects. However, some minimal explanation can be useful in helping managers to improve their IT efficiency. Practising managers put forward three main reasons why IT projects tend to be more irreversible than non-IT projects.

First, IT can be much more pervasive in customer relationships than managers realize. Changing a billing date by two days to save $10m or so, for instance, may not seem like a difficult decision to every manager, but if all your customers rely on billing being done when it always has been, then it's a big issue.

Secondly, IT can be just as pervasive in influencing and shaping internal relationships as relationships with customers. If two rival business divisions have not shared their cost and margin data in the past, and a new accounting system is going to reveal such data for each division to the other rival division, and no political preparation has been done, it is quite possible for the new accounting system to encounter all sorts of implementation difficulties as both rival divisions temporarily unite to kill the initiative. Information is power, and organizational politics recognize the roles that IT systems play in changing the balance of power through changing the distribution and quality of information.

Thirdly, IT and particularly MIS can determine what management knows and doesn't know. For instance, a large US travel company had a department which was responsible for ensuring that customer enquiries were answered. These enquiries were important because they led to sales and because they provided senior management with information about market trends – if enquiries about Cancun, Mexico, were up this week, then it could be time to block-book hotel accommodation in Cancun to meet next week's anticipated demand from customers. As part of Year 2000 preparations, an in-house system central to the department's work was replaced by an off-the-shelf package. Although cheaper, the new package was unable to identify similarities between new enquiries and older enquiries. The system was not a disaster, but it was a step backwards. First, the number of duplicate enquiries for one customer entered into the system increased because the new system made it harder to identify and link similar enquiries from the same customer or customer family.

Secondly, the predictive power of the database declined, which increased management's costs in making forward bookings, because with the new system these were typically done three days later than previously to get the same degree of certainty.

The third way in which the consequences of poorly performing IT projects are worse than poorly performing non-IT projects has to do with the strategic options created by projects. On one view, corporate strategy is all about creating and nurturing a portfolio of options for the future growth of the organization[6] – some spare floorspace in the manufacturing facility here in case demand picks up, an alliance with a Asian partner there in case demand abroad picks up but the home market slumps, and a patent or two on new technology up the corporate sleeve in case the market moves that way. Of course, none of these things will necessarily happen, but one of them probably will and by being prepared the organization has an option which gives it a competitive advantage in that eventuality. The idea is that such strategic options created by the right use of IT tend to be some of the most valuable options to have.

A good example of what this means in practice is in the telecoms markets in the US and the UK. At deregulation most traditional telephone companies had IT systems which could only manage customers by a customer reference number. The new entrants to the market had new IT which provided a range of options for customer relationship management, including the option to manage customers by name as well as by a reference number. Of course it is normal to expect newer technology to offer more options, but of greater significance is that the established telecoms players were better able to afford the new technology than were the new entrants. The way we've described the situation it's obvious the established payers should have adopted newer technology with increased options for customer relationship management, but at the executive level the established players simply didn't see it in these terms, and lost significant market share to new entrants. Equally new technologies can also offer different options.

A US engineering firm had to choose between two different CAD systems in 1997. The technichal differences between the systems on offer were obvious, but less obvious were the marketing consequences of these technical differences. However, by careful management analysis the firm worked out the options provided by the competing systems. They concluded that one would be better if the firm broadened its product range into more work with plastics, as well as its traditional steel business, while the other system was better supported by maintenance in Europe and had many users there. This analysis therefore linked the technology under consideration to the strategic choice facing the firm, and helped the firm to price its two strategic choices, which were to either expand into Europe by acquisition or to stay in the US but expand its range of work and products into plastics.

This engineering firm understood that the decision about IT had far-reaching business strategic consequences. Many firms still take this kind of decision in isolation from any consideration of firm strategy. As this example shows, there is sometimes great value in making sure that the strategic consequences of IT decisions are understood. And most of the time it need only take a two-hour meeting between business management and the IT management followed up by a couple of emails. If you doubt this claim, find out exactly when your organization began to insist that all new software and IT systems purchases had to be Year 2000 compliant. Most companies started to impose this requirement in 1996 or 1997, whereas the Year 2000 problem has been known about since the 1960s or earlier.

Not all IT projects have these problems. Some companies have learnt to manage IT-intensive projects and businesses. Ultimately this is because individual managers have learnt. The firms and managers who can deal effectively with IT-intensive business will open up very valuable portfolios of strategic options for themselves, and will be able to capture that value, as firms and as individuals. If you and your team can improve your company's ability to manage IT, your life and career will only improve.

New systems fail to meet user functionality expectations

Even if an IT-intensive project does deliver on time and within budget, the result can still disappoint the users and customers. Users, managers, suppliers, customers, IT development and IT production may have expectations that are different or incompatible with what was actually built and delivered. However, it is possible to exceed expectations. When technology is used well the results can be extremely profitable. Three examples are Citibank, CIGNA RE and Kodak. Citibank re-engineered its credit analysis system and achieved a 750 % increase in profits as a result. CIGNA RE improved the speed of document-processing while reducing the labour required. Kodak halved new product development time for cameras.[7]

However, in most managers' experience of IT investment, the cases where expectations are exceeded are a minority. The frustration felt when a project fails to meet expectations is only magnified by knowing of the most successful cases, such as Citibank, Kodak and CIGNA RE. Who as a business manager has not seen their firm invest in a huge IT-intensive project that has run into the sand within a couple of years? Who as an IT professional has not been involved in a project that has been forced through because of momentum from unrealistic but embedded expectations in their firm, when the line IT management would have taken a different approach or cancelled the project? Who as a management consultant has not been brought in by a desperate customer to fix an unfixable IT-related project where expectations have been allowed to become totally unrealistic?

It is not just large, complex new IT systems that fail expectations. How easy is it to go to a hotel, plug your laptop into a telephone and connect to your firm's network? Now ask yourself whether this is a reasonable expectation or not. While asking yourself this, also remind yourself how much your organization spends on upgrading desktop PCs. Then ask yourself how easily you can log on to one of your organization's PCs in another country in order to read your email. In some organizations this is absolutely standard and very easy, but not in most. Sometimes failure to meet user expectations are undoubtedly because those expectations are either unrealistic or just plain hard to meet. However, often enough the expectations of users and non-technical managers are reasonable enough but are not met for years. And this doesn't apply just at the low level of hotel connections for computer modems. According to one experienced business manager, when it comes to IT: 'There has been persistent stonewalling of the attempts to produce and implement what the customer really wants: simple, cheap, efficient and scalable networks.'[8]

Microsoft is one of the world's most successful IT businesses with a reputation for delivering. Even Microsoft has difficulties meeting expectations. In 1995 the magazine *Infoworld* was one of many sources expressing concern that Microsoft's Windows 95 product would not meet expectations. It said 'Microsoft describes Windows 95 as a 32-bit pre-emptive multitasking operating system that would run multithreaded applications and 16-bit applications on a 386 processor with 4MB of memory,' and then translated this for the rest of us as 'we're counting on Windows 95, but the problem is that it is a Lexus with a Chevy engine'.[9] If Microsoft faces such difficulties in managing expectations on its home turf for its flagship product, then managers in other businesses may wonder what hope there is for the rest of us in managing expectations of much smaller IT projects.

Reliability

Once an IT system is installed and working, and irrespective of whether it meets the expectations of the various interested parties, there is an issue of reliability. Reliability is probably less frustrating than issues of unmet expectations, cost overruns and time overruns, but poor reliability imposes significant costs on users and owners of systems compared to what a more reliable system would cost. Now of course few things in the world except death are 100% reliable, but we all have an intuitive sense of what it is for a system to be 'reliable enough'. On average cars, the telephone system, television and passenger aircraft are 'reliable enough' for most people most of the time. Cars are not maintenance-free and sometimes break down when in use, but the amount of maintenance required is not onerous and breakdowns are comfortably rare events, although frustrating at the time. The telephone and television are almost always available and work with great reliability. Passenger aircraft have fatal in-flight failures but happen so rarely that such events are headline news. Road accidents, mass murders in Third World countries and domestic accidents each kill far more people than passenger aircraft accidents, but are not generally headline news.

It may be that this state of affairs is morally wrong, but it illustrates the point that passenger aircraft, telephones, and many other pieces of technology are generally felt to be 'reliable enough'. Contrast this with any IT system you use on a daily basis. Is your spreadsheet, your word processor, your email, or your web browser 'reliable enough', or does it crash for no reason from time to time? If it crashes, does it then compound the irritation and inconvenience by displaying a box that requires you to click on an 'OK' button, when things manifestly are not OK? It is as if the mainstream culture of the IT industry is not to care at all about reliability, efficiency or even truth[10] as these concepts are usually understood in other parts of business.

The same kind of reliability issues exist for corporate IT systems as for personal or desktop systems. For instance, Strategic Research Corp has calculated that when airline reservation systems fails, the consequent financial losses are $90,000 per hour.[11] One of the best known airline reservation systems is SABRE. Now SABRE is an excellent system; it provides connectivity to other reservation services, it links to flight operations systems, it is integral to financial control, besides many other functions. It has been very profitable for American Airlines, its creator. And yet despite its great success and capability, it would be even more profitable for its owners and users if it was more reliable. A SABRE crash can last for six hours and delay 200 flights, delaying new ticket bookings and requiring baggage to be manually rather than automatically checked.[12]

The reliability problem is not limited to older systems such as SABRE. E*Trade and Schwab offer Internet-based retail stockbroking services; both are extremely popular because they provide a low-cost, very easy to use but high-quality service – most of the time. These firms lead their field, have some of the best technologists and management in the business, many say in the world, but still have major reliability issues.[13] This is a feature in managing high technology, and is in no way a shortcoming of these firms' management. Both firms are at the very forefront of information technology's capabilities, so of course it is not surprising that there are reliability issues. However, in this book we are concerned primarily with how to manage IT for maximum efficiency, and must accept that managers who depend on technology take it as they find it.

New systems work OK but destroy existing structures

Another major efficiency issue is the impact that new technology can have on organizational structures. Suppose that HumungousCorp is one of the top ten companies in the world by market capitalization, and yet it also has a reputation for innovation and fostering a good work ethics, and furthermore it operates predominantly in growth areas. In short, quite a corporation. Yet suppose now that 90% of what HumungousCorp does can be done on the Internet with half the people, and in a way that disintermediates an entire sub-industry of specialist advisers, consultants, wholesalers, government regulatory agencies and other middlemen that have some reason to depend on the way that HumungousCorp does business rather than the end-product of that business. Is the world suddenly going to let go of a gravy train and welcome radical change on a vast scale? No. As everyone over the age of about 12 knows, the world just ain't like that. Many of HumungousCorp's middle managers will want to preserve the *status quo* and their jobs along with it; the intermediaries will be about as keen to be disintermediated as a chicken would be to make scrambled eggs on toast; any regulatory bodies involved in the business would be far more likely to find intellectual justifications for protecting the consumer from radical change than adopting the true free market approach of *laisser faire*. Of course, the consumer might perhaps be in favour of radical change, assuming that they had a say in things based on information not too distorted by the other interested parties, but often in such situations the consumer is ignored whenever possible.

Why is everyone but the consumer against this kind of change? A useful way of answering the question is in terms of organizational change. Much money and human effort, emotional and practical has been invested in building organizational structures the way they are. Careers have been built, power established, influential relationships hewn out of an often nasty or uncertain political environment. There is too much at stake for those in the established order of things for the majority of those benefiting from it to wish for change. So much is only rational. That arch-revolutionary Mao-Tse Tung understood the theoretical benefits of overriding such powerful vested interests when he preached his doctrine of permanent revolution.[14] However, as every schoolchild knows, he may have kept on preaching it, but after one experiment in permanent revolution he made certain that no further revolution was allowed.

It is easy to see a conspiracy theory in the way organizations tend to react to innovations that threaten their established organizational structure. For as long as man has been a political animal, a perennial rumour has been that someone has invented a great labour-saving device but the establishment has conspired to bury it. However, the conspiracy theorists take a very one-sided view. There is another perspective: senior managers have to work very hard indeed just to keep their organizations where they are, and have little time to think about every new technology that appears on the horizon. Even if it is clear that a particular new technology threatens the *status quo* of an organization, it does not necessarily follow that it is possible for managers to see how the organization ought to change, let alone for all senior management to agree.

In practice the choice may be between smashing the existing organization now and hastening disaster, or playing for time and hoping the new technology will either go away or that someone will work out how to deal with it in time. This is probably a good approach: most new technologies that are trumpeted do fail, and the Internet's uniqueness is as much for being a new technology that really *has* changed the world as for anything else. (In their turn technologies such as helicopters, hovercraft, digital video disks, smart cards, and coin-operated television have all been advocated as the next technology that would fundamentally change the world and all economics.) Nonetheless, the problem managers face is that sometimes a new technology does have the power to destroy an existing organization, and working out how the organization should change, and then making it change, is a very difficult and expensive task.

Examples abound: telephone call centres and the Internet have forced retail banks, insurance companies, stockbrokers, airlines, travel agents and many others into rapid disintermediation and delayering. Ten years ago in the United Kingdom the National Westminster Bank was the leading retail bank, apparently unassailable, and the Prudential Corporation[16] was a sleeping giant of a mutual insurance company. Today NatWest – as it has renamed itself, as if delayering its own name would somehow be enough to help it compete successfully – is a second-tier bank, Prudential had wanted to start buy a retail bank, but used new technology to set up a new bank, called Egg, from scratch and has been so successful it no longer needs to buy a bank, let alone something like NatWest which is long of expensive retail branches and short of new banking ideas such as Internet banking and broking.

But the music industry provides an even better example of the problems organizations face when trying to manage new technology. By 1994 the majority of major music companies were aware that they could use the Internet to distribute music to their target audiences in all the world's more technologically advanced countries much more efficiently than through the existing distribution network of wholesalers and retailers. However, none of the major record companies established websites to sell their music, because this would have compromised their established marketing channels. Indeed, 1994 was too early to have established alternative Internet-based distribution, because in 1994 there was little e-commerce and there were too few potential customers with Internet access.

However, the record companies have perhaps delayed too long, and now, in the new millennium, their business is threatened by three major forces, all based on technology that made record companies behave as if they wished it would just go away. First, Amazon.com and others have started selling CDs and tapes in competition with the traditional retail outlets for music, so the music company's traditional business model has ended up threatened anyway. Secondly, music is being downloaded directly over the Internet, and, thirdly, stored and copied on cheap high-quality digital recording devices. This means that the entire business model of the largest music companies is under threat. A few of them may survive, but several are likely to go out of business in the next five years.

When new technology changes a market, the incumbents are almost always too slow to exploit it, and this is perhaps inevitable.[17] A small start-up with no customers has much to gain and nothing to lose by embracing the new technology. For the incumbents the reverse is true. This was precisely the dilemma facing the major music companies, and it is not clear that they had any easy solution. Why is a potential solution so hard in practice?

It's about more than the distribution chain, that is the problem of new technologies doing away with traditional distribution chains. As well as a distribution chain there is a chain or structure within the music companies themselves, and the real problem lies in the difficulties in changing the internal structure of the music companies. If an executive's skill and power base depends on knowledge and experience of, and personal relationships with, the major music wholesalers, retailers and magazines, then that executive has to be unusually brave to throw away a whole career's worth of experience and relationships and take a gamble on an entirely new way of doing business. And it is hard enough for a single career manager, and it's almost impossible for a whole management team to do. This problem is faced every time a fundamentally new technology arrives – the incumbent market leaders find it very hard to adapt their own organizational structure. IBM made the largest loss in corporate history until then because its managers ignored the arrival of the PC.

When asked in 1997 how to shake up the bureaucracy that was stifling innovation and beginning to show in poor results in the bottom line in one of the world's largest banks, a senior executive said simply 'Introduce firm-wide email.' This executive strongly believed that email alone would break down barriers to communication, get things done faster and enable innovators to outsmart the timeservers and placeholders. This executive wanted to use new technology deliberately to challenge the existing management structures. The point is that all new technology, from the steam engine and before, has upset existing power and organizational structures. This inevitably engenders opposition to the new technology in large organizations. But the biggest prizes go to those who understand how to shape and benefit from the organizational and industry changes that new technology brings.

Management systems problems

Management systems do not exist in a vacuum, but interact with an organization's people and technology. The case given in the previous section of the bank executive hoping to change the management structures and relationships by introducing new technology, email, shows the interaction between technology and management systems. For examples of the interaction between people and management systems, consider the following: in the private sector, the most educated and professionally qualified individuals such as lawyers and accountants tend to work in organizations structured on the partnership model, whereas large labour-intensive organizations such as car factories or infantry battalions tend towards more hierarchical and rule-based structures. It is widely believed that the type of person in an organization partly determines the optimal organizational structure for that organization.[18] Management systems, people and technology all interact with each other, and a change in one can exert pressures on the others. This fact must be recognized by any manager who hopes to make IT investment or IT cost-control an efficient process.

One of the greatest sorts of costs imposed on an organization are costs imposed by its management systems, and technology can magnify the benefits or problems in this area. The sort of problems that impose particularly severe costs in this area are when a piece of technology is implemented that imposes an inefficient way of doing things. We've all experienced this sort of problem, where an old system that was convenient to a customer has been replaced by some badly thought-out piece of computerization that ensures a lower quality of service than in the old system. In 1998 to return a car to one of the major car rental firms in London, you just drove into their garage where an employee would enter your car registration into a hand-held computer, check the mileage, fuel and state of the vehicle, and you'd be out of there in a couple of minutes. But now that a new computer system is implemented, you return the car, then have to go into the car rental office and join a queue, which can take 20 minutes or longer. Whatever the new computer systems does for the firm's management, it does nothing for the customers, except turn them away to other rental companies.

Another example is the despatch computer system installed in a major taxi cooperative in London. This system is so inflexible that taxi drivers who have moved to the new system are less likely to pick up passengers than taxi drivers without the system. This is because the system allows taxi drivers far less judgement than before on what passengers to pick up. Not only is the system worse for passengers overall, the taxi drivers loathe the system, and it forced the cooperative to the verge of bankruptcy. Overall, this system has imposed enormous additional cost on taxi drivers, and indeed on London society, for no additional benefit.

Case study

How Amazon.com used efficient IT to create massive strategic growth

There are many other pairs of companies we could have used instead of Amazon and Borders to highlight just how much value can be created by using IT efficiently. Michael Dell built one of the world's greatest PC companies out of his university dorm by understanding IT and above all how to manage it efficiently. There are many examples of IT companies which are themselves unable to use IT efficiently, however it seemed better to use an example from outside the IT industry. There is, for example, the financial services industry, with firms like E*Trade and Charles Schwab on the one hand, and venerable Wall Street Goliaths on the other, each taking a different approach to the use of IT. Charles Schwab and E*Trade understood how to manage technology efficiently when many of the established houses on Wall Street faced almost uncontrollable IT costs and steadily reducing capability to control the business and respond to new customer demands.

To take a UK example in the same industry, the UK's Prudential insurance company wanted to buy a retail bank. It set up Egg, a savings bank, by appointing a team with great experience of using technology effectively. While much of the UK's retail banking industry wallows in a sea of red ink and complacency, Egg has been very successful, gathering over £5bn ($8bn) of deposits in less than six months after opening for business. Prudential has decided it doesn't need to buy a bank. However, we feel that the financial services industry may not be representative of business as a whole. What could be more everyday and further removed from the computer and software manufacturing industries and the financial service industries than bookselling? Books are a very old product, very simple, and definitely an everyday business. Amazon (see Table 1.1) has shown that you don't have to be in IT or finance for an understanding of how IT can be managed to add huge value to your business, so we have chosen the book industry as the setting for this case study.

Table 1.1 Amazon.com

Sales $m	Amazon	Borders	Amazon's sales as % of Borders'
1995	0.5	1511	<1%
1998	610	2595	23%

Jeff Bezos used to work for DE Shaw & Co. One of DE Shaw's businesses was to finance new technology start-ups. The founder and CEO, Professor David Shaw, is highly qualified in IT as well as having seen how the major investment banks used technology in the early days of his career. One day, according to industry insiders, Jeff Bezos decided to start up his own business, and he approached his employer for funding. DE Shaw are a very professional firm, and were happy for employees to try their turn at setting up on their own, especially in something that didn't compete with any of DE Shaw's businesses. However, for all their expertise, contacts and experience in high technology business and investment, nobody at DE Shaw could see the value in what Jeff Bezos was proposing. His request for funding was turned down.

As everyone knows, Amazon soon became 'the world's biggest bookstore,' and very much the model for retail business on the Internet. It is not that the folks at DE Shaw were stupid not to see Amazon's potential. 'Stupid' is one adjective that applies to nobody at DE Shaw, and that firm has been almost unbelievably successful in its business.[19] The point is rather that it is very difficult to see how to use technology effectively, especially new technology, and if it's difficult for DE Shaw to see these things, then the rest of us should also expect to find it difficult. However, we should try, because there is much money to be made here. Even if we can't foresee the future of new competitors like Amazon, we should watch out for them and be quick to learn from them. Borders woke up one day and found that a competitor had grown up in three years with sales of about one-quarter of their own. Could this happen to your organization?

Does Amazon have any of the four kinds of IT efficiency problem we identified that plague so many organizations today? Look at the fourth kind of problem, which is when new systems degrade core strengths of the organization which acquires them. In fact Amazon has taken the inverse of this problem as the model for its business. In other words, it has built itself around some core strengths, and it has used IT to reinforce those strengths. What are these strengths, and what has Amazon done in using IT efficiently? Amazon's success can be attributed to understanding how the right use of IT could be used to create four competitive advantages: customer convenience, range of products, pricing and service quality. (Some people would add 'brand' to this list, but in a sense it is the four advantages just listed that have created the brand.)

Customer convenience

One of the macro trends in society is that the more money people have the less likely they are to have time to shop. The hard working executive wants to shop when they finish work, which could be at 10.30 pm. Another way to fit in shopping requirements is to shop from the PC at work, say in a lunch or coffee break. Amazon meets these modern convenience needs by using technology. Customer convenience is a customer-focused version of our old friend user-friendliness. It is very hard to get real user-friendliness or customer convenience. It is much easier to just take the technology as it comes. How user-friendly is your organization's technology? Really? How do you know? Is IT intuitive for new users? We can be so used to some once-inconvenient features of software or technology that they no longer strike us as being unfriendly any more. Have you ever seen an elevator that closes its doors and moves to another floor just as you are walking up to it? If a person caused that to happen you'd be offended, but we have grown to tolerate such behaviour in machines. Amazon went back to basics on points like this; and if Amazon ever went into the elevator business you could be certain that they would wait for you as you approached them (unless they were full).

But didn't Borders offer better customer convenience than before? Yes. Borders was one of the pioneers of the book superstore idea, putting a huge range of books into stores equipped with comfortable seats and coffee bars for use by potential customers. All this is very impressive marketing, but Amazon became even more successful (at least initially) by understanding both bookselling and IT. Some commentators have argued that Borders has a unique marketing advantage in the human aspect of the bookselling business. Such commentators claim that bookstores are great places to meet new people and even pick up someone for a date, and say that Amazon, for all its understanding of IT, will never be able to compete on this aspect of marketing. But if the issue here is about meeting new people and making new friends, then already there is evidence that the Internet is a very effective means for doing this, but how many times have you met someone new in a bookshop? Probably once or twice if you're lucky. If you want to meet other people interested in books through Amazon, just write a review of a book that interests the sort of person you want to meet and attach your email address.

It seems that whether convenience for the customer is measured in terms of the ease of buying books, or whether it's measured in terms of the ease of making new friends, Amazon and other online retailers have more to offer than their traditional counterparts. This doesn't mean that all retailing will be online, any more than the arrival of catalogue stores or supermarkets meant the death of all other forms of retailing. But it does mean show the importance of understanding the detailed implications of IT for business management and marketeers.

Range of products

Amazon is 'Earth's Biggest Bookstore' and carries more than 3 million books. At first it seems that this competitive advantage has little to do with the effective use of IT. However, as Lenin said, 'Quantity has a quality all of its own.' There is a significant management and coordination problem in dealing with such a large variety of anything. For Amazon this general problem appears in four dimension: individual titles, publishing houses, customers and potential customers. There are huge numbers of each of these, and all have to be managed. One of the original forces that drove forward the development of some of the first computer technology was the need to handle the huge and increasing numbers of the census in the US. The US government believed that it would be unable to cope with the need for a larger census.

Discount pricing

Amazon sells books for up to 40% off the cover price. In selling books, as in most other businesses,[20] demand rises as price falls. Amazon has been able to use technology to achieve the high volumes and economies of scale which make such discounts possible.

Quality of service

Amazon's quality of customer service is outstanding in the eyes of its customers. How many businesses promise that if a third party defrauds its customers, it will step in and make good any loss to the customer? Yet this is one of the things Amazon has done as part of its launch of its Internet auction business. Amazon's policy is that while fraud is rare, 'if it does happen to you it's our problem . . . Essentially, we're going to take your word for it that you're the victim of fraud.'[21] Is it possible that insurance firms would take this approach to doing business, trying to trust the customer instead of behaving as if all customers are fraudsters? Technology can help here too. Under efficient management, technology such as that used by Amazon can analyze a customer's behaviour and, more importantly, trends and anomalies in groups of customers to make it easier to distinguish between the majority of honest people and the small minority of felons. This approach may be able to reduce actual fraud to below levels achieved by treating all customers suspiciously, and will certainly developed greater brand loyalty in all honest customers.

Table 1.2 Five major projects and their problems

Organization	Project description budget	Original budget	Cost overrun	Overrun	Time slippage
1 NASA	Space station. The view of some in Congress was that NASA was unable to manage large, complex problems effectively.[22]	$17 400m	$3600m	21%	n/a
2 DoD/Lockheed Martin	Theatre missile programme[23]	n/a	$467m *(Excludes a further $265m attributed to DoD's changing requirements)*	Substantial	
3 DoD/Lockheed Martin/Boeing	F22 programme. Plan to build 438 planes, replaces F15	$18 900m	$767m	4%	Substantial. As at 18 March 1999 only 5% of planned test flights complete.
4 Motorola	Iridium mobile telephone project	Reliable 'before v. after' statistics for budget and time overruns are hard to obtain for Iridium, as for most private sector projects. But outsiders estimate the project has cost $5bn and taken 11 years.			
5 Internal Revenue Service	Modernization of IT[24]	$8000m	$2500m	31%	15 years and no sign of many key deliverables

Summary

This chapter sets out the problems caused to organizations if they fail to manage their IT efficiently and effectively. We identified four main categories of problem faced when implementing new IT:

1. Projects go over budget or over time.
2. New systems fail to meet user expectations.
3. New systems have poor reliability.
4. New systems degrade core strengths of the organization which acquires them.

Each of these problems can operate of different levels in an organization. We looked at BlackSystems, a real business that went bankrupt through poor management of its own IT. BlackSystems showed that perhaps unexpectedly, problems operating at a high-level and which are therefore obvious to senior management can be less threatening than IT-related problems operating much lower down in the organization, invisible to senior management. These kinds of problems can be generating operational costs and inefficiencies that can kill a business. Finally, we looked at the amazing growth of Amazon.com in the retail book market, and analyzed its success in terms of its use of IT.

Table 1.2 lists five major IT projects with a summary of their problems.

Endnotes

1   Hess (1999).
2   Widely documented at the time. See for instance Harrison (1994).
3   Morris (1994).
4   Timmins (1999).
5   Coke's experience with its new formula has been covered extensively in management literature. For a recent retrospective see for instance Schuck (1999).
6   IBM is one firm that takes this view of options, and has been extraordinarily effective by doing so. A particularly robust approach to strategy in terms of options is given in Shapiro (1999). As one might expect, the idea is also treated extensively in Trigeorgis (1996).
7   These three examples are from Romney (1995).
8   Alford (1996).
9   Pontin (1995).
10 Software providers regularly state that new features will be available by a certain date or that a new product will have a certain functionality when this is not the case.
11 *Airline Industry Information* (1998).
12 *Arlington Morning News* (1998).
13 This issue is frequently documented, see for instance Horwitt (1997).
14 Tse-Tung (1954).
15 Salisbury (1992).
16 The UK Prudential, not the US firm with a similar name.
17 See Foster (1986).
18 See, for example, Maister (1993).
19 We understand that the firm's sale in 1999 resulted from external political considerations.
20 But not in all businesess. The examples of staples such as bread at the lower end of the market and luxury goods such as fine fragrances at the upper end are well-known to businesses and economists as being exceptions to this general rule, technically the 'price elasticity of demand'. Fans of economic theory who also have an interest in managing IT efficiently should look out for exceptions to this rule in the IT world. It is said that Adolf Hitler ignored his scientist's request for funding for the atomic bomb because the request was for such a small amount of money that he didn't believe any serious weapon would result. Sometimes in IT, projects have to be expensive to be taken seriously. One Belgian firm sold mainframe computers for hundreds of thousands of dollars when it could easily have sold them for tens of thousands. The reason had little to do with maximizing profit margins; it was because in their niche market the

machines would not be taken seriously at a lower price tag. How many mainframes today are running applications that could be run more cheaply on a PC or workstation?

21 Bezos (1999).
22 Vartabedian (1998).
23 Washington Transcript Service (1998).
24 Frank (1998).

2 An IT expense healthcheck

Three tests to check quickly how well your IT department is managing its costs

Aim

The aim of this chapter is to describe three tests that business managers can execute to get a ballpark estimate of the efficiency of their IT support organization. The tests are effective on all kinds of IT support, and it doesn't matter if IT is in its own department, or is integrated into the business unit, or is a combination of both. The aim is that these tests should be relatively quick and easy to implement, rather than being 100% exhaustive or 100% infallible. They should also indicate the main area of inefficiency within the IT support organization, so that management's efforts at improving efficiency can be efficiently directed. Finally, the tests should be readily understood by both IT and business management because many inefficiencies in IT derive from an absence of any shared understanding of the problems or of any common language in which to discuss both business and IT problems. Cooperation and not conflict between the business unit and the IT function is vital if any progress is to be made in managing IT costs.

These aims might be ambitious, but they are achievable, and we want you to know how to achieve them too. For proof that such aims are achievable, consider the outsourcing industry. The essence of outsourcing is straightforward: hand over the management of part of your organization – IT services, say – to third-party management. What is happening here? Put simply, the outsourcer outsources because it judges it can make money on the deal. The customer organization agrees to this because it thinks it too will save money. In short, the proposition is that the outsourcer can manage IT more efficiently than the customer. The CFO of a large investment bank represented the unease that many feel about outsourcing when he said 'I'm not happy with these IT costs, but I'd rather we solved them by managing them better ourselves so that we can keep the profit we'd otherwise be giving away to an outsourcing company.' This bank felt it had management talent available to be deployed in resolving the IT cost issue. If true, it may be that outsourcing was not in fact the right decision for this particular investment bank, however, not all organizations are in the position of having sufficient numbers of skilled IT management and staff.

Whether outsourcers are used to increase IT efficiency or not, the existence of the outsourcing industry shows that the correct identification and remedying of IT inefficiency can lead to massive value creation, and this issue is more important than whether or not to outsource in a particular case. Put another way, the most significant issue is that the very existence of outsourcing as an industry proves that there is the potential for massive value to be created when an organization gets its IT right; whether getting IT right involves outsourcing or not is secondary to grasping the first point, and will depend on the particular circumstances. This point is so important, let's put it a third way: for most businesses there are huge opportunities to make money by understanding IT and managing it better than it is managed at the moment; outsourcing proves that the opportunities are huge.

In an IT organization run at average efficiency it is quite feasible to gain a 20% cost reduction or 20% value increase. This is the typical planning assumption of the outsourcing industry and many of its clients.[1] For instance, Chevron Corporation is implementing a programme to save $50m annually in IT ownership cost, and the main initiative in this programme is simply to standardize the software it uses.[2] Procter & Gamble's Efficient Consumer Response (ECR) has IT cost efficiency improvements as one of its four central themes. The ECR programme is designed to save costs and forms part of its plan to double sales in ten years.[3] In due course we believe that the management techniques used today by outsourcers and other specialists to achieve these massive efficiency gains will become part of the standard management repertoire across all industries and functions. This chapter aims to show you how to take the first steps on the road to getting your organization the massive gain that IT can give.

Introduction

Imagine that as a manager responsible for meeting a budget, you always felt confident that all the money your department was charged for IT was well-spent. Imagine further that the reason you felt confident was that you understood how every dollar, pound or euro was being spent and why it was being spent, and that the IT organization was spending your department's money in the most effective way. Stop reading for a moment and think how this would alter your job as a manager. Would it remove any anxiety about sudden IT charges hitting your budget? Would you be able to focus more on managing, for instance on how to apply IT in radical and innovative ways to improve your businesses' efficiency? This chapter will show you three simple tests which will enable you to judge how well your IT support is managing its costs and your IT costs. The results can be the basis for a constructive dialogue and a change programme that will improve the efficiency of your IT services.

How feasible is this vision? In the next section we will see that some companies have in fact come very close to this vision, and more are well on their way towards achieving it. But first we will check just how feasible this vision really is in the real world of ordinary business life. We will do this by looking at some business support functions other than IT in order to sharpen our understanding of the problems of managing IT.

First, consider office services – that part of the organization responsible for providing, furnishing and maintaining the premises, and which typically includes such functions as vacuuming the carpets, cleaning the windows, supplying desks and chairs. Most managers responsible for budgets do not have an issue with the costs charged for office services in the same way that many managers have an issue with IT costs. Of course you always wish costs were lower and revenues were higher, but apart from this common wish, office services are generally a good example of transparent costs. Almost all managers, if asked, will say one of two things about their office services costs: they are OK, or they are too high. This simple fact is striking. Why? Compare this situation to IT costs.

If asked why their office services costs are too high, most managers will be able to explain their opinion in some detail, and will often be able to explain their opinion by reference to facts. Their explanations will be of no more than two kinds: either that the input costs are too high, or that the management of the office services department is inefficient. By input cost we mean things like rent. If the rent paid per square foot is excessive in the opinion of our business manager, no degree of efficient management in office services will reduce the cost charged per square foot below the cost of the rent. If, on the other hand, our manager opines that it is the inefficiency of the management of office services which is the real problem, he will usually be able to justify his opinion in one of two ways. He might cite lower costs in a comparable business in a comparable area, or, secondly, he might cite specific work practices or instances of overmanning in the office services department which he believes to be inefficient.

What is striking about managers having one of two opinions of their office services costs (OK or too expensive) is that when it comes to IT costs, many managers do not have clear opinions on whether they are too high or not in the first place. And the few that do have such opinions are able to back them up only very rarely with the sort of facts they would use when dealing with office services. Our purpose in making this comparison is to provide a familiar example to managers that shows it is possible to manage IT so that costs are easy to understand.

You may be thinking that this is all very well, but in real life IT costs are at least an order of magnitude more complex than office services costs. If so, you may be wondering how fair the comparison with office services is to the IT department. It is true that the management in office services tends to focus on tangible things – buildings, carpets, wastepaper baskets, lavatories, windows, and so on. This objection, while true, does not invalidate the usefulness of the comparison between managing IT and managing office services for our present purpose. The comparison to the office services department serves to set out the fundamentals of what it is for a manager to understand their costs: the manager will at all times have a clear opinion on whether his costs from that support unit are OK or excessive, and they will be able to support their opinion with some evidence that can serve as the basis for a comparative evaluation. This is not usually the case for IT support units. But let us consider another non-IT support unit, but one that is not open to the criticism we have just made for the comparison with office services. The point of considering office services was to show what it is like to be able to understand costs, and that in some parts of an organization it is in fact quite normal.

So there might be doubt about the validity of the office services comparison because IT costs are much more complex. However, consider how a legal department manages its costs. Unlike office services, the objects and activities managed by the legal department are not tangible objects such as tables and everyday activities such as the cleaning of tables. Instead a legal department manages intangibles; a typical legal department might manage corporate litigation, intellectual property disputes and labour disputes, and it might advise senior management on the requirements of new legislation.

Now remember our 'acid test,' which is to ask whether ordinary managers would be so confused when faced with a department's costs that they would have little instinctive feel for whether the costs were reasonable. Is the average manager as confused by his legal costs as by his IT costs? Probably not. Just as in the case of office services costs, the average manager might hold the view that the charge to the department for legal costs is excessive, but he will also usually be able to back up this opinion, for example, by citing an excessive year on year increase in the cost of obtaining a patent, or of defending unfair dismissal actions. But in such disputes, there is at least a consensus on what the issues are that can serve as a basis for investigation, if the extent of the disagreement about costs warrants such an investigation. Indeed, it is usually easier than in the case of office rental costs to obtain comparative data for legal services because there are so many firms of lawyers offering comparable services, and it is relatively straightforward to get a quote.

We started this chapter by sketching out a vision of what it would be like for a manager to have confidence in the cost efficiency of his IT support department or function. By these examples of other support departments we have reminded ourselves that this vision is achievable not just in practice, but is an everyday reality in non-IT departments, including ones that deal in complex issues such as the legal department. Further we hope to have shown, in principle at least, that cost transparency should be feasible for the IT function also, as indeed it is in a few organizations. The aim of this chapter is simply to provide non-IT managers with a set of basic tools to evaluate the performance of the IT department in the same way that the performance of the office services department, the legal department, or the human resources department is already evaluated. We believe that the only significant difference between this kind of evaluation of other support departments and the IT department is that the rules of thumb and mental habits that managers use for evaluating non-IT departments are so routine for them compared to the techniques appropriate for evaluating IT. In five years' time, we hope it will be as normal for managers to have a ready view on the efficiency of their IT support as it is for them now to have such a view on legal, human resources, or office services support. It is the purpose of this book to try to help bring that about.

At this point it is worth emphasizing that the goal is not to prove or disprove that inefficiencies exist in the IT department. IT departments are typically staffed by very hard-working human beings, who respond in the same way as do other human beings if one makes a show of trying to highlight one's opinions of their personal shortcomings. The goal is absolutely not to apportion blame. Indeed, if one did want to apportion blame, then the rest of business would have to share the blame for the excesses in IT costs, whether they are real or apparent, for having failed to work with IT over the last 40-odd years to educate IT about financial management. Blaming IT, and even abusing behind their backs individuals who work in IT departments is a popular pastime in many organizations today. It might be fun, but it is not part of a solution to the problem of excessive IT costs.

This chapter explains three simple healthchecks to help diagnose the current efficiency in an IT organization. If they indicate cost problems that need to be solved, the process of solving them will be much easier if the findings are delivered sensitively. The fat man who goes to the doctor for advice on how to lose weight needs to be told more than just 'it's because you eat too much.' A good doctor would establish that eating rather than hereditary or emotional reasons were in fact the cause, and would then spend some time reviewing options for weight reduction that fitted the circumstances and character of the individual. More exercise or fewer calories are of course the only real options, but a useful diagnosis will try to determine what balance of these two options is right for the individual, and how each option is best attempted – walking for 60-year-olds, marathon running for the less mature, and gratuitous insults for no-one.

Case study | How organizations have used IT healthchecks to achieve efficiency in IT

RedBank

RedBank is one of the world's most respected financial institutions, and for the past five years has been one of the most successful in Europe. It employs over 20,000 people, and besides Europe, has operations in the USA, Latin America and Australasia. Management considers that the Latin American market is the greatest opportunity for RedBank's growth outside the home market. The bank's management had focused on improving IT management in the home market, and in the late 1990s this had been achieved. But as the pace of globalization in financial markets increased, not least because of the boom in banking and financial services delivered through the Internet, RedBank initiated a priority review of IT management in the rest of its territories. The performance of the foreign businesses was largely satisfactory, except for problems specific to the economies of one Latin American country. Senior management was unaware of any major issues in IT, although from the limited detail in the high-level financial reports they received they still had some concern about IT costs, which had been rising slowly but steadily as a proportion of operating costs for several quarters.

A small team of three staff and three external consultants worked under the direction of a senior manager and were supported by the sponsorship of a main board director. The project team interviewed the country managers for all significant overseas operations, and found a greater level of concern about IT costs than in headquarters senior management. Except for a few managers including the one who was well known for his tendency towards excessive fault finding, no business unit was unduly concerned about its IT costs.

Things as seen from the centre, however, were quite different. When the costs of IT across all foreign branches were aggregated, it became clear that IT costs were significantly higher than competitors'. One of the greatest concerns raised by benchmarking was that the IT costs of the international businesses' operations were significantly higher than the IT costs of domestic operations, and no significant part of this difference was due to the international nature of operations.

A few days later the reasons seemed fairly obvious as the project team compiled RedBank's first consolidated report of IT projects and resources across all the regions: there was little standardization but much duplication of effort. The individual countries were managed as standalone entities, when there were in fact massive synergy opportunities. In the most glaring cases of inefficiency, mainframes which ran the same general banking systems in neighbouring countries in Latin America, for instance, would be running at half-capacity or less, with no thought given to closing one down and using the unused capacity on the other instead. Ten years ago, before cheap international telecommunications and high-speed data networking this would not have been feasible, but by the time of the study such practices were not only feasible but common practice. In other cases, different systems were being used in neighbouring countries to achieve essentially the same task, and in some cases different systems were being used in different locations even in the same country. At little cost, it would be possible to achieve 20% savings by standardizing systems and stripping out redundancy, and even greater savings looked entirely possible given a little investment.

RedBank's senior management therefore started a rationalization scheme which was planned to extend for three years. The approach was evolution, not revolution, with standardization being planned to coincide with software updates and systems changes already planned, for example, Year 2000 and EMU. This would minimize cost and leverage off other initiatives and changes in RedBank, thereby ensuring the greatest chance of successful implementation.

It took the project team just over two weeks to identify and measure the sources of inefficiency. Several of the individual metrics used were then incorporated into a regular management report instituted to enable senior management at the centre and country managers to monitor and improve IT efficiency over the three-year transition period and thereafter. By using healthchecks, RedBank managed to bring the level of IT efficiency in its overseas operations up to the same high-level as it had achieved in its European operations, and gained over 20% cost reduction in the branches covered by the project.

GreenStore

GreenStore is one of Europe's leading retail chains, and the global strength of its brand name has enabled it to expand into other countries. It also purchased a large retail chain in the USA. It employs over 15 000 people. GreenStore has an efficient central IT organization, highly regarded by colleagues in other service lines. Not all IT operations were owned by the central IT function, and when technological and labour law changes made it feasible to re-engineer the business processes of GreenStore's printing and packaging operations, the marketing division, of which printing and packaging formed a part, decided to invest in new IT. A pilot investment of over £1m was approved by the board, with approval for further investments should the pilot prove successful. The aim of the re-engineering effort was to reduce the overall time to market for new products by 50%, where marketing material, packaging and signage were often limiting factors. GreenStore's IT supplier also expected substantial cost savings and efficiency improvements to result, and forecast an IRR[4] for the investment of over 25%.

The re-engineering project was championed by George M., a middle manager, and after board approval George's manager, GreenStore's head of marketing, signed the contract for new equipment. Three months later installation was complete. George M. worked hard to ensure the project succeeded, often working late to attend personally to matters raised by the equipment suppliers instead of delegating them as he would have on any other project. The project ran smoothly, and it seemed to senior management that GreenStore and their suppliers were set to succeed and meet all targets. But just at this point George M. left unexpectedly to found his own business, and the project continued without a champion in middle management. The project seemed to carry on successfully for months after George M. left.

At first the IT suppliers noticed no change in how things were going at GreenStore. The project had been going so well, and such was the strength of GreenStore's reputation and brand that the suppliers reckoned this particular project had been a significant contributing factor in sales of their IT equipment, and was worth at least another £10m in revenue over the next two years. While the project continued to go well immediately after George M's departure, there were other major changes that were to affect the project in the longer-term. First, GreenStore's marketing department was reorganized, and secondly, the technology on the market developed, offering increased functionality at ever-decreasing costs. The longer term consequences of these changes were that by the end of the third quarter after George M's departure, the project was no longer likely to meet its objectives unless something special was done.

GreenStore and the suppliers shared an interest in making the project succeed, although for different reasons. GreenStore wanted to speed up its turnaround time and raise the quality of its marketing material, while also, of course, reducing costs. The IT supplier, however, wanted a flagship customer such as GreenStore, because it was launching new technology and a good flagship customer would enable them to sell the new technology much more easily. Another difference in the reasoning between GreenStore and their IT supplier was that the supplier assumed a much greater degree of automation of GreenStore's processes was feasible than GreenStore itself did; GreenStore was very pragmatic, and wanted to concentrate on getting a few basics right. It is not an exaggeration to say that their suppliers, on the other hand, almost believed that more technology for its own sake was a good thing.

These different reasons led both the suppliers and GreenStore to approach the issue of efficiency tests in different ways. The suppliers either assumed that the problem lay in the operators of the IT system or realized that there was nothing they could do about the weakness of GreenStore's middle management, and either way decided not to test the efficiency of the project. At the time the suppliers behaved as if any problem could be solved by applying more technology. GreenStore, on the other hand, decided to initiate a more thorough management review of the project. GreenStore's board had been monitoring the results of the project because they expected the project to reveal strategic information about changes in the optimal degree of vertical integration in the industry, about the efficiency of the decentralized model of IT and about the risks in business process re-engineering.

A year after George M.'s departure, Peter O., a senior executive, was appointed to review the investment in the project and recommend appropriate action. GreenStore started with an assumption that the decline in performance experienced after George M.'s departure could stem from three possible sources. First, it could be that the relevant processes in marketing and printing had not been re-engineered in the right way. Secondly, the rapid pace of technological change might mean that the equipment was already obsolete and incapable of matching the efficiency of the state of the art, although it was only a year old. Senior management suspected that a third hypothesis was the most probable, and that it was inefficiency in the management appointed to take over from George M. that was the primary cause of the project's difficulties.

Because of the new developments in technology and the internal reorganization, however, GreenStore was unable to be certain that the cause of inefficiency lay with the new project management. The experience of GreenStore's competitors also clouded the picture and neither confirmed nor counted against GreenStore's diagnosis of its problems. One of GreenStore's main competitors had just signed up with the same supplier, but two other competitors had announced they intended to use a newer competing technology to effect their re-engineering, although neither of these competitors had yet installed any of the technology. GreenStore now had about £2m of sunk costs in the project, but stood to benefit by £11m net present value (NPV)[5] if the project could be made to work efficiently. Peter O. set up a one-month project that applied short tests to determine the cause of the change in project performance.

Peter O's enquiry required few staff. The new manager in charge of the project was involved, although the real work of the enquiry was undertaken by one middle manager and one junior manager, both seconded part time from line functions. The enquiry lasted just over three months, the first two of which were taken up largely with developing a set of tests to determine the cause of the inefficiency. After the six weeks it took to administer the IT healthchecks, GreenStore produced its conclusions.

First, it decided that the new management put in place after George M's departure was inefficient. Secondly, it decided that a new investment of £0.5m should be made to adjust the systems to the needs of the reorganized department, but also, thirdly, it decided that new technology was beginning to catch up with the system installed and therefore the new technology's benefits should be monitored. It is important to record that the individual who replaced George M. was a competent manager in their previous role, and one of the findings of the enquiry was that this manager had been asked to perform a task without being given the right management reporting tools to manage the technology. In fact, had the manager concerned had available the tools that the enquiry developed to make its investigation and draw its conclusions, GreenStore felt there would have been no fall off in project performance. GreenStore's IT healthcheck identified the main cause of inefficiency in the project and management were able to make changes, including organizational changes that restored the project to success.

Healthcheck 1: key performance indicators (KPIs)

When evaluating our children's school, most of us instinctively know what information we need. Is little Johnny happy there? Do the teachers show an interest? How does little Johnny score in his end of term exams against the class? How expensive is the school? What proportion of its pupils make it to a good university? Whether this is exactly the right ranking of importance for the criteria depends on the views of the parents concerned. Although the proportion of children passing on to university is important for most parents, it is probable that the happiness of their beloved offspring is more important still. How do schools evaluate themselves? Largely on the same criteria, although the ranking may be slightly different. Even in these modern times of enlightened schooling, schools facing competitive evaluation in league tables may be just that bit more willing to trade a small amount of happiness now for a better grade in public examinations and thus achieve a higher ratio of pupils going on to university. Parents and schools also tend to have criteria that do not figure in the other's reckoning. Parents might want a school within easy driving range. A school may want to teach some fashionable subject to satisfy the academic ambitions of a staff member.

This comparison of parents' evaluations of schools and schools' evaluations of themselves prompts two observations pertinent to KPIs for IT. First, schools and parents have had some time to learn to understand each other – at least a millennium – and during this time the function of the school has changed little. Secondly, even though they agree on many of the criteria of what makes a good school, their respective ranking of these criteria can differ, and they might each have criteria which are irrelevant to the other party. Substitute IT function and business unit for schools and parents and the same issues hold, with only a few complications.

One of the most significant problems in evaluating IT performance from the point of view of an organization's management is that IT can fundamentally change a business, yet IT is so new in society that there has been little time for institutions to learn how to manage it. Compare this situation to the management of mines. It was not until 1816, after several millennia of mining, that Sir Humphry Davy's miner's safety lamp was used in mines, transforming mine management. Computing has been pervasive in business for no more than 20 years or so, and the great advances in technology have not yet been fully matched by advances in skills for managing organizations in which technology is pervasive. KPIs are one of the new techniques for managing IT in organizations. KPIs may well prove to be the Davy lamp of IT management, a tool that signals to business manager whether their IT is OK or whether there is an unseen risk of an IT-induced corporate explosion.

The KPI healthcheck

In seven steps, a manager can get a good initial estimate of the efficiency with which his IT support is run. Each step answers one question about the firm, and some questions focus more on the IT department of the firm, but others ask about overall firm management. The questions are:

1. Do KPIs exist?
2. Are the KPIs relevant to management needs?
3. Are the KPIs accurate?
4. Are there gaps in the KPIs?
5. Are there controls associated with the KPIs?
6. Do the controls work?
7. How can the KPIs or controls be used?

Busy managers will naturally want to answer these questions in the most efficient way possible, and what approach is most efficient will vary from organization to organization. For instance, take the first question – do KPIs exist? In one organization, KPIs may be distributed regularly as management reports, and so the question hardly even arises. In another organization, it may be hard for the business manager to find anyone in IT management who even knows what a KPI is, so getting a definitive 'no' answer will be hard work. Perhaps the most difficult situation arises where IT management know what KPIs are, and have been meaning to publish them for a while, but have deferred until after the year 2000 because of the perceived distraction to IT management. And from here it is quite possible that after January 2000 some will decide to review the original need for KPIs, thus pushing back the timetable even further. In this case the reply to the question might be that KPIs do exist, or that they will exist soon. Of course the business manager asking the question might not be told too readily that nothing has been done on KPIs for two years, or that the IT department knows the KPIs are meaningless because they were designed for the old IT infrastructure. In real life, these things have been known to happen.

In one large US shipbuilder, line management watched as IT costs rose by over 10% per month. The IT department kept the line managers at bay for six months by the simple device of saying that the IT KPIs were under development. In fact no work was done at all during these six months on KPIs. Whenever business management came to investigate, an old report from a well-known firm of IT management consultants was dusted off and presented as work in progress, with a few more pages of the original report at every new management request.

Having put the case for good corporate citizenship and professionalism, the last word should go to a veteran of company management who still has seven years of his career ahead of him at one of the world's leading soft drink brands. 'When it comes to IT's answers to tough questions – be safe, be sceptical.'

Next, for each of the seven questions we set out how to go about getting answers, and give suggestions for interpreting those answers. Use Table 2.1 to score the answers to the seven questions in this first healthcheck.

Table 2.1 Scoring the KPI healthcheck

Result	Score
You or your business unit already receives regular IT KPI reports, and the KPIs are relevant to managing costs (see rest of chapter for details if uncertain)	15
KPIs are sent to you immediately with little or no fuss	13
KPIs are sent after some discussion with IT, and are to some extent relevant to managing IT costs	10
IT knows what KPIs are and they are sent within two weeks, or . . .	8
. . . within a month; or KPIs are sent to you relatively easily, but contain little that aids an understanding of IT costs or their management	5
You receive a consultant's report describing what KPIs are and proposing they are used in your organization	3
Any other response	0

1. Do KPIs exist?

Skip this section and award your IT department 15 points if you are one of the lucky few managers who receive regular reports on KPIs relevant to your responsibilities from the IT department. Otherwise, ask for them; ask the IT department for KPIs relevant to your function, and if none is forthcoming, ask for any KPIs that IT produces, even those by which the IT department is managed. You might wish to delegate the task of asking for KPIs, and also be prepared for the IT department to ask for a meeting with you to find out exactly what it is you want.

2. Are the KPIs relevant to management needs?

Once you have a set of KPIs in front of you, the next question is whether they meet your management needs. In trying to understand and manage your IT costs as a business unit manager, you are essentially interested in two things:

■ How much is your IT support costing overall?

■ What drives IT costs, from within your organization and within IT itself?

You will probably be interested in the overall cost for the simple reason that overall costs matter. But to manage overall costs you will need to get into the detail, and the first step is to distinguish two kinds of IT cost driver. One kind of IT cost driver is external to the IT department, especially things your business unit asks IT to do (see Case study below). Are you creating inefficiencies by asking IT to achieve the results you want in an inefficient way? That is, could you get the same results from IT at lower cost if you had them performed differently? The other kind of cost driver is the efficiency with which the IT department is managed.

Case study **Cost driver**

A design studio was part of one of the largest agencies in the UK, so it had professional managers who knew how to organize workflow, although they had got most of their experience before computer graphic design techniques had become prevalent. The firm had invested almost £500 000 in computer graphic workstations, and in the year after installation work there had been a noticeable reduction in job turnaround times, but it looked as if some areas, such as client presentations, had become more expensive. The management worked closely with the workstation suppliers to investigate this anomaly.

The design studio found that there were two causes. First, the agency's staff were simply asking for more variants in preparation for the presentations than they had before the automation of the studio, simply because they could now ask for and get many more variations. Reflecting on this development later, management commented that to some extent it seemed as if judgement had been replaced by increased variety of output. But most of the unexpected cost arose because the agency account executives who made the presentations insisted on seeing expensive colour proofs of the designs to be presented at all stages. Colour proofs were necessary immediately before the presentation, but when lettering and rough layouts were being discussed, simple black and white line drawings were just as good, and often clearer than the colour proofs. Communication between the studio and the account executives was poor, partly because they were in different buildings, and partly because of poor teamwork. The account executives had no idea of the costs they were incurring, nor were they even aware that crisp black and white line drawings were available. As soon as the account executives started to use the black and white line drawings for initial concept checking, the costs of running the workstations dropped significantly, and workflow sped up. This is often the way with IT – previous work practices have to be modified to get the best cost and quality performance out of new IT systems.

We want the KPIs so that we can understand and then manage the IT costs which hit our departments – cost drivers internal to the IT department, and cost drivers which originate in the business unit we ourselves manage. Of course there are other cost drivers that influence IT costs, the main ones being the drivers originating in other business units. However, our approach is pragmatic; to manage what we can given our position in the management structure of the firm. Later on we can examine the overall management and efficiency of IT resources in all divisions of the firm if the need and opportunity arises. But just before we proceed with reviewing our KPIs, we should be aware that in our focus on pragmatism we are paying a price in ignoring a potentially significant source of firm-wide IT costs, a portion of which may be allocated to our department.

When reviewing KPIs, managers must take account of how the cost drivers work in their particular organizations. This is even more important when designing KPIs, as you might be asked to do if your IT department has no KPIs. The most effective KPIs take account of the relative significance of the three kinds of cost drivers, as they affect costs allocated to your department and how these get allocated to your department. This means you must find out, in overview, what other departments do that generate IT costs, and in greater detail what your department does. This can usually be accomplished in a meeting with a senior manager from the IT department, and if you are lucky enough to have an IT department with its own integral finance people, they will also be useful people to talk to.

Go and meet these people. Aim to draw up on one side of paper in the meeting a list of other business units served by IT, and the main services provided by IT and associated cost drivers (Table 2.2 shows the sort of notes that you might want to

Table 2.2 A typical list from a cost driver meeting to determine IT allocation

Main user departments

Sales

- network support
  - demand peaks 2130 – labour costs
  - due for an upgrade
  - other depts piggyback off the sales network. Allocation?
- nightly data transfer from reps' homes to data warehouse
  - essentially a fixed cost
- laptop maintenance and upgrades
  - salespeople decide what they want. Control?

Marketing

- marketing database management
- data feeds
- call centre IT management/support

Production

- production datacentre management
- customer prototyping support

Shared

- helpdesk
- network management/ shared infrastructure
- year 2000/EMU project

Corporate HQ

- payroll
- general ledger
- MIS datacentre
- R&D support

make.) Mark which ones affect or may affect your department. This is something you or someone from your department needs to do, because the purpose is that you should understand the cost drivers sufficiently well to be able to come to an opinion on the relevance of the KPIs that is informed by a sound understanding of the cost drivers. This is unlikely to be a trivial task, and may take a couple of weeks in elapsed time, as your department and IT build a shared understanding of the

Cost drivers

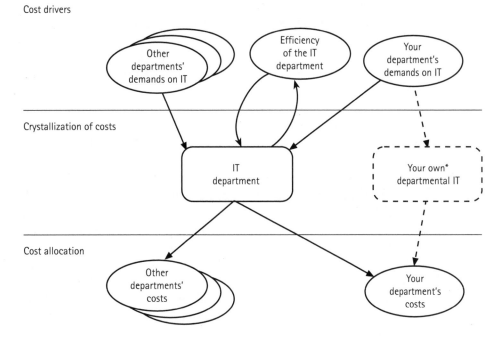

Crystallization of costs

Cost allocation

* Your department's total IT costs will be impacted not just by any centrally provided IT services, but also by IT which your department controls itself. We are ignoring these for the purposes of this chapter, but include them in this diagram for completeness. They can be managed by the same techniques as are being described in this chapter for managing centrally provided IT costs, although in practice because they are integral to the department and are not shared with another group intra-departmental IT costs are usually easier to manage.

Fig. 2.1   IT cost drivers

information needed. The test of whether you have the right information for your purposes is that for each KPI, you should have be reasonably confident in your judgement of whether it will indicate whether the following are increasing or decreasing:

■ the efficiency with which IT manage themselves, given that yours is not the only department they have to support;

■ activities which are not performed in support of your department but for which, through imperfections of the current cost allocation system, you are likely to be allocated cost;

■ demands your department is making on IT that will increase your IT costs.

And this is only half of what's needed. The reader will have noticed that all this work (and anyone who has ever managed a successful IT cost reduction programme will know that what we have just covered in a few paragraphs is hard grind) takes us only to the middle section of Table 2.1, to the point where costs are incurred, in the IT department. Before they hit your budget they will probably go through the corporate cost allocation system.

Therefore similar meetings are needed with a finance function of the firm to understand the principles on which costs are allocated from the IT department to your department. Whether this is the central finance function or a finance function integral to IT will depend on the particular organization. Focus on major IT cost items only. The way to make progress in understanding corporate cost allocations is to be selective. It's been described as rather like controlling football hooligans, where apparently the thing to do is to focus on a few big troublemakers. So it is in allocations, limit yourself to understanding the 20% of allocation principles that account for the bulk of the dollars allocated. (Allocations, how they work and their associated terminology are described in Chapter 3.) Aim to come away from the meetings with the allocations people knowing what your firm's predominant allocation principles are for allocating IT costs, which allocations principles tend to be used for each of the major IT cost drivers, and the views of IT management on the fairness of how IT cost allocations are made.

You should now be in a position to judge the relevance of the IT KPIs. Does each KPI tell you what is happening to your IT costs and why, in such a way that you as a manager are likely to be able to do something about it?

As an example, consider Table 2.3. It shows the period covered, who the report was prepared for, and who prepared it. The period covered and who it was prepared for are not trivial pieces of information, but are exactly the kind of 'obvious detail' that gets left out of such reports, and if it is left out only causes inefficiency when work is delegated or handed over to outside consultants. This kind of background information is itself an indicator of how efficiently the IT department is run. Next, the name of the individual who prepared the report appears. Again, 'obvious detail' – how much easier to make one quick phone call to resolve a simple question about the data in the report than to make a fundamental error in one's assumptions. For example, does what IT spend here include telecommunications and telex costs? In some firms telecoms is part of the IT budget, in others it is not, and in yet others parts of telecomms, such as fax switches and internal line costs are included in IT spend but fax machines and external line rental are not. This is the level of detail required to understand and manage IT costs, and although much of this detail will be uncovered in the course of meetings with the IT department and IT finance people, there will always be simple questions that need answering later. One phone call to Percy Spodder will tell us.

Moving on to the contents of the report, we see that the data is broken down under five headings: expenditure, customer service, user support, staffing and

Table 2.3   Sample set of KPIs

IT Key Performance Indicators			
Period: Month to 31/11/99			
Business unit: North American Region Call Centres			
Prepared for: Charles Suave, Director North American Region			
Prepared by: Percival Spodder (Birmingham X4345)			

	Month actual	Month target	Δ y/y actual
1 Expenditure			
▪ total IT spend	$ 11.5m	$ 10.9m	+9.7%
▪ development spend	$ 626k	$ 650k	+15%
▪ maintenance spend	$ 601k	$ 260k	+0.2%
2 Customer service			
▪ quotes processed	136k	<150k	+102%
▪ MIPS/quote	270	275	+400%
▪ quotes rejected by supervisors	3%	1%	33%
▪ web RFIs processed	201k	<100k	N/A
▪ MIPs/RFI	50k	N/A	N/A
▪ web availability	99.21%	99.99%	N/A
3 User support (internal customers)			
▪ network reliability	98.9%	99.996	+5%
▪ number of tickets opened	4.2k	<1.5k	+203%
▪ average time to respond	2'23"	<30"	−1'34"
▪ % calls resolved within 15 minutes	45%	66%	+12%
▪ % calls resolved within 1 hr	88%	25%	+30%
▪ desktops moved/rebuilt/setup	178	N/A	N/A
▪ systems upgrades	1247	1225	N/A
4 Staffing			
▪ total number of IT staff	23	21	+64%
▪ managers as % total staff	13%	14%	+200%
▪ turnover	19%/yr	<15%	−26.9%
▪ absence	2%	<3%	−0.0%
5 Efficiency			
▪ helpdesk tickets closed/IT staff	480	525	−4.5%
▪ MIPS/$ for month	9.58	10.00	−17%
▪ quotes/IT staff	5913	7000	+8%
▪ deals closed/IT staff	1005	1400	+12%
▪ internal/external bandwidth usage	203%	33%	N/A

efficiency, and under each heading is a further breakdown. For each line of the further breakdown there are three sets of data, the month's actual numbers, the budget numbers of the month and a year-on-year variance, or Δ (delta – a term that technical folk often prefer as shorthand for 'change'.) The year-on-year comparison is interesting, but many managers will want some shorter-term measure of change, for instance a month-on-month comparison or a three-month rolling average trend. Another column of comparative data that will be useful is the difference between the month's actuals and targets or a variance column.

Let us review Percy Spodder's report (Table 2.3) to Charles Suave line by line, with our key question to the front of our mind: does each KPI tell us what is happening to our IT costs and why, in such a way that we as managers are likely to be able to do something about it?

Total IT spend

We know that this means total IT spend on behalf of our department, that is, allocated to our business unit, which in this case is the North American Regional Call Centres business unit. However, if we had not been certain that 'total IT spend' means the total on behalf of our business unit, we should confirm this. In today's large corporation, it is far from simple to get the dollar costs of IT. A consultant from the Gartner Group, a consultancy working in the field of general IT management, has this to say: 'I spoke with many IT managers about this and they are taken aback that we at GartnerGroup do not know what *they* in their organization are spending outside the IT budget. If they do not know what they are spending, how should we know?'[6]

The next lines we see are a breakdown between development and maintenance spend. This is often a ratio that IT managers themselves use for measuring the efficiency of an IT operation, although it is rarely the case that the IT department is able to institute the changes necessary to alter this ratio without the support of the rest of the business. Our interest in these two lines is in the development/maintenance ratio.

The development/maintenance ratio gives an indication of how efficiently an IT organization is able to manage the lifecycle of IT equipment and to some extent, the suitability of the IT infrastructure for business purposes. If too much obsolescent equipment is in use, maintenance costs are likely to be excessively high; and efficiencies now achievable with more up-to-date technology are probably not being captured.

By comparing the development/maintenance ratio in your IT department to best practice among your competitors you will be able to form a fairly reliable view on the efficiency of IT management. (This principle holds whether you actually have an IT department or whether your IT is decentralized or outsourced.) To repeat a warning given earlier, if this test indicates inefficiency in IT it does not automatically follow that the management of the current IT department are at fault. There could be several reasons for this, including previous under-investment in IT infrastructure, which may have led to the present requirement to devote excessive resources to maintenance. The analogy with a leaking roof makes the point: failure to invest in a new roof when the old one becomes obsolete will cause the repair bill to exceed the amortized cost of a new roof. This healthcheck is simply the equivalent for IT of determining whether household bills are excessive because too much is being spent on maintenance rather than structural repairs. But to get maximum value out of this test we need to go a little beyond this analogy and look at some financial and management aspects of IT.

Customer service

Here the creator of the report means the firm's customers, not the internal customers. The manager for whom this report has been prepared (in this case Charles Suave) will know that the call centre is in the business of handling incoming customer calls, making outgoing calls to customers, and maintaining a website.

'Quotes processed' presumably tells us how many quotes were prepared for customers and sent out, a process in which the IT infrastructure plays a key role. This is an example of a transaction-based metric, because processing a quote can be regarded as a transaction. Transaction-based metrics are generally useful when the transactions drive value added, that is when value is created by those transactions. Here we can assume that there is some correlation between the number of quotes processed and the sales volume, or at least sales number.[7] Transaction-based metrics are generally not useful when the transaction measured does not add value to the business. To take an extreme example, staff purchases of cups of coffee are certainly a transaction, but are irrelevant to the value added to the firm (except possibly for staff trying to stay awake to work late at night).

A less trivial example of a transaction that should probably not be used as a KPI might be the number of quality control rejections. In the case of our example this might be the number of quotes rejected by supervisors. This example raises two important issues for transaction-based metrics. First, in our example the point is not the absolute number of quotes rejected, but the ratio of quotes rejected as a proportion of total quotes. This is precisely what appears on the next but one line of the report. Secondly, it is in practice not always easy to make a clear distinction between those transactions that add value and those that do not. Rejecting a quote is not directly adding value because the result of that action is not seen by the potential customer, and no sale results. However, indirectly it adds value by ensuring that the potential customer gets to see a better average quality of quote.

If the reader is unhappy with this example, then consider a metric based on quality meetings held, (that is meetings about quality, not high-quality meetings about other subjects). This metric was used in all seriousness by one of the world's largest software suppliers in the early 1990s; after this firm made record losses a new management team said, in private, that the efforts to count the number of quality meetings held were a prime example of the loss of management focus on the business basics which contributed to the monumental corporate losses produced by the previous management team. The point is that you as a manager need to be satisfied that any transaction-based metrics used cover transactions that most directly add value to your business unit – don't let advice from so called experts override your common sense too quickly.

There are two lines that use MIPs, or millions of instructions per second. This is one of the IT industry's favourite processing capacity measures. Most people are familiar with bytes, as in, say, a 32 Mb RAM or a 1.44 Mb floppy disk. Where bytes measure storage capacity, MIPs measure processing capacity. More prosaically, bytes are the engine size and MIPs are zero to 60 time. Much attention has been focused within the IT industry and by management consultants on whether MIPs are a good measure of processing capacity, and how to adjust MIP-based metrics for the efficiency with which they are used.[8] This is not the place for a detailed discussion of the merits of MIPs as a measure of the processing capacity of a datacentre or individual IT system. If your IT department measures MIPS, and the likelihood is that someone in a datacentre does, and no better measure of processing capacity is available, then use it in the report. If someone can't convince you in five minutes or less that they have a better capacity measure than MIPs, then it's probably not a better measure.

Why might our MIPS/quote have increased 400% year on year, as shown in the example report? If the quotes produced by our call centre have become substantially more complex the MIPS used per quote may well have increased in this way. Quotes may have become more complex because of the introduction of colour or graphics, or perhaps because of regulatory or other legal requirements, as has been the case in the retail financial services in the US, the UK and many other countries recently. So the value of good KPI reporting is not all one way, it is not just an opportunity for business management to squeeze more out of the IT department's management. A good set of KPIs can be at the heart of a partnership approach between IT and the business units.

In our example, IT management might be able to show the business unit that the new requirements for preparing quotes on the call centre's IT infrastructure has led to a 400% increase in processing capacity required, whereas the increase in dollar costs has been just under 10%. And business managers who understand the real potential of IT will not think the figures of 400% and 10% are unusual. These are exactly the sorts of scale by which business and financial efficiency can improve in some areas in any large business if IT and business management work in close co-operation. The more obvious examples that support this claim are E*Trade, Amazon.com, Cisco, EasyNet and other Internet businesses which have achieved even greater cost reductions and capacity increases, to the extent that they are changing the global economy.

The last item under the customer service heading is 'web availability'. This is a straightforward example of an availability statistic. Other availability statistics include network availability, application availability, helpdesk support availability. In contrast to transaction statistics, availability statistics usually measure the potential availability of a service. The key thing to remember with availability statistics is that if that 99% is not necessarily good if the service is needed at all times, as our web presence probably is for this call centre. If this statistic was presented in days or hours of unavailability instead of as a percentage of availability, it would show that that the call centre's customer website was unavailable for just under three full 24-hour days in the year,[9] or about 69 hours, instead of showing 99.21% availability.

User support (internal customers)

The network reliability statistic seems to be another availability statistic, although it is worth checking this kind of assumption. The same observations apply to network availability statistics as to the web availability statistic just discussed. The more distributed the computing environment is, the more important is network availability as little gets done when every workstation and PC depends on the network being up. However, the more distributed a network, the less likely it is that the whole network will be unavailable all at the same time. This raises the question of how to define 'availability' for distributed networks. Why does this matter to you as a manager? Do you really need to bother with what a distributed network is? It matters to the extent that if there is an unclear, or worse, an 'elastic' definition of what availability means, you may find that your IT staff spend time and money trying to measure availability and producing a statistic that is almost useless. This won't be the IT people's fault if management have not been clear about what availability means.

However, having said this we advise against worrying too much about complex definitions of availability. Find a clear definition, find a definition that works for you as a business manager, and don't spend too much time finding the definition, but do get it agreed between the users, the business management and the IT folk. Agreement can be reached in about six emails. Agree to review your definition after, say, six months to see how it's working. One organization which faced this problem had about 1000 users on a distributed network. It simply picked the 100 most important users, and network availability was defined as availability to these 100 users. Simple, somewhat arbitrary, but it worked very well because it gave IT management and business management a clear metric by which to manage and cost network availability.

The next line counts the number of tickets opened. In running a helpdesk, a 'ticket' is often the term used to refer to an incident for which the user requests help. There are obvious difficulties with using tickets as a metric – such as what should count as a ticket. However, users want problems solved, and to them tickets are irrelevant.[10] Suppose that newly installed software contains a bug and that most users will not notice this bug because it is in a little-used function in the software package. The bug might manifest itself as a printing problem, and as a software conflict problem in another application, and as a colour problem on the screen. This could be three or more tickets from the helpdesk point of view, but is really one problem. Another problem is that individuals in the helpdesk may be motivated to open several tickets for problems they judge to be easily resolvable, and just one ticket for other kinds of problems. So it is not clear that the line for 'number of tickets opened' is useful in controlling costs. When starting an IT efficiency programme, it may be more efficient for the firm to concentrate on improving other metrics than to spend too much time trying to find the perfect helpdesk KPI. Once the rest of IT becomes more efficient, users often tend to perceive the helpdesk as having become more efficient.

The average time to respond to a user probably refers to helpdesk operations. This is certainly a measure of the quality of service, but it is not clear that it passes our test question: does this KPI tell us what anything about what is happening to our IT costs and why, in such a way that we as managers are likely to be able to do something about it? Probably not. This criticism also applies to the two lines measuring the time to respond to calls.

It may seem that the criticism can also apply to how many desktop PCs are moved or rebuilt, or set up as new staff are taken on. This will depend on the particular firm concerned. Physically moving a PC from one desk to another can take half an hour for two support people. Such costs soon add up, and this is before the cost of any technical specialists setting up the machines moved. If a firm is undergoing rapid change or reorganization, the cost of moving desktop PCs or workstations can be substantial, and in several cases freezing desktop PC moves has been an effective way to reduce IT costs, if only in the short-term. Even measuring this cost can help reduce overall costs if it helps in the financial analysis of the business case for new remote desktop software management tools or the introduction of technology to enable any member of staff to work at any PC – so-called 'smart desking'.

The merit of 'systems upgrades' as an IT cost KPI is less obvious. In some cases this will pass the usefulness test for understanding and managing costs, for instance where upgrades initiated by individual users are a significant variable cost. An example of such an environment is a pharmaceutical research laboratory, where individual research teams might need constantly to upgrade specialized research packages or install new packages on their PCs and workstations. On the other hand, where upgrades are performed *en masse* for most of the workforce by an automated process that delivers the software at night over the network with little manual intervention, it is much less likely that a systems upgrade KPI will be useful.

Staffing

Our main interest in IT staffing derives from the fact that a significant cost of IT will be people-related costs. We immediately notice that under this subheading there are no dollar costs. Of course we cannot expect any dollar-cost data that would enable the user of this report to deduce an individual employee's remuneration, even approximately. But given that there are 23 IT employees covered by this section of the KPI report, it would be useful to see an indication of the fully loaded cost per head of IT staff. If this is too sensitive, given the circulation of the report, the manager using this report should certainly obtain this figure if he does not already know it. As an example of actual numbers, in the investment banking industry in 1997 it was normal to assume that the average fully loaded cost of an IT staff member was in the $90 000–$110 000 range, exclusive of bonus payments. This came as a surprise to many managers in that industry, and also to professionally qualified staff working in departments other than IT, such as the legal departments, whose average costs were considerably lower.

The turnover and absence figures in this section of the report are presumably included as they are a major cost driver for the IT department. However, unlike IT staff remuneration policy, which is a firm-wide issue, or the complexity of quotes produced, which is largely a front office management issue, staff turnover and absenteeism within the IT department is probably more within the direct remit of IT management. It is unlikely to be anything that the business unit manager can influence, so probably has no place in this report. However, if there is a big restructuring project in IT, or if staff turnover in IT has been raised by firm management as an issue, it might be sufficiently informative to warrant inclusion. These are also circumstances where the management-to-staff ratios might be sufficiently informative to warrant inclusion in the report.

Efficiency

The efficiency metrics in this report are all ratios, because this is what efficiency is, namely the relationship between inputs and the relevant output. The problem as we have seen throughout the rest of the report is that it is rarely clear exactly what the inputs are and what the output is. It is often even harder to specify these in an accurately measurable way. This is no reason not to try to measure efficiency; an inaccurate measure is often better than no measure at all, and with experience accuracy can be improved. There is an argument that a watch that is five minutes slow is never accurate, whereas a completely broken watch will be exactly right twice each day. But from a practical point of view, most business managers, for example, would find a watch that was accurate to within a few minutes far more useful than one that was precisely right only twice each day. How is this point relevant to controlling IT costs? The point is to go for useful, practical metrics and not to distracted by complete precision. Isn't this just good management sense? What's slightly different about IT is that to succeed in their discipline, IT people are trained to be completely accurate. This requirement can colour the way that IT departments think, and they wouldn't be good IT departments if they didn't.

Some senior managers can be too quick to veto any metric which is unlikely to be completely accurate, whereas in managing IT, some costs can be significantly reduced even if the only management tools are inaccurate.[11] For example, some managers refuse to estimate how much IT projects cost because they feel the estimates are inaccurate. But even if they are inaccurate, even two hours spent trying to estimate the costs can be valuable in controlling costs. A two-hour planning exercise can identify the major sources of cost, and identify which can be controlled and which cannot be controlled. Management can then focus attention on controlling controllable costs, and not expend effort managing uncontrollable costs. Costs which are controllable are new purchases of standardized equipment, such as PCs, telephone services and travel. Costs which are not usually controllable are depreciation on existing equipment, fixed-dollar contracts for services (until the next break clause) and rent (in the short-term). Some costs may be controllable or not controllable depending on the nature and deadlines of the project; an example is overtime costs.

The measure of how many helpdesk tickets were closed per IT staff member raises three points. First, why is it separated from the metric several lines above 'number of tickets opened'? If both these quantities are know, they must have been measured at some point, and so it cannot be too much trouble to provide the average time taken to close a ticket. Secondly, is the right denominator being used here? If this is a measure for cost control, wouldn't 'tickets closed/helpdesk staff member' be better than 'tickets closed/IT staff member', as there will be many IT staff who have nothing to do with the helpdesk.

The fall in $/MIPS year on year seems impressive at first sight, and more so because this month's figure is below budget. However, if the average cost of MIPs is declining at 25% per year, a reasonable assumption, a 17% decline is less spectacular. Of course, MIPs are only part of the departmental cost, staff costs being a major costs unrelated to MIPs. In the lead up to the year 2000 AD, it has not been unusual for IT staff costs to inflate at 20% p.a. or more. On balance, this line is useful but needs to be considered with some judgement and understanding of other factors at work in the firm's IT cost structure.

The next two items, 'quotes/IT staff member' and 'deals closed/IT staff member' are less obviously useful in managing IT costs. Although they are interesting, they probably fall more properly under the exclusive remit of IT departmental management.

Finally, an interesting metric that is just beginning to be used is the last item in the report, 'internal/external bandwidth usage'.[12] It is too early to have heard much comment from business unit managers about the usefulness of this particular metric, but the rationale stems from senior management's concern that staff may be spending too much time looking at the Internet and not enough time working. While there is no evidence that staff do abuse access to the Internet and the World Wide Web more than they abuse access to telephones, paperclips and other office supplies, or even access to employees of the opposite sex, it is a senior management concern in some companies that excessive personal use of the Internet is a major cost driver. We doubt it, but if you don't, this is probably a KPI for you, as it tries to measure the Internet equivalent of incoming versus outgoing calls, and there are software tools to measure this.

Review of Table 2.3 – Sample set of KPIs

Overall, the set of KPIs shown in Table 2.3 is not bad. (For a not so good set of KPIs, see Table 2.4.) You are a lucky manager if having no KPIs you can make one telephone call and receive something like. However, it has a number of weaknesses, which we have reviewed in detail above. Here is a summary of improvements that could be made to this from the point of view of a business unit manager interested in managing IT costs allocated to their business unit:

1. Clarify the meaning of 'total IT spend'. Show spend that hits our department.
2. Show the ratio of development to maintenance costs, including a target figure.
3. Show IT dollars spent per quote, and per request for information (RFI).
4. Remove the lines about helpdesk tickets and the two lines showing percentage of calls resolved, or at least replace all of these with a single line showing the average time taken to resolve issues raised in the tickets. Make it clear that a ticket pertains to the helpdesk.
5. Show the average fully loaded IT staff costs.
6. Combine turnover and absenteeism into a single metric, or delete entirely.
7. Insert a column for the variance between budget and actual.
8. Insert a column showing short-term trends, to supplement the year-on-year trends. Possibilities include a three-month moving average, showing direction of momentum, or a month-on-month change.

3. Are the KPIs accurate?

There is a famous online bank in the UK that advertises itself as being open 24 hours a day seven days a week. Whether this claim is accurate or not depends on whether one ignores several periods a year when no service is available at all, either by telephone or Internet, because 'the computers are upgrading' or 'the computers are offline'. So how accurate is this claim? If the standard of accuracy is set by the standards of what is acceptable for marketing purposes or advertising puff, it doesn't matter that this bank in fact runs a service that is unavailable quite often. However, if the standard is a higher standard of strict legal liability where a customer regards the claim as being material to a contract, then unavailability several times in a couple of months probably does matter.

The point of this anecdote is that what counts as accurate depends on the purpose of the measurement. There are several reasons why as a manager you might want KPIs. For example, you might want KPIs:

Table 2.4 Sample set of KPIs from Superficial Inc.

IT Key performance indicators	Month actual
1 People	
■ IT headcount	23
– of which helpdesk	7
2 Hardware	
■ servers	$36 000
■ clients	$42 000
■ tapestores	$7 100
3 Software	$72 995
4 Networks	
■ access points installed	17
5 Moves and changes	23
■ moves	13
■ changes	10
■ new joiners	5

■ to indicate emerging trends – in effectiveness of equipment, efficiency of staff, in new or in test markets;

■ to ensure that your firm does not trigger expensive penalty clauses in service level agreements;

■ as 'quick and dirty' substitutes for other KPIs that would be more expensive or more difficult to collect.

The accuracy required of KPIs differs in each of these cases. Excessive accuracy is not necessarily a good thing. Often greater accuracy imposes greater cost, and if a more approximate but inexpensive KPI will do just as well as an accurate but expensive KPI, why pay extra? Consider the case where a system has been set up to produce a KPI that shows the trend in the amount of memory used by employees connected to a network of PCs. The purpose of the KPI is to forecast demand for storage so that extra memory can be added before the network hits its capacity, but without wasting money buying unnecessary storage too soon. One way to get the KPI is to record the amount of memory used by all users, but another way is to use a sampling technique to reduce the amount of data used in creating the KPI.

In those cases where we need maximum accuracy in KPIs there is the question of whether the actual KPI data are accurate, or whether errors have somehow crept in.

Usually you probably won't want to second guess the team that provides the KPIs – organizations have to trust their own staff to be competent. But sometimes there may be occasions where it is essential to audit the accuracy of a KPI. Where the original team is trusted they can simply be assigned to do some more work to verify their original findings. One way to do this is for them to show other metrics that are consistent with the KPI: for instance, by having changed in the same way over a period of time, and for them to show under what conditions an error could exist in a KPI, and why those conditions do not apply. Where the team that created the original KPI cannot be trusted or where the original team is no longer available, a team of outside IT consultants or accountants can usually help, for a fee.

4. Are there gaps in the KPIs?

KPIs evolve. The set of KPIs that were perfect for management's requirements two years ago will not be perfect today, even if there have been no changes to the organization, its people, its product or its customers. This is a corollary of the old management saying, 'manage what you measure.' As people or organizations learn that they are being evaluated according to a set of criteria, their behaviour will generally change to avoid the disadvantages of this fact or to take advantage of it. This is not limited to the IT world. Trains in Britain in the 1980s were often late, so people bought cars and drove themselves about their business instead of taking trains, which caused congested roads, pollution, and greater losses than ever for the train companies as fewer people bought tickets. The government researched the problem and found that people would use the trains if they were more punctual. So new regulations were introduced whereby the railways had to compensate customers if the trains were late beyond a certain degree. For a few golden years in the early 1990s, it was possible to travel extensively by taxi at the railway's expense because paying for customers who were waiting for late trains to go by taxi was far cheaper than paying the compensation. While this was great for the customers, it was not good for the train companies, whose trains were now not just late but also empty because the customers were travelling by taxi at the train company's expense. Then they padded out their timetables so that a journey which had once taken just over two hours would be transformed into a three and a half hour journey, the extra time allowing for almost all delays that were normal in the original timetable. This meant that the threat of having to compensate customers no longer had any effect on the train companies, as they would no longer have to pay for expensive taxi journeys. It also meant that all the people who had started using the train again because it had become a reliable way to travel stopped using it. The system had moved from having timetables showing fast trains with trains that were often actually slow to having slow timetables with trains to match. At the time of writing, the timetables are back to the fast speeds of 15 years ago, and the trains are fairly punctual, but so many people try to get on them that they are too crowded and passengers often have to stand for their whole journey. The train companies and the train regulators each evolved new strategies to deal with the old rules. And the same applies in IT management: IT and the organization it serves will both evolve and adapt in response to each other. This means that a KPI that was very effective two years ago may be ineffective or even counter productive now, just as the UK train companies added hours to timetabled journeys to ensure they could be 'punctual' without ever having to be competent.

IT has another dimension to this co-evolutionary race between the IT infrastructure and the organization it serves. IT advances very fast, as everyone knows. This means that some KPIs become obsolete just because new technology makes them irrelevant. Twenty years ago computers were very expensive, but now PCs are cheap and plentiful: twenty years ago, there may have been good reason to take CPU time per user per week as a KPI by which to manage the efficiency of a data processing centre. Conversely, three years ago, there was far less need for KPIs to measure the effectiveness of an organization's anti-virus measures, but as the potency and pervasiveness of viruses has increased there is now a need for an appropriate KPI in many organizations.

As a rule of thumb, practitioners seem to indicate that they believe that at least 5%–10% of KPIs used should be changed every year in a well-run organization that already has KPIs and has several years' experience of managing them. In those organizations where the state of KPI usage is more fluid, anything up to a total change of KPIs may be in order.

5. Are there controls associated with the KPIs?

Indicators are pointless if the indications are not acted on. Just as there is no point having a computer or any other asset that sits ignored and unused until obsolescence: there is no point going to the trouble and expense of creating and implementing KPIs if there is no control mechanism put in place to ensure that the message from the KPIs is used. For example, an organization might choose to set up a KPI of IT cost per head, but this will be a waste of time if all that happens is the IT cost per head is presented at a quarterly management meeting and be forgotten about.

One approach to checking that controls are associated with KPIs is given in the matrix in Table 2.5. The purpose of such a table is to check that each KPI is actually doing something. It does assume a knowledge of the intended purpose of each KPI. For instance, the KPI of Total IT Spend has the associated control of cutting discretionary IT spend. This means that if total IT spend breaches some limit, for example as a proportion of total firm expenses or as a proportion of net revenue, then IT spending should be cut. It is easiest to cut discretionary items; specific examples include:

- a freeze on the purchase of new PCs, printers and fax machines;
- postponement of mainframe or router purchases;
- a freeze on moves and changes;
- skipping the next software update on software that constitutes major cost;
- reducing service levels in maintenance contracts;
- postponing routine functionality upgrades to custom software.

An alternative to freezes in this list is to require a higher sign-off authority than before, which usually has the effect of reducing demand for the item or service in question.

In short, KPIs indicate whether or not management action is required. A KPI is not worth having if no action is taken when a KPI indicates it should be, and such redundant KPIs should be replaced or scrapped unless management will change to act in response to the KPI.

Table 2.5   Example report showing controls associated with KPIs

KPI	Associated controls	Who is responsible for implementing control?	When last used	How effective is the KPI/control pair?
Total IT spend; IT spend per employee	Cut discretionary IT spend	Finance Director; IT Steering Committee	October 1998	Effective; there may be special cases (e.g. Y2K) when big projects cause a blip in IT spend, but these can be stripped out of the figures by the IT Committee
Ratio of development spend to maintenance spend	Find new IT capital projects that will reduce overall maintenance need	CIO; IT Steering Committee	September 1999	Works reasonably well, although there is a constant risk that budget squeezes cut new projects which are projected to reduce maintenance spend considerably
Website availability to customers	(1) Invest in band width availability (2) E-commerce team incentive bonus	E-commerce team; CIO	Used almost every month	Could be more effective, but problem is the unpredictability of demand on our site and recent problems with hackers. Incentive bonus control needs to be used lightly

6. Do the controls work?

This question is an extension of the previous question. Take the example of cutting discretionary IT spend in response to a KPI that measures total IT spend: the control action initiated by a KPI must be effective. This point may seem obvious, and it may seem that question six is not worth including in the list. We include it because managers are often adept at evading controls. In one London bank, when a reduction on discretionary IT spend was applied and the purchase of all new PCs was explicitly prohibited for a period, dozens of machines were in fact purchased with the costs being expensed as entertainment. The result was that there were controls associated with KPIs, but the controls did not work.

7. How efficiently can the KPIs or controls be used?

KPIs and controls cost money to implement. They also risk the credibility of those involved in creating them, and the process of setting them up uses up goodwill in an organization. This is true of many managerial activities, but it should be born in mind when creating KPIs, and in particular it is a reason to try to leverage good or proven KPIs as much as possible. Where a KPI exists or is to be implemented, what else can it be used for. Can two controls share one KPI? Can different KPIs validate each other? Can two KPIs be merged into one? Do any existing KPIs overlap? Six months after KPIs have been implemented, it is often worth comparing all KPIs and asking these questions. The process need not take more than half an hour for an individual or a small team. Often the IT steering committee will perform such a review.

Healthcheck 2: standardization/variety test

Generally speaking, in IT standardization reduces costs and variety increases costs. This fundamental principle has been used to drive costs down and increase efficiency in mass production. Eli Whitney won a contract to provide the US army with 10 000 muskets in 1798[13] because he standardized parts, which allowed mass production, in other words, low-cost production. Standardization has been called 'the decisive and most American innovation'.[14] Standardization applies just as much to intangible engineering such as software as it does to more tangible engineering such as disk drives, silicon chips or bridges and cars. One way to understand the mechanism of standardization in lowering costs is to approach it from the model of the learning curve and minimum efficient scales,[15] and this shows why standardization is a major factor in managing IT, including software, as it is in longer-established branches of engineering.

It is easiest to think of the standardization of industrial and consumer goods, things that hurt if they drop on your toes, but standardization has been applied also to intangibles other than IT software. In the 1950s and 1960s General Electric of the US standardized management training,[16] so that its business would be run no longer by specialists in the business performed by the unit, but by 'general managers who would transcend functional specialisms.'[17] There were at least three potential sources of efficiency in General Electric's approach here. First, reduced cost of management training by applying mass production techniques. Secondly, increased utilization of managers because managers who have undergone a common, standardized training are more easily interchangeable between jobs and more easily replaced by a fellow manager should the need arise. Thirdly, improved teamwork among managers from better communications arising from a shared understanding of common concepts and models. In this last point, the words 'synergy' or 'efficiency' or 'critical mass' can be substituted for 'teamwork' as taste requires.

Of course, none of these claims is entirely uncontroversial, and the extent to which anything in human nature can be standardized through training is a rich field of debate.[18] For the purpose of managing our IT costs, let us not get distracted by this debate; we need assume only that there is at least some efficiency to be gained in management and the production of intangibles, in our particular case in IT, by learning from standardization and other techniques of mass production. Even firms of lawyers have started to adopt standardized training for junior lawyers instead of the old apprenticeship system.

Consider the case of an international retail and commercial bank, with branches predominantly in the Americas and Europe. The core business of the bank was taking retail deposits, running current accounts (checking accounts), and making commercial loans. These activities ran on a kind of system generically known as the SBS, or standard banking system. Peripheral products such as letters of credit and foreign currency transactions were handled by various plug-in software components. Each country in which the bank operated had two mainframes running SBS, one of which was a backup to the other. The bank's strategic planning department conducted an efficiency review, which began by investigating why each business needed two mainframes. Usage statistics showed that only one of the mainframes was used at any one time in each country. This was because the second mainframe was kept as a backup, or in the language of IT, for 'disaster recovery' purposes.

The sort of disaster envisaged as most likely in the risk management plan of the bank was fire, although in some countries earthquakes, sabotage and terrorist bombs were also judged significant risks. It was disconcerting for the strategic planners to find that many of the disaster recovery machines were close enough to the primary mainframes to stand some chance of also being affected by the risk envisaged. With recent improvement in telecommunications and data networking, it would be a better management of risk as well as a massive cost reduction to use the spare capacity of a primary machine in one country for disaster recovery of another country's machine, as well as saving money by eliminating all back-up machines. At first this looked an easy change to make, because there were only two kinds of mainframes used and enough of each kind to provide the necessary disaster recovery capacity. However, the data protection laws of some of the countries involved prohibited the transmission of personal data such as that in the SBS to other countries. This was solved by relatively inexpensive data encryption. The cost of installing the necessary data transmission and encryption technology was $3.5m in the current year, and the savings that would accrue were about $15m over three years.

The problem was that each country used either a different operating systems or version of operating systems, or a different version of the SBS software. A short investigation showed that there was no significant economic benefit to any local branch in using its own preferred software version, this situation had arisen merely because there had been no standardized approach to software procurement and upgrading. It took some effort to get all the branches on to one of the same two sets of software, and an investment of a further $3m. However, the result was a cash windfall of $2.3m from the sale of surplus mainframes, a reduction of over $4m a year in maintenance and running costs, and the elimination of several expensive-looking projects that would have had to have been initiated in each local branch to ensure Year 2000 compliance, and the elimination of some projects to ensure EMU conversion. Such are the benefits in IT cost management of standardization.

How standardized is your IT support organization?

Ask your IT support for details of the variety of systems supporting your business. This is a straightforward exercise. You want to end up with something like Table 2.6. This is a fairly typical chart for an organization where there has been no strong culture of standardization, or 'techno fascism' as it is sometimes rather chillingly termed. In a large firm it is not always possible to obtain a complete inventory of hardware and software, hence the estimates and approximations in this chart. On the other hand, in gathering this data always make a note of intentions for new equipment purchases and equipment retirement as they are discovered. Like all management, the trick in managing IT costs is to manage the future, not the present.

Similar charts should be produced for software, including software tools and operating systems. Does diversity really drive costs so much, and does standardization really reduce costs so much? It does, absolutely. Management literature is full of examples that support this claim;[19] veterans of managing IT costs will be aware of even more from their own experience; and there is a view that the big management consultancies, have made their fortunes because of their clients' reluctance to standardize software. Consider the case of a large US manufacturing operation – call it X-Corp – with regional plants in the US, the UK, Hong Kong and Singapore. X-Corp made essentially the same product in all three locations, and it sold products from one manufacturing utility to the markets in other regions as temporary shifts in demand necessitated.

Despite the plants all performing the same function, and despite the IT hardware being mostly of the same series from the same manufacturer (over 80% commonality), different software was used. Europe and Asia used two different versions of proprietary software, and the US used a third piece of software, from a third-party

Table 2.6 Standardization/variety chart for IT hardware

Equipment	Canada/US	Latin America	Europe
Mainframes			
IBM 9670	1 (request for funding +3)	22	6 (5 from August)
DEC VAX 4000 series	16	3 (to be eliminated Dec.)	8
DEC VAX 3000 series	6	0	2
Fujistu	3	1	–
LAN servers			
HP	22	7	12 (probables)
IBM		8	6
Tandem		5	3
PCs			
Apple Power PC	200	3	26 (corporate finance only)
Dell	853	–	–
IBM Thinkpad	70 approx	unidentified number	652
IBM Desktop	many	many	34
Compaq	–	771	some??

manufacturer. Whenever standardization was mentioned, senior management would be told that Europe and Asia used the same software. This was true to the extent that the software and hardware had been the same in 1982, but in the intervening years the two versions had each been modified independently and had therefore grown apart. They had become about as different as Karl Marx and Groucho Marx; they share the same name, but not too much else. In fact, whenever there was a need to prove to senior management that the two versions were the same, it was pointed out that they had the same name. This distracted senior management so much that senior management never really bothered about the third version in the US that not only had a completely different name but was also a third different system doing the same job.

Before laughing too loudly you may wish to check that the same kind of problem is not costing your organization several millions of dollars a year in unnecessary costs. Middle management in IT in X-Corp knew that it was wasting millions of dollars per year from two main inefficiencies. First, three sets of maintenance costs were being incurred instead of one. Secondly, the Europe and Asia systems ran on a proprietary operating system instead of an industry standard system. This meant that maintenance of the proprietary operating system was shared with no other company; in fact all the programmers had retired from the original vendor, and now worked as freelancers, at three to four times the normal rates because they knew they were indispensable to X-Corp. In short, X-Corp had one of the most expensive production systems in the world. So why didn't senior management do anything? For two reasons. First, as we have seen, they never really had the confidence in their own understanding of their own IT organization to get beyond the fact that two of their systems had the same name. Secondly, they were distracted by Year 2000 costs, which had ballooned to more than ten times the original estimate and by then dominated the rest of the IT budget.

By now the argument for standardization as a means of cost control in large IT organizations should be clear. One of the aims of this chapter is to answer this question: does the information from the healthcheck tell us what is happening to our IT costs and why, in such a way that we as managers are likely to be able to do something about it? This question is addressed by our next healthcheck, and is about the diversity or standardization of IT systems, and requires more judgement, and perhaps rather more work than the last healthcheck. The aim is simply to measure diversity and determine whether excess diversity in the IT support for which your business unit pays is causing excessive IT costs. Put another way, is there a significant opportunity to reduce costs by imposing standardization? If there is, the opportunities for cost reduction will mainly fall in the following areas:

1. a reduction in the requirement for hardware, operating systems and applications as synergies are achieved by moving to fewer different models and versions;

2. a reduction in maintenance costs by using more industry standard software and relying less on custom software (in effect, the maintenance and development costs of standard products are shared over a much greater customer base than proprietary systems, leaving your business unit able to concentrate proprietary resources on the areas offering greatest value add);

3. increased labour flexibility as you can recruit from a larger labour pool and deploy staff on a wider range of tasks when standardized equipment and software is used rather than proprietary software;

4. potential balance sheet improvements as standard equipment is more easily re-sold, or at least priced in a market, than proprietary equipment.

The business unit manager must derive his own measure of systems variety, but the IT department will usually have someone who has done this kind of work before, and probably even has someone working on it right now. If not, there are any number of IT consultancies or management consultancies who will be happy to help. An example of the kind of approach required is the scoring chart shown in Table 2.7.

Scoring the tests

It might take a month or two to get to the point where you have scores for the tests. If you have used scoring similar to the charts for the two healthchecks shown in Tables 2.1 and 2.7, then it is likely that your IT support charges are in the state of health shown in Table 2.8.

Table 2.7 Systems variety: scoring chart

Result	Score
For all software applications and operating systems used for the same purpose, at least 80% are the same type and version	12
For each type of mainframe and midrange computer, at least 80% are the same model or series; and at least 60% of PCs and laptops are of from the same manufacturer	18
At least 80% of LAN/WAN servers are from the same manufacturer	5
For all software applications and operating systems used for the same purpose, at least 50% but less than 80% are the same type and version	6
For each type of mainframe and midrange computer, at least 50% but less than 80% are the same model or series; and at least 25% of PCs and laptops are from the same manufacturer	4
At least 30% of LAN/WAN servers are from the same manufacturer	2
There is a plan in place supported by the IT director and at least either the CEO or the CFO to start moving towards the above state of affairs in the next 12 months	8

Remember that these scores are only ballpark indicators of some parts of the IT efficiency investigation. The more qualitative aspects have been covered in the tests and we suggest that they be summarized in a paragraph above whatever scoring approach the reader decides to adopt. Above all, remember that to reduce costs as quickly as possible, the whole exercise must be conducted in an attitude of partnership with the IT function.

Table 2.8 Scoring the tests

Score	Result
>50	Your IT department is exceptionally well run
40–49	Your IT department is very well run, and you should probably have no major concerns
30–40	Your IT department is reasonably well run, although there are a few opportunities to make cost reductions and the tests will have indicated areas for management focus. Find out what is being done in these areas, and what the inefficiencies are costing
20–30	There are probably major opportunities to reduce IT costs
< 20	There are almost certainly major areas for IT cost reduction, and it may be worth investigating outsourcing of parts or the whole of your IT support

Healthcheck 3: inspect the physical IT assets

We have seen that a large part of improving IT efficiency is about eliminating duplication. In practice, management tends to eliminate duplication in tangible assets more readily than duplication in intangible assets, and this causes problems especially when it comes to information technology resources. Imagine how long 100% duplication in traditional manufacturing plant and equipment would be tolerated – those hundreds of expensive spare machine tools, pristine but undriven forklift trucks, and mountains of stock turning over barely once per year would soon be axed by management, with or without the help of just-in-time, total quality management, business process re-engineering or some other technique of the moment. Many managers today find it much harder to recognize inefficiencies in their IT than they would find it to recognize inefficiencies in warehousing, distribution, manufacturing processes or more established administrative procedures such as human resources.

It can be a salutary experience for a non-IT manager to visit a datacentre, the place where mainframes and servers are located. Go there and ask what each box does, maybe even count them. More than one manager who has made such a visit has found boxes being maintained which supposedly supported businesses sold off, closed down or transferred to a sister company a long time ago. One manager in Europe found that his department was paying for equipment that recorded the telephone conversations of his competitors. Before it was sold off as a separate entity, the competitor had been part of this manager's own organization. When the business was sold off, no one had made any plans to do anything with the backup telephone call recording equipment, and ever since all calls to and from the call centre had been taped on equipment paid for by this manager's department. This cost was completely avoidable, possibly exposed both firms to considerable litigation risk, and would have been avoided had someone made a simple physical inspection of the IT assets earlier. It is not unknown for such visits to count a number of machines one day, and one more the next, when no purchase orders had been signed for an extra machine. In such cases the extra machine has been made up from spare parts, if so this suggests poor management and cost controls, and also money wasted in carrying an excessive inventory of spare parts.

There is a tendency in large organizations to rely on staffwork and reports, and to leave physical inspection to others. We believe that even for the manager who feels little acquainted with IT, perhaps especially for this manager, spending a few hours having a look around the datacentre or its equivalent can be valuable. If the datacentre is a continent away, it is probably still worth somebody with a fresh perspective making a visit. An executive once travelled half way around the world partly to make such a visit, and found that because so few people made such a long journey, the local management had been running IT as if no one but their own small team would ever make a physical inspection of hardware. As it happened they were running an efficient operation, but their reports back to head office did not represent the full picture of their IT operations. This was a pity because this operation was one of the best in the whole group and the other businesses could have leveraged off many innovations and practices developed by their remote colleagues.

Site visits are usually very easy to arrange, not least because the managers of datacentres rarely receive any attention from the rest of the organization, and are usually regarded as little more than the guardians of a dull collection of boxes, whereas the fact is that if they did not do their jobs well the whole organization would suffer severely. Any IT line manager should be able to arrange a visit to one of your organization's datacentres.

Possible questions to ask or things to have in mind when making a site visit:

1. What does each box do?

2. How many computers are there, and how many different models of computer are there?

3. Could space utilization be improved, for instance by stacking boxes differently?

4. Where are the spares kept?

5. Are there any significant items of equipment not in use, for instance special printers or back-up tape drives? How essential are these?

6. What ideas do the datacentre staff have for cost reduction? Who else has asked for their input recently, and what has been done as a result?

Summary

This chapter described three tests that the business manager can use to estimate the efficiency of their IT support. By using these tests you should be able to form your own view of the value of your IT support. The chapter gave many real life examples, for instance, RedBank and GreenStore, which show that significant improvements in IT efficiency are possible. The chapter also emphasized that it is unlikely to be the IT department that is to be the most to blame for inefficiencies in IT, and moreover the issue should not be to look back and find fault, but to focus on how to make IT usage in future more efficient, and this is as much if not more the province of business management than IT management alone. Many organizations have brought about big improvements in IT efficiency not by large, unwieldy and expensive programmes of change, but by small teams supported by senior management, which can often deliver huge value at low cost.

The three tests introduced in the chapter were:

1. KPI healthcheck

2. standardization/variety test

3. physical asset inspection.

KPIs will make managing your IT much easier, and if you already have a good set of KPIs then you are ahead of most managements. Don't expect new KPIs to be perfect from the start, it takes time to optimize them and to get used to using them for their greatest value, and imperfect KPIs are better than no KPIs at all. KPIs should become a standard management tool for IT, and will help your IT become highly efficient.

As in other areas of business, variety in IT creates inefficiencies and limits your ability to change how you do business. Your organization needs some degree of variety in order to be able to do its business, but do you know how varied your IT is, and what costs are being generated by needless variety? Management tends to focus most on the variety of IT hardware, but the variety of operating systems and other software is at least as important from an efficiency point of view as IT hardware.

It is often worth making a personal inspection of those IT assets for which you pay. Few managers ever make such inspections, but they are easy to make, and will give a very quick but reliable feel for how efficiently IT is being run. Many managers who have done this have found they were paying for too big an inventory of spare parts of too many systems.

Good managers have all the skills necessary to conduct these simple tests. These three tests have saved hundreds of millions of dollars and ensured that opportunities worth hundreds of millions more have been available through efficient IT organizations instead of being lost forever. These tests can make a difference to you and your organization.

Endnotes

1 The figure of 20% is based on standard outsourcing industry assumptions, readily obtained from those in the industry. In addition, ie see, for instance, the comments of Everest Software Corp. (1996) ; Asda and IBM (Hollinger, 1997); Eastman Kodak (Foremski, 1997).

2 Johnston (1996).

3 Karolefski (1997). The other three elements besides IT are design and manufacturing, go-to market system, and organizational structure.

4 Internal rate of return defined in Appendix.

5 Net present value defined in Appendix.

6 © 1998 by GartnerGroup, Inc. (Potter, 1998).

7 The distinction between number and volume can be significant in thinking through what drives costs, especially IT costs. Volume = number x price. If a bookstore sells one $5 book each to ten customers, the number of sales is ten, and the sales volume is 10 x $5 = $50.

8 For a term that is relatively widely understood within IT departments and often used within them for management and control purposes, surprisingly little of the great MIPS debate has been documented in the standard texts. However, for a thorough overview of the controversy and key issues, see Strassmann (1995).

9 (100% − 99.21%) x 365 days = 2.88 days = 69 hrs, 12 mins.

10 This claim can easily be tested in your organization. Next time you call the helpdesk, don't record the reference number you are given, and see whether it takes any longer to fix the

problem. Most helpdesks can easily find the fault log from your name or telephone extension number. In fact, if you log two problems in separate calls to the helpdesk and each is assigned a different log number, some helpdesks will initiate two separate actions to fix the problem. One way to immediately make helpdesks more efficient is simply to abolish numerical logs of problems and track all faults by username. Bureaucracies like assigning human beings numbers, but successful growing businesses tend to treat people as people, and it seems that this is as much a point about sound business practice as about morality.

11 A historical example of the success that can be achieved with even the crudest metrics is the French direction finding service in the Great War (1914–19). Ideally a direction finding service consists of two separate radio receivers which show the direction of an enemy signal. The directions of the enemy signal from the two receivers are then plotted on a map, and the enemy is located at the intersection of the signals. France lacked suitable radio receivers, but was fortunate enough to have very good management of its codebreaking service. Using no metric other than the radio operator's perception of whether a signal was faint, loud or very loud, the French had correctly located most German radio stations within two weeks of the outbreak of war simply by drawing concentric circles. This is the best example we know to show that effective measures don't have to be accurate. (Kahn, 1996).

12 I am grateful to H.J. Nokes, late of the high technology investment bank Quartz Capital Partners, for drawing my attention to the emergence of this metric in KPIs.

13 This example is from Shapiro (1999). Any history of the industrial revolution or standard economic history will cover this issue in detail.

14 Landes (1998) p.301.

15 A good treatment of the learning curve from the perspective of IT in business is Sichel (1997), esp. p.108.

16 It is not difficult to think of earlier examples. Several MBA courses predate the GE management training scheme, but the earliest plausible answer we know of is the standardization of military staffwork by the Prussian general staff, which was first permanently established in the 1790s (Schellendorff, 1893). One could trace standardization all the way back to the beginnings of recorded history, via the Spartan standardization of schooling their children, but it is perhaps more useful to distinguish standardization where the principal aim is to increase efficiency from standardization aimed at other ends, such as political or ideological objectives.

17 Kay (1993) p.339.

18 And has been since at least Plato (360BC). Plato's *Phaedrus*, discusses the extent to which human knowledge, including knowledge of how to do things, or skill, is codifiable, and at least one well-known Swiss investment bank has used *Phaedrus* as inspiration for its approach to intellectual capital management. Codification is the preceding, and hardest, step to the standardization of knowledge, one of the goals of so much of the present 'Intellectual Capital Management' movement. (See, for example, Stewart 1997.) However, Dilbert (Adams, 1996) is probably the most recent analysis of the limitations of this approach to human behaviour and its management by applying the techniques of mass production.

19 See, for example, Grindley (1995) *passim*. For a less staid, in fact a less accountant like approach to this issue, see Kelly (1994).

3 Cost allocations

What they are and why they matter

The smell of all money is sweet.

Vespasian

Introduction

This chapter will help you win the cost allocations war over who ends up overpaying for IT costs in your organization. Cost allocation is the process by which general business costs are charged back to specific business units, and a more detailed description is given below. Cost allocation is one of the most tedious subjects on the planet. However, despite being dull, allocations are vital to the profit and loss position of your department, which is a good reason for understanding them better. Water purification is also considered a fairly dull subject, but just as a town which neglects to purify its water will vanish from the map of the country, so a business unit which fails to watch how costs are allocated to it will vanish just as certainly. Your organization is full of other business units who, wittingly or unwittingly, would love to offload some of their costs on to your department. One of the most effective ways to do this is through the allocation of IT costs. By the end of this chapter you will be able do three things: first, determine whether your department is being charged more than its fair share of IT costs, secondly, if it is being so overcharged, to identify what mechanism is enabling those excess costs to be charged to you, and finally, to make your case for changing your IT cost allocations. This approach is simple, and has worked for many businesses in the US and the rest of the world, and it can work for you also.

The chapter is in three main parts. First, we look at what allocations are and why they are important; many readers will be familiar with this, and can skip to the next section. In the middle part we look at IT-specific issues in cost allocations, covering the difficulty in applying the general principles of sound cost allocation to IT. In order to do this, the main kinds of IT cost will be explained, together with problems specific to allocating each kind of IT cost. The last part of the chapter sets out an action plan to achieve our aim; that is, to identify whether your department or business unit is being unfairly allocated IT costs: if you are being unfairly treated we need to define the exact form the unfairness takes, and then decide what steps to take to get fairer IT cost allocations.

At this point it is also perhaps worth briefly considering the question 'What if everyone did that?' – meaning, what if all the people involved tried to reduce their IT cost allocations? Wouldn't the organization as a whole suffer? This issue concerns senior management, strategic planning departments and policymakers, who have an interest in the health of the organization as a whole. There are two quite independent answers to the question 'What if everyone did that?' Both show that it would in fact be a good thing if all managers in a firm took a keen interest in cost allocations. From the practical point of view, it is simply a fact of business life that most business unit managers do fight the allocations 'war', so it is already almost the case that 'everyone does that.' What happens in this case is that the few individual managers of business units who don't play the allocations game see their departments vanish as more and more of the rest of the organization's costs are loaded onto them. It is not necessarily a good thing for the business units to be subsidized, because it will lead management to make poor capital allocation decisions. Secondly, from a theoretical point of view, if every business unit competes to reduce its allocation, then the efficiency of the internal market for resources within the organization increases. It is better to have an efficient internal market for resources than a market that hides valuable resources from those best able to use them.

What are cost allocations and why do they matter?

There are two objectives in allocating IT costs. First, allocations are a means of controlling the underlying costs of an organization. Secondly, allocations are vital to ensuring accurate performance measurement. If your organization has a significant IT spend, then one of your interests in how IT costs are allocated will be to ensure that IT costs are properly controlled. Besides this, if you have any input to the assessment of the IT management's performance, you will have a further interest in ensuring that you base your input to this process on reliable information. Otherwise some fault in the allocation process could mean that you unintentionally reward poor IT managers while discouraging effective IT managers. Similarly, if IT affects any processes by which you or your department are evaluated, then you may have an interest in ensuring that nothing in the way IT costs are allocated diminishes your reputation or remuneration.

Within a company there are two kinds of costs, direct costs and allocated costs. Direct costs are those where the business unit that has incurred the cost is readily identifiable. For instance, if Mr Jones of the Sales department of SuperGizmo Inc. makes a video specifically to help close a sale to a client, and then the client goes ahead and places a large order, then the cost of making the video should be charged directly against the cost of this sale. But consider the cost of running the head office of SuperGizmo Inc., or even of just paying its CEO. The CEO helps out in some sales, but he also contributes to research, development, marketing, human resources, financing and general management. It's not possible to keep an accurate, detailed tally of where the CEO's effort go; it's not possible to do this at the same level of detail as, say, it is for where the cost of the sales video should go. Such 'overhead' costs are nonetheless real costs and are necessary to the business. The CEO's work is spread over too many projects, too many parts of the firm, and the pay-offs are far less quantifiable (although probably far larger and in a sense, more important). The CEO's costs are therefore allocated. Figure 3.1 shows the scheme at a high level. Now it is important to know how this general scheme is in fact implemented in your particular organization, but if you start with the high-level scheme in mind, then it is straightforward to work through to the detailed implementation. It is particularly important for managers with budget responsibility to understand what principles are used to allocate IT costs, and how those principles are implemented, or to have a deputy who understands. Later in the chapter we look at just how to develop the sort of understanding needed in such situations with a simple one-page form.

Case study | Theory and practice in allocating IT costs – an example

As an example of the difference between the principle a company may believe it is using to allocate IT costs and what actually happens, consider the case of a leading US bank. Department heads had agreed that the cost of all modifications and changes to the bank's core banking IT systems should be allocated on the basis of hours spent programming for each customer department. So if, for example, the foreign exchange department had requested a modification to the core banking system to handle euros, then this work would be billed internally to the foreign exchange department. The intention was that each programmer or other IT professional would fill in a timesheet with the project code number, and the financial controllers would allocate the costs according to which customer department owned that project code.

However, there were two problems in implementation.

■ First of all, the financial controllers were working off an out-of-date list of project codes, so they allocated 15% of total costs to the wrong departments.

■ Secondly, IT staff would write down on the forms that they had spent more time on Year 2000 related projects than they really had done, and far less time on all other projects.

In this way the Year 2000 project subsidized all other projects in the firm. The problem was that some of the large but low-margin departments had been allocated fixed percentages of the Year 2000 costs. When the Year 2000 project came in at over four times the estimated cost, the effect was that large, low-margin, departments were subsidizing smaller, high-margin departments for not just a few percentage points, but for fully 60% of all IT costs. According to one senior manager, these large departments had been 'stuffed'. She and others responsible for P&L in the large, low-margin, departments had only token bonuses. And all because the allocation system had taken money from them and given it, free of charge, to the IT infrastructure in small, high-risk and high-margin, new departments.

The cost allocation process and its problems

The problem in allocating fixed costs tends to be different from those in allocating variable costs. One difference is that by their nature, fixed costs are often more predictable than variable costs. The rent for premises on a datacentre, a fixed cost, is usually more predictable than, for instance, the cost of overtime payments, a variable cost. A second and related difference is that, often, fixed costs are less controllable than variable costs. For example, little can be done in the short-term about the depreciation charge on a mainframe, but overtime payments in the helpdesk can be eliminated by suspending overtime working for a limited period.

One of the problems in allocating fixed costs is the withdrawal problem. Suppose that three business units share premises and split the costs equally. If one business unit were to vacate the premises, then either it must continue to pay its one-third share of the cost of the premises, or the other two business units must increase their share from a third to a half of the premises costs (unless another occupant is found). The danger then is that a race develops not to be last to vacate a building where other business units are starting to leave. This is just one example of the way in which poorly designed allocation principles can induce bad business management. Well-designed though poorly implemented principles can have exactly the same effect.

Some fixed costs, such as floorspace in use, are easy to attribute to a business unit. Just as with variable costs, the common sense principle is to charge these costs back to the business units according to actual usage. However, it is often difficult in practice to see exactly how much of a particular fixed asset is used by a business unit.

For allocating variable costs within an organization, the general and commonsense principle is to allocate costs to those business units that cause the variance. It's only right that if a particular business unit incurs travel costs – a classic example of a variable cost – then it should bear those travel costs itself. This much is obviously right and fair. In this way all variable costs would be allocated to the business units generating them according to how much actual cost each generated.

The main problems that you are likely to encounter in cost allocations are typically especially severe when it is IT costs that are being allocated. This means that IT cost allocations can significantly reduce the profitability of your business unit. The example given earlier, of when the organization is paying rent for unused floor space, illustrated the practical difficulties of deciding who bears what proportion of costs when there is no obvious allocation principle. Keeping with that example, there are many good reasons for having unused space: an organization may take a lease on larger premises than it needs in anticipation of future needs from growth, or the most suitable and economical office space available may be larger in total than is required. But having a good reason for the organization's incurring additional cost is not the same thing as having a principle on which to allocate that cost.

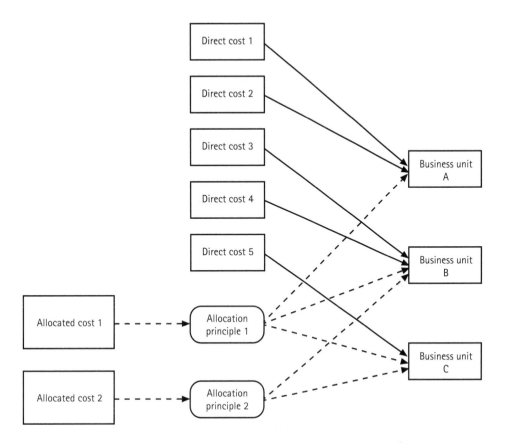

The key point is that whereas direct costs fall against a business unit directly, allocated costs need to go through some process, based on an allocation principle, in which they are divided up between several business units. It is vital to understand the allocation principle and how it is implemented in as a business process, at least at high level, for your major IT costs. Note also that not all allocated costs go to all business units.

Fig. 3.1 Directly charged costs and allocated costs

Sometimes there simply is no good allocation principle, and one of the consequences is that business units can always make a plausible case for changing the allocation principle in use.

The three main problems you are likely to encounter in cost allocations generally are:

1. It may be unclear which business units should bear costs.

2. There may be many good allocation principles to choose from, each of which has a different effect.

3. The distinction between fixed and variable costs may be unclear in practice.

Unclear which business units should bear costs

The second kind of problem is where it's not clear where the allocated costs should go. How does this differ from there being no obvious way in principle on which to allocate costs? We saw earlier that costs must ultimately be matched to revenue. Suppose that for some costs, it is agreed within an organization that the best way to allocate a certain cost is on the basis of usage. An example might be the problem of allocating the cost of a subsidized staff restaurant, in which case this principle would mean that the subsidy would be allocated according to who ate meals, or some combination of who ate the meals and their cost. The problem here will be that although costs must ultimately be matched to profit centres, many departments in an organization will not be profit centres. This principle tells us how to allocate the costs incurred by employees of revenue-generating departments to those departments, but does not tell us how to allocate the costs incurred by employees of non-revenue-generating departments.

Recent examples of the problem of having an agreed allocation principle but disagreement on which business units should pay include corporate Internet projects. Everyone agrees that the company should have a better website, and that costs should be allocated to those business units that benefit. The problem is deciding who benefits.

Many good allocation principles to choose from

The third kind of problem is where there clearly should be an allocation, but there are many principles on which costs could reasonably and fairly be allocated. Take our example of the staff restaurant again. Suppose that some staff need to stay late regularly. Further, suppose that the staff who need to stay late are from support units and not revenue-generating business units, and that they provide support to all functions of the firm. Now because of overtime costs, it is more expensive more to run the restaurant early in the morning and late at night than at midday. So there is a cost allocation issue because it appears that in money terms, greater charges per head would need to be applied to support unit staff than to revenue-generating staff, overall. The issue here is how to allocate the restaurant costs. In many ways, IT costs are just like staff restaurant costs: everyone needs IT, support functions can make heavier demands on IT than revenue generating units, and it is not clear how the benefit of IT is apportioned as it flows through the support unit staff to revenue generating units.

This cost-allocation issue could be solved in a number of ways. The restaurant could charge higher prices in the early morning and late at night; the restaurant could be given a subsidy by the firm as a whole, or by those parts of it deemed to benefit most from having the employees concerned available 24 hours per day; or the restaurant could charge slightly higher prices throughout the day, so that in effect the daytime diners subsidized the nighttime diners. The advantages and disadvantages are summarized in the table shown in Table 3.1. This shows that there is a trade-off between transparency of how the costs are allocated, and fairness. Ideally allocations would be transparent and fair, but the reality is that there is often a trade-off, and it is not obvious what the extent of the trade-off should be. The example of the restaurant costs illustrates a major problem that applies to allocating IT costs. There are often many different ways in which IT costs could be allocated, and while none of them is entirely perfect, none is much better than the others either.

Our aim here is to set out the general problem of cost allocations, using simple, non-IT examples. This will help to understand most of the key issues you are likely to face in how IT costs are allocated in your organization. Is there agreement on a fair and reasonable way to allocate costs? If there is, is it clear to which specific revenue-generating business units these costs should go? If there are several principles, all equally fair and reasonable, on which costs could be allocated, how will your organization choose among them?

Often, one way to get a better understanding of an organization's IT cost is to consider two aspects of your IT costs. Are they fixed or variable costs? And are the costs hard or easy to predict? Figure 3.2 illustrates this approach. Some variable IT costs can be predicted reasonably accurately, for example outsourced costs where the terms of the outsourcing contract ensure predictable costs. Another example of a predictable fixed cost is in-house maintenance of stable legacy systems running in standard languages. A variable cost that is hard to predict is the cost of application development for a new kind of application, particularly if new application development technology is being used. Easily predictable fixed costs include depreciation costs for mainframes. If a company is expanding rapidly and decides to equip its workers with mobile computing capabilities, then it might find that the cost of new PCs is hard to predict, but each one bought will add to the fixed costs of the firm.

Analyzing your IT costs according to these two aspects can help you see where the allocation problems are greatest, and where to focus management effort to resolve allocation issues with the least effort. As we saw earlier, good allocation processes can actually add value to your company by improving IT resource allocation. This effect is greatest for those fixed costs that are hard to predict. A manager will pay more attention to the decision on whether to buy another PC for the department if it is a fact that the department will end up bearing the full cost of that PC. The point is to align the IT cost allocation principles with the business strategy of the firm. This two-aspect analysis also shows that it is easiest to find acceptable allocation principles for predictable fixed costs, and hardest for unpredictable variable costs.

Figure 3.3 shows how a Chicago company used this two-dimensional analysis in practice. The Chicago firm reviewed its major items of IT expenditure, totalling $20.2m in the current year (1998), and determined where each fitted in the two-dimensional matrix. Senior managers in this firm had become very worried that the issue of cost allocations had become a source of friction within management, was obstructing good teamwork and was distracting managers from more productive

Table 3.1   Staff restaurant: solving the cost allocation issue

Allocation solution	Advantages	Disadvantages
Charge higher prices in the early morning and late at night	Transparency – actual costs are passed on to the diners at the time	Complexity – the restaurant staff would have to keep changing the prices, and might make mistakes in charging at around changeover time. Unfairness – or at least perceived unfairness. Why should a cup of coffee cost most late at night?
Whole firm contributes to a subsidy	Simplicity	Unfairness – if only part of the firm benefits why should the whole firm pay?
Those parts of the firm felt to be benefiting most from the 24-hour workers contribute a subsidy	Fairness – those who benefit pay	Complexity – working out and agreeing which profit centres benefit and by precisely what amounts will be a long and expensive process, and may be impossible to resolve to everyone's satisfaction
Slight increase in prices throughout the day	Simplicity	Unfairness – why should daytime diners subsidize the nighttime diners? Unfairness – this may push the costs of eating in the staff restaurant above the costs of eating out nearby

work. The analysis summarized in Figure 3.3 not only helped senior management understand the problem quickly, but also pointed the way to a solution. The problem was that 42% of IT costs were in the top right quadrant, that is, they were the hardest costs to allocate. After less than six months of analysis and internal debate, the firm decided to make two changes as shown in Figure 3.4.

1. First, the firm adopted a new approach to tactical IT development work. The firm had made a detailed study of the development work it had undertaken in the previous 12 months. The study found that one-third of development work categorized as tactical development was more accurately described as strategic development work. That is, this development work was vital to the long-term interests and survival of the firm, but weak senior IT management and lack of a coherent IT strategy had meant that this vital work was being done as well as possible and piecemeal under tactical development rules. For instance, a new price optimization application that had implications for the profitability of every division was being led by the northwestern sales director, and not an experienced project manager or senior executive. Consequently, the wider implications of pricing strategy were completely ignored. This third of development work was

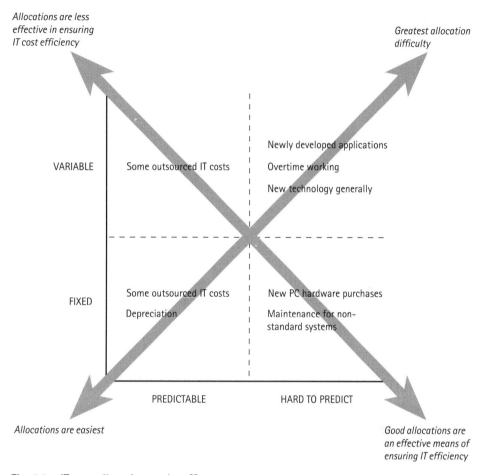

Fig. 3.2 IT cost allocation trade–offs

removed into a strengthened central IT function and incorporated into the three-year IT strategy. The result was that these costs became highly predictable. The remaining two-thirds of tactical development work remained a variable cost, but became subject to strict budgeting rules at the business unit level. In return for imposing greater accountability for IT costs, the business units received greater autonomy in the type of tactical development work they could initiate.

2. Project Jazz was a project to equip the salesforce with better home and mobile working technology. The first phase of Project Jazz was outsourced to an external IT consultancy. The consultancy had better experience of this type of project, and was prepared to co-invest with the Chicago firm in order to develop its credibility in a new industry sector. This change meant that the costs of Phase 1 of Project

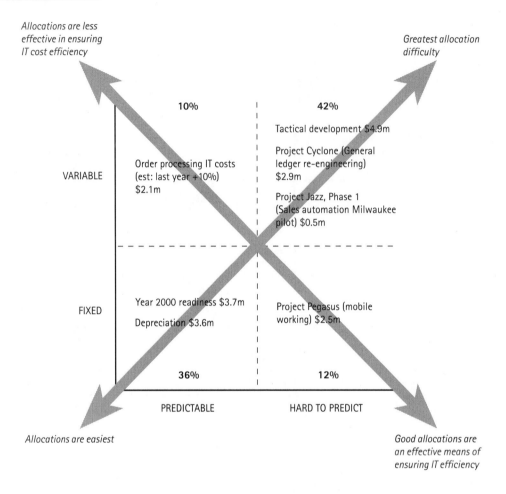

Fig. 3.3 The Chicago company – the problem

Jazz ceased to be variable and unpredictable, and became fixed and completely predictable. Even better, a no-win, no-fee clause was added, so that if Phase 1 of Jazz failed, the Chicago firm would not incur any further costs.

In this way the Chicago firm improved the efficiency of its IT, and stopped IT cost allocations from generating internal political heat that distracted managers from managing the business. It would be an exaggeration to say that the study of IT cost allocations was the only reason for these changes. However, it is true that the allocations study catalyzed a number of other initiatives and clarified the findings of those other initiatives, so that the changes in the way IT was managed and planned and had its costs allocated happened much faster than would otherwise have been the case.

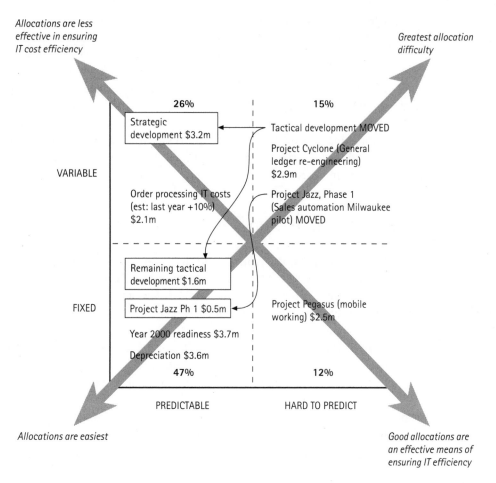

Allocations are less effective in ensuring IT cost efficiency

Greatest allocation difficulty

26%

15%

Strategic development $3.2m

Tactical development MOVED

Project Cyclone (General ledger re-engineering) $2.9m

VARIABLE

Order processing IT costs (est: last year +10%) $2.1m

Project Jazz, Phase 1 (Sales automation Milwaukee pilot) MOVED

Remaining tactical development $1.6m

FIXED

Project Jazz Ph 1 $0.5m

Project Pegasus (mobile working) $2.5m

Year 2000 readiness $3.7m

Depreciation $3.6m

47%

12%

PREDICTABLE

HARD TO PREDICT

Allocations are easiest

Good allocations are an effective means of ensuring IT efficiency

Fig. 3.4 IT cost allocation trade-offs

How fixed are fixed costs, how variable are variable costs?

A further problem in cost allocation is the assumption that the distinction between fixed and variable costs is itself clearly defined. This is not so, and ignore any accountant who tells you otherwise. Much work in finance and tax is about converting fixed costs into variable costs or *vice versa*. Buy a photocopier outright and it's a predominantly fixed cost. But take the same photocopier on a lease where you pay per page and it's now a variable cost. But it's the same piece of equipment, doing the same job, giving your business the same benefits. Many costs are aggregates of fixed and variable costs.

Even within the cost of running the photocopier, some variable costs are more variable than others. The photocopier will be dusted every week by the office cleaner whether it is used or not, so the cost of dusting is more of a fixed cost in some respects. However, we decide that as an economy measure the cleaner should come only once every fortnight, which gives this cost a variable characteristic. Paper is a variable cost, in that one sheet is used for every copy (although less variable for double-sided copying). We are now delving into minute detail of cost allocations, but the whole point is that detail matters for cost allocation, just as detail matters for writing code that makes a software program run well and just as detail also matters for making sure that a company's accounts are straight. It is especially true of IT cost allocations, and to control how much of IT costs your department is allocated, you need to understand the detail of how your IT cost allocations work.

How do cost allocations work?

We have seen that the point of cost allocations is to distribute costs to profit centres, in those cases where the costs do not arise directly from the operations of those profit centres. There are two fundamentally different approaches that commercial organizations tend to take to allocations.

In a minority of organizations, a small group of senior executives meets periodically, usually once a year, and simply decides how much of the total allocated costs each business unit will be allocated. There is no attempt at explanation or justification. In a variant of this approach the allocated costs may be broken down by category, for example so much for general management overhead, so much for IT, so much for rent, and so on. This is the 'black box' approach to cost allocation, and will be covered in more detail later in this chapter.

The other way to allocate costs, followed by the majority of organizations, is to have some sort of pre-specified allocation process to determine precise dollar or percentage allocations for each category of cost. We will concentrate our discussion on this second approach. In most cases IT cost allocations follow a process along the following lines. A principle for allocating IT costs is agreed by the firm's senior management or a committee designated for that purpose. The principle is then implemented as an approach or methodology or operating procedure.

The major categories of IT cost and how they are allocated

So far we have set out the problems in allocating costs generally within the organization. Let us now look at the specific problems in allocating IT costs. We will approach this by looking in turn at each of the main categories of IT cost, as they are commonly found in organizations. One way to look at IT costs is to distinguish between development costs and production costs. Development costs are those costs associated with developing new IT capabilities, primarily new applications, as in the term 'application development'. Application development includes not just actually writing the computer program, but designing, testing, and, to varying degrees, implementing the program or application.

Many organizations incur not just these two but three main categories of IT cost. These are development costs, just described, maintenance costs, which are incurred when maintaining something already developed, and network or infrastructure costs. Network costs are costs relating to the network (physical and virtual) over which the IT runs. Sometimes network costs are included in maintenance costs. Another term for maintenance costs is 'production costs'. These terms are not precise. For each of these categories, we will first review what kinds of IT cost are in each category, then we will discuss what drives these costs, which will then enable us to discuss issues in the allocation of the costs in each category.

Development

What are development costs?

Development, or Application Development, means creating new systems or parts of systems. If you need a spreadsheet, you would buy that software from a supplier, such as Microsoft or IBM/Lotus. You would not get your IT department or a subcontractor to custom-build a word processor. However, if your organization needed some special purpose program not available off-the-shelf, then creating that program would be application development work. Examples of typical application development work include:

- aerospace – air traffic control systems;
- agribusiness – crop yield management systems;
- communications – switching and routing software; micropayment systems;
- defence – missile guidance systems;
- entertainment – ticket distribution systems; billing systems;
- government – tax and census administration systems;
- investment banking – derivative pricing; trade processing;
- manufacturing – automated production line control;
- retailing – stock control systems; predictive reordering systems; shelf yield management systems;
- software – developing retail systems (using spreadsheets and word processors);
- transport – reservation systems; passenger yield management systems.

What drives IT development costs?

Development is expensive, and the best way to avoid development costs is to avoid doing development work. The alternative is to buy software, which means that someone else will have developed it; in business terms this is the classic 'make or buy' decision. No-one would build a word processor today, instead this is bought 'off the shelf' from a supplier such as IBM, Microsoft or Oracle. Three points about IT costs and allocations follow from this observation: first, applications that need to be developed today may be purchased as packaged software in future; secondly, development is a high-risk business activity and needs to be managed accordingly; and thirdly, development can be outsourced.

The kinds of applications that can be bought as off-the-shelf software packages changes with time. In the 1980s there were still some organizations or even departments that developed their own word processors, but no-one would do this now, because since the 1980s the cost of word processors has fallen, and their capabilities have increased greatly. At lower cost and with greater functionality, there is no longer any business case for developing your own word processor.

The development of software as a commodity means that for more and more kinds of application, buying an off-the-shelf package will be better and cheaper than developing in-house. In 1993, if you wanted to set up a website, then you would have needed a PC, a high-capacity Internet connection and some graphic design skills. The total cost would have been several thousand dollars, and would have been expensive to maintain because you would have needed a highly skilled IT technician to perform the site maintenance. Much of your total cost would have been application development. By 1995, Web hosting services were starting to be offered. (For some reason many of them were in South Africa.) For these services you paid a fee, often highly negotiable, for which someone else managed the maintenance of your Internet site, but on their machines and their high-capacity Internet connection. However, at that time you would probably still have needed your own PC and Internet.

By 1999, Yahoo, IBM and many other companies could design, host and maintain your Website without your even needing a PC, all for a flat fee of around $20 per month. It takes under an hour to have a website up and running, and all this can be done from the comfort of a terminal in a cyber café – you don't even need your own PC. For a few dollars more the Web host will provide an e-commerce service to take and process credit card orders for your site. What would of necessity have required application development less than ten years ago can be done better and at lower cost today through a standard service. Word processing, spreadsheets and Web hosting are just a few specific examples of the general point that as the software industry develops, so more kinds of application which would once have required development are now marketed as standard packages.

Issues in allocating IT development costs

Some application development work will be for applications that benefit one business unit only. Other development work will be benefit the whole organization. A corporate website (or, in times past, a word processor) is an example of a cost that might need to be allocated over several departments, because it benefits all of them. In reality, a website is a very simple piece of development work, and is unlikely to be a large enough cost to create a significant allocation issue. However, larger business-critical applications that must be used by many business units and have to be developed rather than bought as packaged software will tend to create allocation issues. Currently a common example in many large corporations is in applications designed to provide all business units and senior management of an organization with access to all client data across the whole organization.

Datacentre costs

What are datacentre costs? The term 'datacentre' means different things in different organizations, and can even mean different things within different parts of the same organization. At one extreme, a datacentre is a room full of IT equipment, which may or may not include telecoms equipment. At the other extreme, a datacentre is a 'campus' or greenfield site, with several rooms full of IT equipment and offices housing those who administer the datacentre. In either case, the role of the datacentre is to provide the computing services for the organization. Datacentres are typically, although not always, associated with central IT functions. In an organization, applications and databases can be run on PCs, workstations or larger machines. Datacentres tend to be the places where these larger machines are housed, although it is not unusual to see banks of PCs also in datacentres.

What drives datacentre costs?

The alternative to having a datacentre is that the machines that would be in the datacentre would be dispersed throughout the organization. This would mean, for example, that the mainframe used for payroll would sit near the payroll department, the mail servers would sit anywhere, the MIS mainframes would sit in the finance department's offices, and so on. The theoretical advantage of having a datacentre is that it is inexpensive to connect computers remotely by high bandwidth networking. As a consequence, these machines don't need to be co-located with their users, and a number of machines can be grouped together in one place to realize economies of scale in running them. These economies of scale are the usual ones, and include:

- **lower maintenance costs**: co-locating machines of the same type should mean that fewer maintenance staff are required in total, a lower level of spares inventory need be carried, and maintenance contracts can be renegotiated at a lower cost per machine;
- **efficient use of available processing power**: not all applications are used evenly over a given period; for instance, payroll tends to be run at the end of a fortnightly or monthly period, and machines used for running payroll may be free or lightly used at all other times. If several applications run on the same hardware, then co-locating the machines can facilitate a better use of processing capacities over a period of time as the utilization of processing assets can be optimized;

■ **increased reliability**: sharing back-up facilities can reduce the back-up cost per application or machine while increasing the back-up facilities available.

Despite the force of the theoretical arguments in favour of datacentres, which are essentially reducible to economies of scale and economies of scope, datacentres are not always effective in reducing costs. One of the world's largest banks found that the same application cost 35% more when run from the datacentre than when run from outside the datacentre. Why? In this case, for two reasons. First, it is easy for data-centre management to become a little too relaxed about managing efficiently, and allow costs to increase unnecessarily. Secondly, a datacentre is another layer of potential cost allocation, so it introduces another variable into the cost allocation formula. In short, it is another opportunity to allocate costs unfairly among the applications supported. None of this means that datacentres are a bad idea, it just means that they have to be managed carefully when it comes to allocating costs of the IT they support. As datacentres were originally designed, built and managed more with technical efficiency in mind than financial efficiency, it should not be too surprising if there is a need for refocusing on financial management in datacentres.

The factors that reduce costs in a datacentre are those enumerated above, to do with efficiencies of scale and efficiencies of scope. The four factors that tend to increase costs in a datacentre are:

■ IT diversity

■ inappropriate skill levels

■ non-standard user demands

■ bureaucratic inertia.

As in non-IT areas, diversity of plant and equipment generates cost. We saw, above, that not all applications are needed at the same time. A payroll application, for instance, is needed at the end of the month or fortnight more than at other times, so if it runs on the same hardware as other applications, there is the potential to share machines more efficiently. The fewer kinds of hardware and software the fewer skills sets will be needed in the workforce to maintain the machines. Also, a few large service contracts can be placed with suppliers instead of a large variety of low-value service contracts, giving greater scope for negotiating volume discounts.

It is naturally important that the staff in a datacentre have the right skill sets. If there has recently been a major systems upgrade, say a new version of an operating system, have staff been trained to support it? One of the world's biggest telecoms companies won the contract to supply the Internet backbone service for Microsoft in the late 1990s. However, the datacentre staff in the telecoms company received little training appropriate to the task of running an Internet backbone for retail customers. Within a year the deal was cancelled, and a potentially huge revenue stream was diverted away from the company.

What about non-standard user demands? Surely the business user in the front line should be able to demand, within reason, whatever is necessary from the datacentre to meet client needs? The issue here is to identify the main drivers of datacentre costs. We are not evaluating whether these drivers are justified or not; it is simply a fact that as datacentres are set up like mass production factories, any changes to the standard processes will tend to incur high one-off costs. Sometimes the even higher one-off revenues that follow from meeting one-off demands will justify these costs. At other times, management of the datacentre and of the business units will need to consider whether either the datacentre's standard capabilities should be enhanced, or whether some types of non-standard request should in fact be rejected by the datacentre.

Case study

Example: non-standard request

A major American furniture supplier had a datacentre that produced invoices every two weeks for furniture ordered by retailers that it supplied. The supplier sourced furniture from a number of countries, including many in Central and Latin America. Some retailers wanted the invoices to contain data on the ecological status of the wood used in making the furniture – including whether the wood was from a sustainable source and if so, where. The supplier had much of this information in its data files, but the invoicing systems was not configured to generate the data. It could easily be done with manual intervention in the process. This did not matter when there were only one or two requests for invoices to include ecological data. However, when many requests for invoices to include such information came in, it did begin to push up costs noticeably and also caused delays in getting invoices out to customers.

Instead of tolerating the resultant rising costs and delays, management realized that it had to decide between refusing all such requests or investing a moderate amount in adding this capability to the standard invoicing system. The actual decision made by the supplier was to refuse any further requests, but the two key points from this case are, first, that management realized it had to make a decision and then set about making one, and secondly, that either decision would have been sufficient to keep costs down and eliminate the delays that had started to occur.

The term 'bureaucratic inertia' could cover a wide range of management problems, and it does. Put simply, it is usually harder to keep costs low and efficiency high in a large support function operating in isolation from the front line of the rest of the organization, than in a support function located in amidst the front line of the business. However, while it might be harder, it is not impossible, and there are many good reasons for trying to centralize many support functions away from the front line of business. We considered some of these reasons above in the argument for having datacentres. There is a tendency among some champions of the datacentre concept to think that datacentres have to be greenfield sites. And if a new site is being built, then it makes sense to have decent quality buildings and facilities. This is sensible, there is no point in building a new site to look and feel like a dowdy old cramped building.

The dilemma is that if the datacentre has significantly better facilities than the rest of the organization, perhaps a better canteen, better furnishing and better car parking, then it will be even harder to convince visitors from the revenue-generating part of the organization that maximum value is being added. This is a genuine problem and one that management often finds hard. One option is to build datacentres in 'brownfield' sites, that is, in regenerating areas in the centre of the city or towards the edge of the city. Indeed, this is what a number of banks in New York are beginning to consider doing, partly to avoid the appearance of having expensive-looking datacentres.

Issues in allocating datacentre costs

The single biggest issue in allocating datacentre costs is transparency. We've seen, above, that in one company the same application cost users 35% more when it was run from a datacentre than when it was run outside the datacentre. Suppose you have a small department, say 100 people, and you run your own intranet web server. The box with the hardware sits underneath the desk of a junior member of staff, and it's part of that person's job to maintain the site, although only a small part. However, if you now use the datacentre to host your intranet website, two kinds of cost emerge.

First, there are costs that you used to bear but that are now made explicit. Many data centres allocate cost according to the floorspace taken up by the machines, so if your server that's now in the datacentre takes up one square metre of floorspace, then you will be charged whatever the datacentre charges for a square metre of floorspace. And in a similar way you will be charged for the time taken to maintain the server, or perhaps for a fraction of the staff costs in the datacentre. Note that these were costs you were paying anyway. Your junior staff member had to maintain the web server and site, although this cost was probably not broken down as an individual line item in your departmental budget. And the same principle applied to the floor-space; although it hasn't necessarily saved you any costs in your department by not having the server sitting there once it had been moved to the datacentre, the floor is freed up for use by something else.

The second kind of costs are costs that you would not necessarily have borne had you not moved your intranet web server into the datacentre. The datacentre will have certain technical, safety or staff training standards that it applies to all equipment. These standards cost something, and if you had not applied the same standards in your own department, it may be that you end up paying for standards you don't want when the server moves to the datacentre. There is a question of whether it matters that you don't want the standards applied. Sometimes there will be corporate interests such as control standards or risk management requirements that are good reason for your personal or departmental wishes to be overridden, at other times not.

Allocating datacentre costs

Another cost allocation problem when standards are applied across all IT in the datacentre is when a standard reduces overall costs to the organization but increases costs to one business unit. A New York bank had a corporate finance department which used Apple Macintosh PCs almost exclusively. The rest of the bank used IBM standard PCs. As part of a firm-wide implementation of IT strategy, the corporate finance department was required to abandon the Macintosh standard in favour of the IBM standard. Whereas two people in the corporate finance department had maintained all the Macintosh PCs and their entire infrastructure for a department of about 60 people, the new IT strategy called for such support to be provided centrally, with much of it from a datacentre. Overall the firm would reduce costs, improve system reliability and improve management controls. The corporate finance department, however, would see increased costs. Against this, the corporate finance department did expect to find it easier under the new IT strategy to share data and documents with the rest of the bank. (However, it was far from certain that this was desirable from a compliance and regulatory point of view, given the separation that was supposed to exist between the corporate finance department and the rest of the firm.)

This example thus illustrates one of the real dilemmas of allocating datacentre costs. When the firm benefits overall, at the price of an increase in costs to one or two departments, what is to be done? Sometimes a rebate is given to the affected business unit, for a limited period of time, but more often no allowance is made.

Helpdesk costs

What are helpdesk costs? Helpdesk costs are those associated with providing a helpdesk for users. Another name for helpdesk costs is 'user support costs'. Helpdesks can be arranged in several ways. A fully centralized helpdesk has one helpdesk, which all users call for help on all applications, no matter where the users are in the world. This is rare, but some examples do exist. Some specialized software that supports petrol pumps used in retail gas stations all over the USA is all supported out of one location in New Zealand, for instance. A more common model for helpdesks is to have one helpdesk per country or per region, but within the country or region the helpdesk is responsible for help for all applications. This is how many large corporations structure their helpdesks. A third model is to have different helpdesks for different IT applications. This is becoming less common, but can still be economic where there are standalone systems using uncommon technology dispersed within an organization.

A variant of the first two models is to have different helpdesks for different kinds of staff. Senior staff, for instance, might have an executive helpdesk, staffed by more experienced or more capable technical support people, on the basis that downtime in the IT support to senior management will cost the firm more per minute than downtime for more junior staff. Or the division might not be based on seniority, but on function: key revenue generators or safety critical functions could merit a superior quality of helpdesk support. Some hospitals have separate helpdesks for technology in the operating theatre and intensive care wards because this is more critical than, say, the hospital administrator's support system. Note, however, that having separate helpdesks is only one of several possible ways to solve the issue here: another way is to prioritize calls for help within a single integrated helpdesk.

What drives helpdesk costs?

Helpdesk costs are mainly people related costs for helpdesk staff. Besides compensation, this will include training helpdesk staff in the systems they are expected to support. Staff turnover in the helpdesk is usually high, as much of the job entails dealing with users angrily saying that their IT has just crashed or has failed to do what the menu promised it would do. The high staff turnover adds further to costs. Besides the usual IT office equipment, a helpdesk is likely to have specialized call centre and helpdesk ticket tracking applications.

Implementation

We saw, above, that applications come to exist in two ways. Applications can be bought, or they can be written. If bought, they tend to be referred to as packages; if developed, then the work involved is called 'applications development'. In practice, in an organization of any size even when packaged software is bought off-the-shelf there can be a considerable amount of further work required before all users are able to use the package efficiently. This work is called 'implementation'. A simple example is implementing a new version of a word processor. At home you would probably install a new word processor yourself, but in an organization of any size no-one would consider sending out hundreds or thousands of boxes of new software, one to each user. First, to do so would be expensive, as many copies of CDs, manual, user licences and packaging would be required. Secondly, there would be a significant control issue, as not everyone would in practice fill in the necessary paperwork for the licensing. Thirdly, as there is some choice as to how installation is completed (for example, what dictionaries to use, what network settings, where the default temporary storage resides, and so on) and there can be compatibility issues; and finally, it may be that not all employees actually have the skill to install the software. For these reasons, and other more technical reasons to do with efficient maintenance and upgrades of the network, even a simple package such as a word processor needs to be implemented by properly trained and skilled IT staff.

Whereas a word processor is virtually ready to use once installed, many more specialized business applications need considerably more work to be implemented. Implementation is a significant IT cost, and is incurred every time software is upgraded.

Network costs

Network costs are simply costs associated with the network connecting the various machines in your organization. Traditionally, organizations had two kinds of networks, one for voice and one for data. While many organizations will have two distinct networks, it is no longer necessary, as for over ten years the technology has existed for telephones, fax machines, PCs and peripherals all to share the same network. At its broadest, network costs will include the following:

- **hardware** – cables, sockets, router and network-related server hardware, telephone switches, and back-ups for each of these as necessary;
- **software** – router software, switch software, network management software;
- **services** – network management, maintenance and back-up services, and services to extend the network as new users and devices are added.

The four most common IT cost allocation principles

In this section we will cover the four most common principles used in US corporations for allocating IT costs, and list the main advantages and disadvantages of each. However, a cost allocation principle that works very well in one company when used to allocate a particular kind of IT cost can work very badly when used to allocate the same kind of cost in a competitor company. Indeed, where there is a decentralized model of IT, it is possible for the same allocation methodology to be quite acceptable in one operating division but anathema to another. So when considering the most common allocation methodologies, you will need to take a view on how they work in your particular organization, and whether a particular approach is good or bad for you and your department. The positive and negative points set out under each allocation principle can then be used in any case you may need to make for hanging the basis of your allocations.

'Black box'

In the 'black box' approach to IT cost allocations, a small committee decides the amount of money that each business unit should contribute to cover the IT cost. The meeting is secret and the rest of the organization is bound by its decision. No justification or explanation of the rationale for the decision is given, so that there can be no debate about the way in which the allocation was reached.

The 'black box' approach works well when the judgements of the individual members of the committee that decide allocations are well-regarded throughout the organization. This approach to allocations tends to be seen in smaller and more collegial organizations, and is probably more suited to them than to larger organizations (see Table 3.2).

Table 3.2   Advantages and drawbacks of the 'black box' approach

Advantages	Drawbacks
■ Minimizes time spent in the allocations process ■ Minimizes the political heat that can be generated by corporate debates about the merit and appropriateness of different possible principles and mechanisms for cost allocations ■ Easily controlled and adjusted by senior management	■ Eliminates transparency of the underlying principles of cost allocation ■ Business unit managers might feel that they are unable to manage IT costs ■ Requires above average intelligence and trust among the organization's managers

In a major entertainment company, network costs were allocated on the basis of headcount in a large, old business division, but in a newer, more entrepreneurial business division, network and all other IT costs were allocated according to the decision of a small, secret committee that met for the purpose of allocating costs once per year. This is an example of the 'black box' approach to cost allocation described above. In the entrepreneurial division, the committee members were highly regarded and trusted by all management to come to a fair solution. In the older division of this entertainment company, the bureaucratic culture that had developed required evidence and a justification for any cost allocation decision, and a headcount-based allocation methodology satisfied this need. Neither division paid much attention to the question of how the other allocated IT costs – after all, it is scarcely an exciting management issue – until the two divisions were merged. Both divisions agreed that after merging they should use the 'black box' approach, but ten days before the merger took place the managers in the older division changed their minds and insisted on an approach they could vet and argue about.

Headcount

Where IT allocation principles are based on headcount, there is an assumption that headcount drives IT costs (see Table 3.3). And indeed this is usually a reasonable assumption, as far as it goes. Potential problems arise with headcount-based allocation principles when they are implemented in a way that introduces complexity, and this might be unavoidable. The simplest way to implement a headcount statistic is to take the headcount in each business unit. Suppose an organization has two business units, called 'US Sales' and 'Foreign Sales'. If US Sales has 45 people, and foreign sales 15, that is 60 people in total. Then IT costs allocated on the basis of simple headcount would go 75% to the US Sales unit and 25% to the Foreign Sales unit, because the US Sales unit has 75% of the total headcount and the Foreign Sales unit 25%. The problem becomes more complex if some of the IT costs to be allocated come from non-revenue generating units.

Table 3.3   Advantages and drawbacks of the headcount approach

Advantages	Drawbacks
■ A simple headcount statistic is easy to understand and apply ■ Headcount usually is one of the main drivers of IT costs ■ It is easy to compile headcount data ■ Allocating IT costs on the basis of headcount encourages managers to minimize their headcounts	■ In practice, for many IT allocations where non-revenue generating departments incur IT costs, simple headcount is unsuitable and must be weighted by some other factor. This introduces complexity, which obscures the allocation process and can lead to sub-optimal management decision-making

Now suppose this organization has another 20 people in its corporate headquarters. As discussed previously, costs must ultimately be allocated against revenue generating parts of the organization. So how should their IT costs of the non-revenue generating corporate headquarters be split between the US Sales and the Foreign Sales departments? They could be split 75:25 on the basis that this is the ratio of staff in US Sales to staff in Foreign Sales, so in effect US Sales would pay for IT support for 15 of the head office staff and Foreign Sales for five. But what if in fact 15 people in the corporate headquarters are supporting Foreign Sales and only five US Sales? This might be because Foreign Sales are more complex than US Sales and so require more time from head office functions such as legal, finance and planning. In such cases, the principle of allocating costs on the basis of headcount becomes complex in implementation. Often a weighting is applied to the simple headcount formula, perhaps a weighting on the basis of margin, or sales volume, or some agreed number. In many cases the effect of such a weighting is to complicate the headcount principle to such an extent that it is hard to understand and is likely to become unfair to some business unit as business circumstances change over time.

Fixed-cost related

In a fixed-cost related IT allocation principle, IT costs are allocated on the basis of how much of some other, fixed, cost is apportioned (see Table 3.4). For instance, IT costs might be allocated on the basis of floorspace used. What has floorspace got to do with IT costs? Nothing. However, the management thinking behind this principle is that as floorspace, for example, is the greatest cost of doing business after people-related costs, allocating IT costs on the basis of floor space will encourage management to reduce their use of floorspace, thus driving down the firm's largest cost after people-related costs. This works when any resulting inefficiencies in IT are more than offset by gains from rent and other premises savings.

This allocation principle is used in a number of companies both in the US and elsewhere, and seems particularly popular in The Netherlands, for some reason.

Table 3.4 Advantages and disadvantages of fixed-cost-related approach

Advantages	Drawbacks
■ Very simple conceptually ■ Easy to implement ■ Effective in controlling the fixed cost, at least over the medium term	■ No connection with IT efficiency, and can encourage inefficient use of IT ■ Working environment tends to become very cramped as more people are compressed into a smaller space

Volume

By volume-related cost allocation principles, we mean any principle based on a measure volume or quantity of IT usage. This is the most common way to allocate IT costs (see Table 3.5). Examples include allocating the cost of:

■ providing an email service on the basis of the number of email messages sent or sent and received;

■ providing Internet access on the amount of data accessed or downloaded (measured in Kbytes);

■ application development on the number of lines of code written;

■ application development on the basis of the number of function points created;

■ helpdesk on the basis of the number of calls answered;

■ datacentres on the basis of the number of transactions processed (in the securities industry this means allocating costs on the basis of the number of trades processed; a variant is the number of trade tickets processed).

Volume-based allocation principles are usually good in theory. As a manager, however, you should probably ensure that you also understand how the idea behind any volume-based allocations hitting your budget have actually been implemented, as well as finding out what the theory is. Let's consider an example.

Suppose that in your organization the cost of providing email is allocated on the basis of the number of email messages sent. The underlying principle here is that business units should pay for what they use. Behind this principle is the implicit

Table 3.5 Advantages and drawbacks of volume approach

Advantages	Drawbacks
■ Conceptually simple ■ When implementation is straightforward can be a very efficient and effective allocation methodology	■ Often implementation is complex and difficult ■ If poorly implemented, can generate the greatest internal politics of all methodologies

assumption that there is some marginal cost to sending email. Another implicit assumption is that the cost of providing email is distinct from other IT costs. Depending on the details of the IT infrastructure in your organization, there can be several issues in allocating email costs on this principle. First, often the marginal cost of sending email is close to zero. Secondly, the infrastructure used by email may also be used by many other IT services, such as voice traffic for telephones, data traffic for faxes and non-email Internet data, and network management functions. Thirdly, one of the biggest costs incurred in many organizations by the use of email is the cost of cleaning up after a virus has been imported through email, and this cost is not reflected in this allocation principle. So there are at least three potential flaws with email usage as a principle on which to allocate the cost of running an email service.

There are further issues depending on how the principle has been implemented. The most significant is how email usage is measured. Is it the number of email messages? Is it the volume of data sent by email? Is there a weighting for the priority with which each message is sent? Each of these questions may or may not matter, depending on the particular circumstances of the organization concerned. Then there is the issue of how reliable is the data – are all messages really being counted? Or is there sampling, in which case is there a bias to the sampling? It might be necessary to go into this level of detail for some of your allocations if there is a significant amount of cost involved. In a large corporation it is not unusual for such investigations to reveal unfair allocations in the order of tens of millions of dollars per year.

The approach taken in this example was first, to identify the allocation principle, and ensure we understood not just the principle or rationale itself, but all implied assumptions behind it. Then we looked at what problems there might be from a purely theoretical basis. Finally, we looked at how the allocation principle has been implemented in the organization, to identify possible issues that might undermine the stated allocation principle. As a manager it would be nice if you could contact your finance department and ask for a list of all IT allocation principles and how they have been implemented. It is very rare for such data to be available. If you get a complete list of all principles and the costs to which they are applied, you are lucky. To assist, Fig. 3.5 is a form that is useful as a basis for understanding allocations in your organization, particularly volume-based allocation.

How to reduce your IT cost allocations

This section sets out how to minimize your IT cost allocations. The steps given here have been used in a wide range of companies, both in the US and elsewhere, to help managers to reduce the IT costs allocated to their departments. The results have been benefits not just to their departments, but to other departments in the organization, including the IT department and the finance department. The flagship department of one very large New York firm found that after using this approach, not only did its

Allocation assessment

Allocation principle		
What is the principle?	Function points	
What kind is it?	Headcount ☐ Volume ☐	
	Fixed cost ☐ General ☐	

IT costs being allocated

Rationale for this particular principle

Underlying assumptions

What principles do competitors use for these kinds of costs?

Implementation issues

Overall assessment			
Is the effect of the principle fair?	Yes ☐ No ☐	Estimated $ impact on business unit	
What would be a better principle, and why?			

Fig. 3.5   Template for an allocation approach assessment

Allocation assessment

Allocation principle		
What is the principle?	Function points	
What kind is it?	Headcount ☐ Volume ☒ Fixed cost ☐ General ☐	

IT costs being allocated

The cost of applications development.

Rationale for this particular principle

The number of function points in an application is a function of programmer productivity. Previously we allocated on the basis of the number of lines of code written, but it was felt that that was not much of an indicator of programmer productivity, and may have encouraged inefficient programming.

Underlying assumptions

1. That function points are definable in a way that means something in practice;
2. That function points are a measure of productivity.

What principles do competitors use for these kinds of costs?

- Lines of code written;
- Hours spent in applications development (AD);
- 'Black Box';
- Just agree an allocation case by case among the internal customers.

Implementation issues

None of the assumptions underlying this allocation principle appears to be true. Everyone agrees we are no better off than we were with measuring lines of code, except that using this principle takes much more time than simply counting lines of code.

Overall assessment			
Is the effect of the principle fair?	Yes ☐ No ☒	**ESTIMATED $ IMPACT ON BUSINESS UNIT**	**$2.5m**
What would be a better principle, and why?	This is a hard one. It is not clear that there is a principle that yields a better result, but the same quality of result can certainly be achieved at lower cost in management time. We recommend that managers of business units concerned agree an allocation principle on a case by case basis at the start of each AD project, and review quarterly.		

Fig. 3.6   Example of a completed allocation assessment

Table 3.6   Possible ways to structure an organization's IT function

Structure 1

    Application development

    Network and systems

    Infrastructure

Structure 2

    Datacentre

    Development

    Helpdesk

    Implementation

    Maintenance

    Network

Structure 3

    Package selection and implementation

    Network design and management

    Database planning and management

    Technical planning

    Datacentre operations

    Systems rationalization/integration

Structure 4

    IT strategy and management

    Business process improvement/business process re-engineering

    Data network

    Voice networks

    Business recovery services

    Applications development and management

    Hardware cluster management

IT cost allocation fall as a percentage of its costs, but its overall spend on IT also fell. A year after starting the initiative in just that one department, all departments agreed that IT costs were more transparent, and IT was making a greater contribution than ever to the profitability of the firm. You can achieve the same results.

There is a simple three-step approach:

1. Understand how your cost allocation principles (that is, how allocations are supposed to work) and how the principles are in fact implemented (that is, how allocations actually work, in practice).

2. Determine whether your department should be allocated less IT cost.

3. If appropriate, build and make your case for change.

Understand your cost allocation principles

We have seen in the earlier parts of this chapter what allocation principles are, how they should work and how they work in practice. The first step to reducing your IT cost allocations is to develop your own understanding of how IT cost allocations work, in theory and practice, in your own organization. Figure 3.5 is a form which can be used by someone familiar with the ideas presented earlier in this chapter rapidly to capture the information necessary to understand how IT costs allocations work. The way to use this form is to go to your monthly management financial data, or the general ledger, or wherever your most recent IT costs are shown. Go through them and identify the main categories of IT cost. Figure 3.6 shows an example of a completed form. Complete one such for every major category of IT cost or cost allocation principle. Table 3.6 is useful as a checklist of some of the ways that IT departments, and therefore costs, are commonly structured. You might find it helpful to go through your IT costs with someone from your IT function, ideally someone from the IT department's own finance team, although not all companies will have such a function.

One of the main differences in the structure of IT departments is between those which are centralized and those which are decentralized. The structures set out in Table 3.6 can apply within either.

Determine whether your department should be allocated less IT cost

The issue here is about allocations, not total IT cash spend. There exist many analyzes that provide a basis of opinion on whether your department is spending too much, in cash terms, on IT, or too little, and as many again to get an opinion on the fairness of your IT cost allocations. However, we will propose just one simple analysis that shouldn't take more than a few hours of work and not more than two or three days of elapsed time at the most, and half a day if all the data is available.

Simply look at the three key trends for your department against the organization as a whole: headcount, revenue, and IT cost. When you have these data, ask two questions: first, what trend has there been for your department's IT costs as a proportion of the firm's IT costs over time? Secondly, if this trend has been one of an increasing share of the overall IT costs, is there any reason your department deserves to bear the greater share?

Table 3.7 shows data where it seems there is an unreasonable increase in the department's share of IT costs. In 1997 the department bore just 20% of the firm's IT costs, but for the year 2000 it is estimated that the department will be bearing 27.5% of the firm's overall IT costs. This is an increase of over a third. During this period the numbers of staff employed by this department decreased. Given that staff employed is often the major real driver of IT costs, a third increase in IT costs looks very suspicious. In addition, the share of revenue generated by the department has declined. These are usually the main broad trends that indicate whether your cost allocations have become excessive.

Table 3.7   Department shows unreasonable increase in share of IT costs

	1997	1998	1999	2000 (est.)
IT cost (in $m) – your dept	15	22	27	33
IT cost (in $m) – total firm	75	85	99	120
%	20.0%	25.9%	27.3%	27.5%
Heads – your dept	203	198	195	190
Heads – total firm	5553	5779	5903	6000
%	3.7%	3.4%	3.3%	3.2%
Revenue (in $m) – your dept	198	202	210	220
Revenue (in $m) – total firm	994	1010	1202	1400
%	19.9%	20.0%	17.5%	15.7%

Table 3.8   Department not being allocated excessive IT costs

	1997	1998	1999	2000 (est.)
IT cost (in $m) – your dept	15	22	24	25
IT cost (in $m) – total firm	75	99	119	125
%	20.0%	22.2%	20.2%	20.0%
Heads – your dept	203	198	195	190
Heads – total firm	5553	5710	5770	5860
%	3.7%	3.5%	3.4%	3.2%
Revenue (in $m) – your dept	198	202	210	220
Revenue (in $m) – total firm	994	1010	1202	1400
%	19.9%	20.0%	17.5%	15.7%

There might be other trends in your industry or organization; for instance, if your firm has been implementing IT to enable employees to work from home, then it is also informative to record the number of employees thus equipped each year. The point is to ensure that you can see the trend in IT cost allocations over a period of time. You should also check for special circumstances that might explain the trend; for instance, if it were only your department being equipped by IT to work from home, then you would expect to have greater IT cost allocations. So identify the trends and any special circumstances that could justify the trends, discuss your initial thoughts with the IT department and the financial controllers, and then judge whether your department is being allocated excessive IT costs. It might also be that there is nothing unfair about the proportion of IT costs that your department is allocated.

Table 3.8 shows a case where the department is probably not being allocated excessive IT costs, although again you should consider any adjustments to the data required to make allowances for specific projects in this period.

To summarize this part of the process, you should first identify the trends. Next consider any adjustments to the raw trends that should be made for any specific items or projects related to IT. Discuss the findings with IT and the finance department, and then finalize your view on whether you are bearing excessive IT cost allocations.

Build and make your case for change

Assuming that there is evidence from the previous step to show that your department is being allocated excessive IT costs, you will want to get things changed. If so, you will be in one of two situations. Firstly, it might be that the allocation principles are fair, but have been implemented in a way that gives unintended effects, so the principles are not really being applied. Alternatively, the application of the principles will be valid, but the principles themselves will be at fault, and you will need to argue the case for changing the allocation principles.

In making a case to argue for changing either situation you should, of course, exercise some basic company political foresight. Your department stands to gain, so consider which departments will lose, and what the view of the IT and financial controller's departments is likely to be, as they will be closely involved in any changes.

Getting the implementation of allocation principles changed should be straightforward. Your case should show what the intention of the allocation principle was and how it was the organization's original intention that the allocation be implemented. For instance, a major US multinational services business had an allocation principle that allocated IT costs according to projects that each IT professional worked on. The intention was that the IT professionals recorded a project code on their time sheet, and if, say, project X52 belonged to the Special Projects division, then the fraction of X52 hours as a proportion of all IT professionals' hours would be used to allocate IT costs. Put another way:

$$\text{X52 IT cost allocation} = \frac{\text{Total X52 hours}}{\text{All IT work, hours}} \times \text{Total IT costs}$$

This should have worked, but detailed inspection of the timesheets showed that the firm's systems were adding extra hours from other projects to the total of X52 project hours. The reason was simply that the other projects were constrained for billable hours, and project X52 was seen by many as being the easiest way to 'acquire' extra hours to record on the timesheet. By showing clearly what the error was, the department responsible for X52 costs made a clear and irrefutable case to have the costs corrected, and this was also done retrospectively, although not all organizations do make retrospective changes to cost allocations.

If the allocation process is working as it should, but the allocation principles need to be changed, then it is even more important that you understand what the interests of other departments in the firm are. Turkeys don't vote for Christmas, and it takes a well-prepared case and some argument to persuade other business units to approve a firm-wide change that results in a potential increase to their costs. However, a well-prepared case can often win the day. Remember that good allocations align the resource allocation and incentives of the organization's IT assets with the strategic interests of the firm. You should aim to prepare a presentation showing that the existing allocation principles distort this ideal to an unacceptable degree. Show in detail how this happens with one or two cases that you turned up in your research into your costs. The worksheet in Figure 3.5 is a good starting point for this part of your case.

Then consider the sorts of IT project that will be required to support the firm's business strategy over the next three to five years. If there is a large IT project that has strong senior management interest, even better: show how this project would deliver better results under the proposed allocation principle, but worse results under the existing arrangement. Finally, outline, at a high level, how the changes to the IT cost allocations should be implemented. Often an organization will have a cost allocation committee that oversees and arbitrates on such decisions. If so, your aim should be to present the case for change to the allocation committee.

When the organization does decide to change, don't lose interest. The final step is to keep yourself informed about how the changes are being implemented, to ensure that your department gets the maximum value from the changes, and these can sometimes be in excess of $10m per year.

Summary

Cost allocations are by their nature tedious and yet this is the area where business units are most likely to be unfairly penalized in IT costs. It is also the area where a manager can probably improve the performance of a business unit most easily; this will take some detailed work, although much of it can be delegated. The three main points in the chapter were:

- Allocations are necessary to ensure that the costs of an organization are at some point reconciled to its revenue. Direct costs are costs charged directly to a profit centre. Allocated costs are those costs which for some reason cannot be charged directly to a profit centre, typically because they are not directly incurred by the profit centre or because there is no uniquely obvious basis on which to charge the costs back.

- There are three major common IT cost categories: development, maintenance and network costs. These terms are not precise and there is often considerable room for overlap in practice. Your interest in understanding the different categories is that they are usually allocated on different principles. Development costs are incurred in making something new, for instance a new price optimization application. Network costs are costs associated with running the network infrastructure. Maintenance costs may or may not include network costs, but generally refer to the costs of maintaining applications once built, making tactical or minor upgrades to applications, and sometimes to implementing new packaged applications.

■ The chapter finished by describing a three-step approach to getting a reduction in allocated costs, if feasible, for your department. First, understand your cost-allocation principles (that is, how allocations are supposed to work) and how the principles are in fact implemented (that is, how allocations actually work, in practice.). Next, determine whether your department should be allocated less IT cost. Finally, and if appropriate, build and make your case for change, using the analysis and facts from your investigation of your IT costs. Changing poor implementation will almost always be easier than arguing for a new allocation principle, where an awareness of the political realities of your organization will be key.

4 Starting to increase IT cost efficiency

Introduction

'No pain, no gain' is the hearty maxim from the football field. 'No pain, no change' might be the considered maxim from all those who have tried to reduce IT costs in an organization of any size. This chapter introduces five initiatives that have been proven over many years and in many well-known organizations to be effective means to cut IT costs while at the same time improving business effectiveness (see Table 4.1). However, senior management must be prepared to be firm in implementing these programmes. All of them are based largely on common sense, and many of your colleagues or employees will have experience of at least some of them previously in their careers. Gaining support for implementing these programmes firmly in your organization is vital, but should not be difficult if a few managers in your organization have previous experience of successful IT cost reduction initiatives. And an organization which is feeling pain from increasing IT costs or IT-related control problems tends to find implementation easier than when no pain is felt – no pain, no gain.

Table 4.1 The five most effective IT cost efficiency initiatives

Tactical – short-term (this chapter)
1. Immediately start tactical efficiency/cost reduction initiatives.
2. Institute a cost monitoring unit.
Tactical – medium term (Chapter 5)
3. Identify key performance indicators (KPIs).
4. Benchmark against competition.
Strategic – medium/long term (Chapter 6)
5. IT strategy.

We present the five most effective ways to increase IT cost effectiveness with the 'quick wins' first, and the more strategic ones later. It would be ideal if all efficiency projects would yield great increases in efficiency and could be implemented quickly. In practice of course things are not like this, and there are some things that can be done quickly, but that tend to yield either smaller efficiency gains or less long-lasting efficiency gains than other initiatives that require longer-term planning. In other words, there is in general a trade-off between short-term or tactical initiatives and longer-term ones. Besides this trade-off, there is another, between projects that the management of the IT department can probably implement successfully themselves, and those that require the cooperation of several or all departments' management teams. To maximize the increase in IT efficiency, a firm needs to optimize its mix of short-term v. long-term initiatives – the classic strategic/tactical mix of projects. The main trade-offs are summarized in Table 4.2. The best solution to the trade-offs depend to a significant extent on the capabilities of the IT and other departments in a firm, and on the internal politics, as they affect getting the support or buy-in necessary for cross-departmental projects. This means that each firm should decide the priorities for its own various efficiency projects, perhaps using the sort of matrix in Table 4.2.

Table 4.2 Trade-offs in IT cost efficiency initiatives

Initiatives that require cross-divisional support to implement	■ Start as soon as there is sufficient cross-divisional buy-in ■ Many results seen in short term	■ Start as soon as there is sufficient cross-divisional buy-in and planning capacity ■ Results tend to crystallize over the medium/long term, and some individual divisions may might try to capture most of the benefits
Initiatives that IT management can implement themselves	■ Start immediately, ■ Many results seen in short term	■ Start immediately if possible, or if resource constrained, start after initiating the tactical projects. ■ Results tend to crystalliseize over the medium/long term
	Tactical/can be implemented in the short term	Strategic/require longer analysis and planning stage before implementation

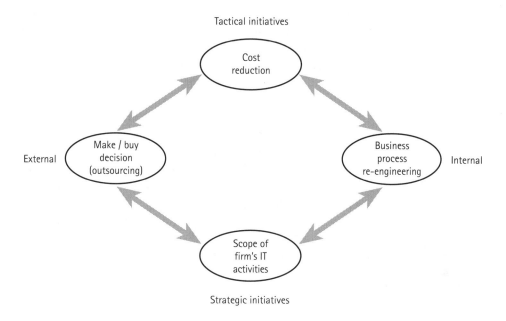

Fig. 4.1   Interaction between tactical and strategic IT efficiency initiatives

We present the two tactical IT efficiency initiatives first, then the two intermediate techniques, then the strategic technique. Each of the five initiatives also works perfectly well in isolation, and individual circumstances, for instance, resource constraint or political considerations, can mean that it is simply not feasible to follow all five techniques. If it is possible to implement all five initiatives in your organization, we recommend so doing because there are significant synergy benefits. One reason there is synergy is that the lessons learned in implementing the tactical projects will be valuable in the planning of the longer-term projects, and *vice versa*, some of the deeper thinking undertaken to plan for longer-term initiatives can result in new quick-win initiatives being identified. For instance, the work done by a cost-monitoring unit (technique 2) will enable an IT strategy (technique 5) to be determined more quickly and in more detail. This is because the understanding of the interaction between your IT organization and its costs and the capabilities of your firm at large gained by the cost reduction unit will most likely be much more detailed than the understanding arising from data gathered for the same purposes in an IT strategy projected started from scratch. Table 4.2 shows how the tactical and strategic initiatives interact.

A real-life example of the synergy between the longer-term and the shorter-term projects was at RedBank. One of the 'quick wins' identified early in the project was to implement the standard approach to project management used in the European region to the other regions of the bank. Another was to reduce the cost of data transmission by changing from several service providers to a single global provider, which would reduce prices in return for a higher volume of data traffic. Implementing these two quick wins together made it obvious to the project team that there was a strong case to consider rationalizing the IT strategy of the firm to adopt a single model for technical support to the business. In this way, the ensuing strategic review of how IT was designed, delivered to the business and managed started from a number of bases. These were a good set of cost and benefit data, experience of some of the key changes required, and a set of specific hypotheses about what should be changed, which could be tested on firm-wide management. The alternative to this approach would have been to consider the issue of IT strategy in isolation. This would probably yielded a similar solution, but with the twin disadvantages of taking considerably longer and starting from an unfocused view of the practical needs of the business.

Focus

Whether you are able to attempt all five techniques for increasing IT efficiency or are constrained to implement fewer, there will be a question of where to focus the effort. Experience suggests that firms with less well-managed IT functions will benefit the most from concentrating effort in the tactical initiatives, and, conversely, firms with better-managed IT functions will best focus on the strategic initiatives. This seems to be because rather like tennis, IT efficiency is a winner's game at the higher end, and a loser's game at the lower end. That is, averagely run or badly run IT departments can achieve the greatest efficiency gain by concentrating on avoiding simple mistakes, but very well-run IT functions make the greatest gains in efficiency by focusing on strategy. (More prosaically, one should learn to walk before running.)

Loser's games and winner's games

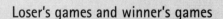

A loser's game is one where success depends on focusing more on not making mistakes than on improving one's strategy or trying to outwit the opponent. Noughts and crosses (tic-tac-toe) is the classic loser's game: even an Einstein playing against someone of modest intelligence cannot win if both players merely block each other's last move. Chess, on the other hand, is the classic winner's game. In chess, a Kasparov will beat an opponent of modest intelligence every time. In a winner's game, success depends more on focusing and refining one's strategy or play.

The distinction between winner's games and loser's games was first proposed for tennis. Professional tennis is a winner's game, but amateur tennis, especially at the lower end, is much more a loser's game. This means that the strategies that must be followed to succeed are quite different in the two games.

A number of senior executives in Fortune 500 and other companies believe that effective IT management is similar. Only the top quartile of IT departments should adopt a winner's game strategy to managing IT and IT costs; most firms should recognize that for them at the start of the first decade of the 21st century IT management is a loser's game. This does not mean the majority of firms are bound to lose in the attempt to manage IT well. On the contrary, it means that winning at their level is quite easy, just focusing on getting the basics right will deliver the greatest improvement. It is harder to get an improvement for the top quartile of firms. These firms have already focused on the basics, and will have to work much harder to achieve improved efficiency.[1]

Another way of summarizing the lesson for IT cost effectiveness to be drawn from the research into winner's games and loser's games is that most firms should focus on getting the basics of IT management right first.

Tactical/short-term IT cost-efficiency initiatives

1. Immediately start tactical efficiency/cost reduction initiatives.
2. Institute a cost-monitoring unit.

These two initiatives potentially lead to many of the same actions, the difference between them being in the management structure required. There are two main differences in the management necessary for these initiatives:

1. First, a cost-monitoring unit requires a dedicated management structure with authority over the whole IT department, and it is desirable for the unit to have formal links into the main business units and departments of the firm. Setting up a cost monitoring unit may therefore take some time, although it should be effective within a month, or perhaps longer in a large public sector organization. Tactical cost efficiency initiatives on the other hand are initiatives that do not require a new management structure for their implementation. They are the sort of things individual managers can implement, or start to implement, within their own areas of responsibility. It will usually make sense for the cost monitoring unit to coordinate tactical initiatives once the unit is set up and operating effectively.

2. Secondly, a cost monitoring unit may require the support of a small accounting staff, whereas no such support is necessary for most tactical initiatives.

From the point of view of the corporate headquarters, the need for cost reduction is often in practice spurred by some external shock – for example the loss of a key client, a hostile takeover bid predicated on the target firm's costs being excessive, or the collapse of a key revenue stream. Similarly at lower levels of the firm, a business unit may decide on a cost reduction programme in response to some more localized negative shock to the business unit. The immediate response to these might be a general instruction to all managers to review all expenses and identify opportunities for cost reduction. As we have seen before, however, cost reduction is only half of the equation for efficiency. One of the strategic functions of the firm's management in the context of IT cost efficiency is to link initiatives for cost reduction into longer-term programmes for overall efficiency improvement. The benefits of implementing an immediate cost reduction initiative include first, communicating a sense of urgency to everyone in the organization, and secondly, encouraging individuals at all levels to think of things to do to reduce costs. There is no requirement for delay while new management structures are set up or a firm-wide approach is worked out (see Table 4.3).

Immediately start tactical efficiency/cost reduction initiatives

Table 4.3   Tactical efficiency/cost reduction initiatives

Savings achievable (as % of IT budget)	Time to achieve savings	Resources required	Critical success factor
c. 10–15	6 months to 1 yr	■ IT cost reduction taskforce: 6–8 people max. ■ 1–3 financial analysts available as needed from finance dept if this capability is not in the IT dept	■ Support of CEO, CFO ■ IT costs data and high-level analytical capacity

1. Initiate the project

One way to start the tactical initiatives is to send out a general instruction for all managers to start reviewing costs. This can be narrowed to a review of IT costs specifically. Such a general instruction can be made more effective by asking for three ideas per week from each manager, to be sent to a designated individual.

Within the IT department itself, a tactical cost reduction initiative can be left to individual managers but it is usually more effective to identify a small task force to oversee the activity. This task force is in fact the nucleus of the IT cost-monitoring unit to be set up in the second efficiency initiative. The task force will also be a convenient contact point for the ideas generated by other managers in the firm for IT cost reduction. The task force should be composed of the head of IT or his designee, and managers who understand all of the sub-departments of IT and those IT assets of the firm that are not controlled directly by the IT department, such as, in many firms, desktop PCs.

A typical IT department[2] will have sub-departments such as: Networks, Data-centre, Applications Development, Helpdesk/User Support, Executive Support, and Database Admin. Whatever the exact structure of your IT department, ensure that any sub-department, group or function within IT that spends more than 10% of the IT budget is represented on the task force. You will probably also want non-IT people on the task force. A representative from any strategic planning function or the CEO's Office can be valuable in ensuring the project acts in a way that produces results sooner rather than later and keeps focused within the firm's overall policy and strategy. If your firm has outsourced a significant part of the IT function, it can be useful to have a representative from the outsourcer on the task force, either full-time or part-time. The task force should be small, about six people, and eight at the most. More people will decrease the effectiveness. If you really are tempted to have more people, start with six and bring the others on board later, at least four months later. (If you still want more than eight people on this team, you are probably the wrong person to be driving an efficiency task force.)

Agree the aim

We suggest that the aim of this task force is simply to reduce IT costs by 10% against the current IT budget, or perhaps 15%. Note that taking into account the run rate, a 10% cut may be a substantial reduction.

Run rate

The *run rate* is the rate at which expenditure is increasing. In many firms the run rate for IT is substantial, which means that for example if the budget for IT had been $100m for the financial year 2000 it could be that halfway through the financial year IT costs were running such that the actual IT spend would be $115m, which is a 15% run rate. This means that a 10% reduction against budget ($10m) would in practice be a reduction from $115m to $90m, which is 22%.

It is vital that all members of the task force are clear and in full agreement on the aim. There is likely to be an issue in most firms of whether the IT department can implement changes in IT that affect all parts of the firm. For example, a decision to change the specification of everyone's desktop PC or to standardize on one brand of word processor will impact the way everyone works, whereas a decision to change the overtime rates for night duty of the IT staff who repair mainframes won't. There will always be different levels of visibility or impact for any changes made in IT. In some organizations, it will be necessary to make this difference explicit in the stated aim of the IT efficiency task force, but experience suggests that it is best to have the simplest possible mission statement, such as 'To cut IT costs by 10%.' The task force and its leader will understand their organization well enough to know which changes need approval from a high-level, firm-wide body, such as the board of directors or management committee, and which won't.

It might seem that such a simple aim, which focuses only on cost, is at odds with the intention of increasing efficiency, as cost is only half the story of efficiency. However, although it is true that only half of efficiency is cost, the other half of efficiency, output, is related to cost, because as resources are finite, spending less on unproductive assets and activities leaves more to spend on productive assets or activities. In IT in particular, it seems to be a feature that the way to raise productivity is to concentrate more on ceasing to do the wrong things than on trying to do very clever things, at least until a firm's IT organization is in the top quartile of world class IT organizations. Another way of putting it is that IT efficiency is a loser's game rather than a winner's game.

> If we could just avoid half, only half, of the IT projects that cost a lot and deliver no business value, the value added to the Corporation by IT would suddenly become clear to everyone.   *Managing director, large manufacturing corporation, USA*
>
> In 20 years I've never seen a case for IT investment that didn't promise the earth. What makes me sick is that after 20 years I still have simply no feeling for which IT projects will be a waste of money and which might do some good. At least with other capex projects I've got some feeling.   *Finance director, top ten global charity*
>
> One day in the last recession, we cut our IT budget by 10%. Everybody complained for five minutes. But do you know, the funny thing was the business carried on just as efficiently. So we did the same the following year, and again the business carried on. Just think how much fat we had been carrying!   *General manager, international brand retailer*

So, in short, the message from many firms that have been been through a successful IT efficiency initiative is that if you concentrate on the costs, most of the efficiency gains will also appear. So pick a simple cost reduction aim, make sure each member of the task force understands and is committed to the aim, and then implement.

Implement cost reduction

The task force should start by doing three things:

- set up a cost reduction hotline together with a mechanism for following up on the ideas;
- review a list of all IT-related projects, current and planned;
- review the cost benefit of all functions or activities undertaken by the IT department, or, where the IT organization is very decentralized, by any other group with significant IT responsibilities.

Cost reduction hotline and follow-up mechanism: a cost reduction hotline is simply a channel for ideas from any employee, consultant, or anyone else who has ideas about how to reduce IT costs. There should be an email hotline, and some companies also provide fax and voicemail hotlines. Your firm must think about the balance between anonymity for those contributing ideas to the hotline and the tendency of senior management to want to know where certain ideas arise. It is important to encourage staff to contribute their best ideas, and not to be put off by the fear that they will be penalized if their ideas are perceived by senior management to be criticising some existing policy.

Case study	**Cost reduction ideas should be taken seriously**

In one of the world's largest software testing firms, which was close to bankruptcy in 1995, a junior employee was fired for suggesting, in response to a plea from senior management for ideas on cost efficiency, that the firm started taking the Internet seriously. He showed in a business model how it could be used to cut costs immediately in distributing software and in the longer-term how testing Internet applications was likely to be a huge market. This employee's opinion contradicted high-profile statements by the CEO and head of research, who believed that the Internet was a waste of time. Soon after firing the junior employee, the CEO and head of research were themselves fired by angry shareholders, after which the company went bust. (The Internet, however, started to boom.) It is in every senior manager's power to behave like this, and in fairness in this example, the CEO was only trusting in the views of his head of research. Everyone knows that in general ideas hotlines must encourage the most junior staff to contribute ideas, but those who have experience of managing any business or project with a substantial IT component know that in IT, the people who understand the newest technology are exclusively the junior staff. IT changes so fast that five years after graduating, an IT professional is a dinosaur in terms of understanding IT architectures and operating systems. Europe's leading universities did not include the Internet as a mandatory subject in degree courses until well after 1996, but by then it was already obvious that the Internet was going to become one of the most fundamental forces to change how firms extract value from IT. The take-home message is that getting your most junior IT staff to contribute ideas is vital to cutting IT costs.

The attitude to new ideas about efficiency and even IT strategy from junior level employees displayed by the management of this software testing firm is in sharp contrast to the attitude of management at the most successful firms. Bill Gates and Microsoft senior management likewise did not see the importance of the Internet, but their approach to managing IT ensured that although they might not have seen its importance to begin with, Microsoft still exploited its potential. Bill Gates said, 'The impetus for Microsoft's response to . . . Internet did not come from me or other senior executives. It came from a small number of people who saw events unfolding . . . smart people anywhere in the organization should have the power to drive an initiative.'[3]

Generating ideas will not by itself achieve any cost reduction or efficiency gains. The ideas must be evaluated and then those that pass the evaluation must be implemented. Staff quickly sense whether their ideas are being evaluated and acted on, or whether the request for ideas from management is just another instance of tokenism.

The mechanism to manage the flow of ideas from the cost reduction hotline must address three needs; the needs to:

■ manage the flow of information;

■ evaluate ideas;

■ ensure implementation of ideas that pass evaluation.

Figure 4.2 shows the path along which information flows, and key implementation questions at each stage.

Managing the flow of information means putting in place channels through which staff can transmit ideas to whoever is designated to receive them, which may be a central cost reduction or efficiency committee, or a single individual, or, in the case of an IT-specific initiative, the IT task force. Examples of channels include telephone hotlines, which can be voicemail boxes or human operators, an internal mail address or an email address. For organizations that have a good firm-wide email system, email is usually used for more than 95% of suggestions, and should be a sufficient channel on its own.

Evaluating the ideas may be done in two stages, with an individual responsible for pre-screening the ideas before the remainder are evaluated by a committee. Pre-screening might involve contact with the originator of the idea to clarify the idea or obtain further information needed to make a proper evaluation.

At either stage, it is necessary to agree evaluation criteria. Considered in the abstract, the net pressure value (NPV) for each idea should be calculated and ideas evaluated accordingly. There are at least three practical difficulties that rule out such

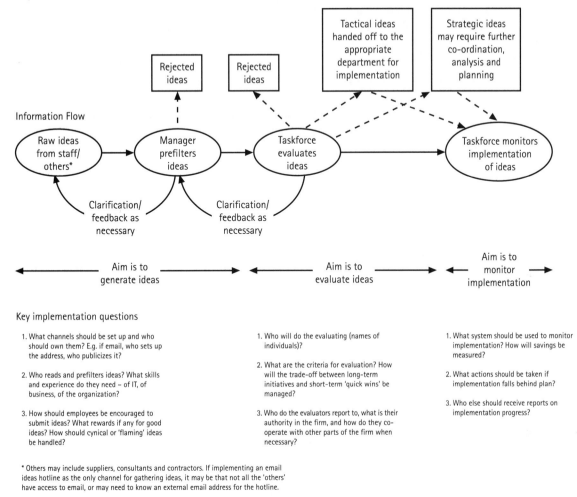

Fig. 4.2 Information flows along the cost reduction hotline

an approach, at least in the early stage of evaluation. First, many of the ideas generated will be unsuitable to the organization or politically unacceptable for a variety of reasons, for example, because such an initiative was tried last year and found unsatisfactory. Secondly, the effort required to calculate NPVs for all but the simplest ideas is not trivial, and such analytical resources as are available need to be focused on calculating NPVs for those initiatives that are more promising than others (this is a pragmatic point more than a circular argument.). Thirdly, even when it is worth making a formal investment appraisal and calculating NPVs, the firm will probably want to start analysis of 'quick wins' before working on more strategic projects with longer-term payoffs.

One framework for evaluating projects that has been used in several organizations is shown in Table 4.4.

Ensuring implementation is about assigning responsibility for implementation to an individual manager, after getting their commitment to undertake implementation, and then monitoring implementation against the implementation plan.

Review list of all IT projects, current and planned: if your organization has a complete list of all IT projects underway firm-wide, then you are already on your way to managing costs well. In many organizations such lists still don't exist. IT projects are a major source of cost, and risk, in the modern firm. The management team running a business would expect to have a complete list of employees, of legal actions against

Table 4.4   Framework for evaluating cost reduction ideas

INFORMATION	Details/data	Evaluation comments
Idea serial number		
Date submitted		
Short title		
Date reviewed		
Originator		
Originator's dept		
Estimated $ payoff		
Short/medium/long term?		
Are > 2 man days of further analysis – Y/N		
Ease of implementation – H/M/L		
Has anything similar been tried before?		
EVALUATION		
Critical success factors		
A Immediate action B Limited further analysis required C Refer for strategic review X No further action		

the firm, and of customers among its management information. These are all potential sources of critical risk, revenue and cost. IT projects are also major potential sources of critical risk, revenue and cost, and as such should be recorded and available to the firm's management in the same way as other sources of risk, revenue and cost. When IT was still something of a novelty in senior management circles 20 years ago, there might have been more excuse not to document such information, but today it is harder to explain why some corporations are poor in tracking major items of spend and risk in IT. The firm needs to know what projects it has, what they cost, why they are being undertaken (ideally with an NPV estimate) and who is responsible for them. A large US telecoms company saved over $100m by simply terminating all IT projects for which no business case or sponsor existed. It found that many IT projects were continuing long after anyone ceased to be properly in charge of them, and when no-one in the firm, and even no-one on the project, could state the business benefits of the project.

What is a project? Definitions and observations

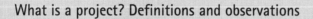

1. 'The principle identifying characteristic of a project is its novelty.'[4]

2. A project is used where a faster than normal rate of change is required in an organization, and requires a management system other than the normal management system of the organization.[5]

3. 'An endeavour in which human, material and financial resources are organized in a novel way, to undertake a unique scope of work of given specification, within constraints of cost and time, so to achieve unitary, beneficial change, through the delivery of quantified and qualitative objectives.'[6]

4. A project will have a defined and measurable objective, which, once achieved, marks the end of the project.

5. 'The most successful projects are those which allow the manager to . . . achieve a personal business objective.'[7]

All IT employees should be working either on 'business as usual' or on a project. Typical projects include Year 2000 projects, systems enhancement projects, application development projects, legacy systems elimination projects, new equipment rollout projects and feasibility studies. All projects should have a sponsor, an end date, a project plan, a business case and a project manager. Get a complete list of all IT-related projects underway or planned in the firm, and for each project show all the details just listed.

Gathering this data will be time consuming, a mini-project in itself, lasting perhaps three weeks in a firm with fewer senior IT managers or less-experienced senior IT managers. In a firm with much IT project management experience, it will be relatively straightforward. (Note that the level of experience in managing IT functions depends not just on the senior IT management but on the whole firm; it is possible that IT management would have liked to increase the use of project management techniques, but have been discouraged from doing so by the rest of the firm.) Typically, it should take one to two weeks to gather all the data. In best-practice firms, there is a centrally maintained list of IT projects with all relevant details. These might even be reviewed regularly to increase or decrease effort expended on projects according to the business cycle. There might be more control-related projects in hard times but overall a reduction in project expenditure, or expenditure as planned, with a shift away from control-related projects towards marketing or R&D support projects in good times.

Categories of project

Many organizations that run reviews of IT projects aim to classify all projects into something like the following categories:

1. Keep the lights on/business critical.
2. Must do/regulatory.
3. Highly desirable.
4. Need to be done at some point.
5. Others.

These categories are to a large extent self-explanatory. The key in categorizing projects is to ensure that projects are in the lowest classification possible. The risk is always that all projects end up being classified as 'keep the lights on' or 'must do'. To manage this risk, it is useful to know certain things about projects, and these are summarized below in Table 4.5. Examples of this format in use are given in Tables 4.6 and 4.7.

Once you have the data on projects, the IT cost reduction task force should review each project case by case to recommend to the firm's management whether projects should continue unchanged, be modified in some way or be terminated. This requires an understanding of the rationale and business benefits propounded for each project. It is likely that once you have the basic project data, someone from the IT cost reduction team will have to make enquiries to the sponsor, project manager or others about individual projects. For instance, the rationale for a Year 2000 project is self-

Table 4.5   Key data on IT projects

Project name	
Project sponsor	
Project manager	
Deliverable	*Summary of the final project deliverable, for example 'Installation of the firm's Internet home shopping order fulfilment system with a capacity for 50 000 customer orders of $100 average value per day*
Deliverable due date	
Next milestone	*Date*
Weeks project ahead/behind schedule	*Most practically determined by reference to the next project milestone*
Rationale for project	*This should be a $ NPV or, in the case of a regulatory requirement, the name of the regulation that requires the project*
Estimated total cost	*$ cost of project, if possible broken down into project staff and non-project staff/resources*
Dependencies	
Major issues and risks	
Category	*That is one of :* 1. *Keep the lights on/business critical* 2. *Must do/regulatory* 3. *Highly desirable* 4. *Need to be done at some point* 5. *Others*
Reason for category, with contact names for supporting evidence	*This is to try to ensure the proper categorization of projects*

Table 4.6   Example of key data on a Year 2000 project

Project name	Global Year 2000 compliance project
Project sponsor	Jean Brody
Project manager	John Mahatir
Deliverable	All IT hardware and software, including OS, used by the firm is to be either certified as Year 2000 compliant or eliminated from the firm by 9/99. Where a system is to be phased out, a phase-out plan is part of the deliverable.
Deliverable due date	9/99
Next milestone	7/99 – All non-2000-compliant systems switched off.
Weeks project ahead/behind schedule	(16 weeks)
Rationale for project	Year 2000 is not just a functional deadline but is required by the regulatory authorities (e.g., health and safety) for many of the firms' functions.
Estimated total cost	$ 420m
Dependencies	Industry-wide agreement on new data interchange standard by 5/99
Major issues and risks	
Category	*Must do/regulatory*
Reason for category, with contact names for supporting evidence	Main board directive of 2/95

Table 4.7 Example of key data on an e-commerce project

Project name	E-Firm
Project sponsor	Yolanda Kumar
Project manager	Michael Bryer
Deliverable	A pilot implementation of an Internet shopfront for 50% of the product line in the firm's consumer division, including all associated order fulfilment and credit card merchant services. To be capable of handling 20,000 orders/day.
Deliverable due date	1/00
Next milestone	6/99 – Stress testing of secure servers
Weeks project ahead/behind schedule	1 week ahead
Rationale for project	1. Most major competitors have similar initiatives 2. Estimated $11m NPV
Estimated total cost	$0.5m
Dependencies	Input from marketing, purchasing and strategic distribution partner
Major issues and risks	E-Firm programmers being transferred to the Year 2000 project to meet critical business needs
Category	Highly desirable
Reason for category, with contact names for supporting evidence	All major competitors have similar initiatives. The CEO approved this project at the 12/98 main board meeting.

evident, but the project managers might have useful information about how to gain efficiencies by adjusting the timing of other projects to enable them to take advantage of the great number of staff released as the Year 2000 effort winds down. For example, if your Year 2000 effort is releasing 120 staff in November 1999 and another project was due to initiate in October 1999, there can be opportunities to save on hiring costs and organizational learning curve costs by delaying the October project.[8] But the feasibility of this cannot be determined by a paper exercise – the two projects might need quite differently skilled IT staff. Someone from the IT cost reduction task force will need to identify the opportunities and issues in individual projects.

Ensuring that managers stay honest – the ranked menu

Often it is necessary to rely on information provided by IT managers and others regarding whether a particular project or activity is vital ('keep the lights on') or is merely desirable. One tool that can be used to try to keep the process honest is the ranked menu. This is simply a list of all projects and activities ranked with the most essential first, and the least essential or least urgent last. No item can be ranked in equal place with another: all items must be placed in order one after the other. When this ranking exercise is performed in a group, perhaps a workshop of senior IT managers, it forces a comparison of each item with another, thereby minimizing the chance that one individual will be able to label a merely desirable project as a 'keep the lights on' project. Next, the value of cutting each activity or project is written alongside each item. In this way whatever percentage saving is required can be gained by cutting or deferring the bottom x items from the list.

There will often be other projects where increased spending will lead to disproportionate savings. This can be because new information that was not available when the original business case was undertaken has come to light. One multinational printing group ran a project to install electronic design workstations throughout Europe to reduce the cost of creating regional variants of its magazines. And cost savings of $4m annually were achieved. However, nothing had been done to automate the production of printing plates, which were still being produced in Germany and shipped by courier all over Europe, and in some cases to the US and Asia as well. Extending the project by just two months enabled printing plates to be produced locally, saving another $3m annually. The project would not have been extended if there had been no IT cost reduction task force, because the design and origination side of this particular business had no interest or awareness of the cost drivers in the production side of the business, whereas to the cross-functional IT cost reduction team, the opportunities for massive savings were obvious. (The moral of the story is don't assume that all obvious cost reduction opportunities in IT are already known to the right people in your organization.)

So Table 4.8 shows a checklist of the kinds of things you need to know about individual projects to identify all possible areas for efficiency increases and cost reduction.

The IT cost reduction task force should review all projects once they are sufficiently well-understood and make a recommendation to the firm for action. Typically the actions to reduce IT project costs will be one of:

- increase spending and increase the NPV of the benefits to be realized;
- no change;
- merge two or more projects;
- reduce the project budget;
- delay the project or postpone indefinitely;
- cancel the project.

Table 4.8 Efficiency increase and cost reduction checklist

1. Is the project still worth doing?	- Is the business case on which the project was originally approved still valid? What were the assumptions? Have they changed?[9]
2. Can the project be delayed? Should it be delayed?	- How will delay change the business value of the project? 3 months/6 months/1 year delay? - What would be the advantages and disadvantages of delaying the project?
3. Are there potential synergies among projects?	- Why are there synergies? Who thinks so? Approximate value. - Can the project be combined with another to reduce project management overhead? - What other projects have similar aims? Are all necessary?
4. Should the structure of the project be changed?	- Have the aims, explicit or implicit, of the project changed? - Should the scope of the project be altered? - Should a more senior/more junior project manager be appointed? - Should the sponsorship of the project be changed?
5. Could the project deliver more value if there were increased investment?	- What other projects would benefit from this project? - Should this project be more ambitious? - What has been learnt about the risks and feasibility of the project so far?

Once the firm has approved the recommendations, the IT cost reduction task force should monitor and if necessary intervene to assist in the implementation of the changes. It is also vital that someone keeps a log of all changes and their associated cost savings, and the IT cost reduction task force is ideally placed to do this.

Review the cost benefit of all IT functions: as stated earlier, everyone in the IT department (or its analogous entities where IT is very decentralized) should be either working on a project, or on routine business. So, by logic alone, there should be no third possibility. This means that everyone on the payroll or hired as a temp or contractor whose value to the organization has not been addressed by the review of all projects, outlined above, must be covered by the task force's review of what the IT organization does in its routine functions. This is the purpose of the review of the cost benefit of all IT functions.

This is straightforward in principle, and should also be straightforward to implement. The starting point is an organizational diagram of all IT sub-departments and groups with budgets. Each group is reviewed on the criteria of cost/benefit – is each particular group worthwhile to the firm, and can they deliver whatever it is they deliver to the firm satisfactorily with a reduced budget? There are really three areas to focus on: headcount, contractors and equipment. It is a sad fact, but nonetheless a fact, that cost reduction means headcount elimination to a great extent. People are expensive, and they use equipment. One approach to reviewing the cost benefit of all IT functions is simply to interview all sub-department managers and ask them to explain how they would implement two or three degrees of cuts to their budget – say 5%, 10% and 15% – and with what consequences to the business.

The main task of the IT cost reduction task force at this stage is to keep the process honest. Good IT managers will adopt the right attitude to this initiative, and will suggest cutting less critical items from their budgets before more critical items. No one likes cutting staff or budgets, but it is part of every manager's duty when times are tough. There will often be some managers who either through misguided loyalty to their staff or through incompetence propose making the first cuts to more critical areas of their budget, perhaps in the hope that by doing so their department will be spared. Of course there might be some projects that simply cannot be cut at all, perhaps safety critical projects in nuclear power stations, but there are probably fewer than senior management imagine. In the run-up to the Year 2000, many senior managers have ringfenced Year 2000 IT projects, when the majority of managers and staff on such projects would agree in casual conversation that the average Year 2000 project was at least comfortably overmanned, and in some firms a positive bandwagon for any casual worker who needed an easy life and IT training thrown in.[10]

Keeping the review of the cost benefit of IT functions honest: three experiences

1. The schemer

The IT cost reduction task force asks the schemer to prepare impact analyzes of three scenarios, showing the effect on the business and what in his department would be changed to achieve a 5%, 10% and 15% cut. First the schemer ensures that all his direct reports know about an impending attempt by head office to cut their department by 10%, 20% or 30%, as if the decision had already been made, and ensures that none of his department are in a cooperative frame of mind. Next, he concocts some imaginary dependencies among his pet projects, which are adding little value to the firm, and the firm's major IT projects. Finally he ensures that his assistant will delay any meeting with the IT cost reduction team for as long as possible. The schemer is all set to make his contribution in the firm's hour of need.

2. The casual manager

The casual manager rose to his management position in the IT department by luck; indeed he is still surprised every day to find that no-one has noticed how little suited he is to the job. But he's not complaining, and generally works reasonably hard, although IT has always been a bit of a mystery to him. He relies on more competent junior staff, and delegates most of his work. This is fine for day-to-day management of his department, indeed many in IT do a far worse job of management than he does. But his staff know that he isn't on top of his job, and take advantage by hiding things. The casual manager has prepared as best he can for the urgent request from the IT cost reduction task force. His report looks good, although even the casual manager knows it is superficial in one or two places. Unbeknownst to him, his staff have kept back vital information about two obvious productivity gains that a more knowledgeable IT manager would have spotted. It will be up to the IT cost reduction task force to find out what these are.

3. The keen veteran

The keen veteran IT manager is a very rare breed. There are many keen young managers, and veteran managers, but keen veterans are rare. (They are not cheap either, but are invariably good value. Cutting them or reducing their benefits is invariably a false economy.) A junior member of the IT cost reduction task force had been despatched to interview the keen veteran about cost reduction opportunities in his department. Within minutes the keen veteran had pulled out a list of all employees, and a second list of all projects in his department. Both lists had dollar costs down the right hand side. It so happened that the keen veteran had precisely enough contractors and consultants working in his department to be able to make a 15% cut in costs without having to let go of any of the firm's permanent employees. (In fact the veteran was intending to lose one underperforming employee who had also made no attempt to fit in over the past two years, and replace him by offering a newly married freelancer who had done excellent work in the past 18 months a permanent supervisory job.) The veteran was a remarkable manager: five economic cycles had little dimmed his keenness, and he had learned after a couple of economic cycles always to manage his department and budget with sufficient flexibility to make changes, in both bad and good times. The meeting finished in just under ten minutes.

This phase of the IT cost reduction task force's work finishes when it has drawn up a list of actions to reduce costs by whatever percentage or percentages the firm requires. Or it might be up to the task force itself to recommend a percentage cost reduction.

Case study | Eliminating unread reports at a large German bank

After the 1998 crash in the Russian financial markets, banks around the world instituted crash cost reduction programmes, which naturally tended to focus on IT costs because these are usually the largest non-interest expenses of banks after premises and people-related costs. Mr DBR had been hired into the IT department to undertake a strategic review of IT costs several months before the Russian crisis erupted. The day following Russia's default, he was re-tasked to lead a more urgent and tactical IT cost reduction initiative.

This German bank was typical of most banks in that it produced a very large number of reports regularly. The daily reports, weekly reports and monthly reports produced each year numbered several thousand. Each report incurred costs in many ways. A system would have to be maintained to capture the data, and users might have to be trained to enter data into the data capture system where there was no automated data capture. Often the data capture systems would not be linked to the system creating the report, resulting in much manual re-keying of data. For instance, data on foreign exchange trades were often printed out in overseas offices from one of the bank's own computers, and then faxed to headquarters, where a graduate trainee diligently typed the data into another of the bank's computers, in fact, the same model running the same software as the one in the overseas branch. (The best graduate trainees tended to leave after a few months to work for big American banks, where they found temporary staff and secretaries fulfilling much the same role instead of graduate trainees.) The majority of reports were printed on to paper, some reports being so long that new equipment had to be purchased by the postroom to deliver the reports because they were so heavy that they contravened new health and safety regulations introduced by the European Union governing what could be carried by hand.

DBR had in fact been a graduate trainee at the same bank 12 years before, and was one of the many who had left to join a US bank after a few months of retyping data. There was less retyping of data now, but not much less. In DBR's original project to undertake a strategic review of IT costs he had planned to re-engineer the processes within the bank to eliminate the intensive re-keying of data. He knew that banking was not alone in this. As a management consultant he had seen similar large-scale inefficiency in a global car hire firm, a major US airline, and even a 'Big 6' accounting firm. However, the urgency to reduce costs created by the Russian crisis would not allow a business process re-engineering approach, which would require heavier investment than the firm could bear and in any case would show no results for at least six months and possibly a year, given the constraints on resources and capacity for change imposed by the twin demands of the EMU and Year 2000 projects.

The CFO had made it clear to DBR personally that his own job would be axed if he did not produce results very soon, but it was not at all clear what could be done to make massive savings. After four days of brainstorming around this problem, reading up on all the IT projects underway to see which could be cut and working closely with the finance people, DBR was still no nearer any solution that looked like it would achieve the savings the bank required. DBR was now starting to worry less about the bank and more about his own job. He had a wife and a newly born daughter to think of.

At this point DBR was sent to New York for a confidential meeting with the head of IT of a suitor who was interested in making an agreed takeover bid for the German bank, and wanted to understand the effort that would be involved in melding the IT organizations of the two banks. With the problem of the bank's costs still heavy on his mind, DBR found himself sitting next to an IT manager from another firm in business class. This was no surprise, as on every flight at least half of business class seemed to be IT professionals flying around the world. DBR failed to notice the irony that this little fact in the age of IT enabled instantaneous global communication by video and voice, but what he did notice was that his neighbour was reviewing a draft of a radical plan to cut IT costs. He struck up a conversation with his neighbour, a Canadian, who soon provided the answer to DBR's and DBR's firm's needs: cut all reports.

The Canadian had also been trying to fix the re-keying problem, but had figured that most of the reports were simply never read, or read much less frequently than they were produced. At first he had removed three daily reports from the pile near his desk waiting to go to the mailroom for distribution. No-one had complained, according to the employee whose only job was to produce these reports every day. The Canadian had then approached the management committee of his bank through his boss. It was agreed that all reports should be stopped for one day, but people would be on hand to receive any angry telephone calls demanding the reports. This was done the following week after all the necessary arrangements were made. In fact about 10% of reports were sent out, being those that were most obviously necessary to running the bank. Of the remainder, about 40% were never requested. Over 35% of reporting eliminated overnight! On further investigation it was found that many of the people who did ring up demanding reports were not the users of the reports, but administrators whose responsibilities included checking that a report had been received. More work was done to identify and talk to the ultimate users of the reports, with the result that by the end of the project just under 50% of reports had been eliminated or substantially reduced in size. There had been no formal quantification of the benefits, but everyone from senior management downwards agreed that millions of D-marks had been saved.

DBR proposed this initiative in his own bank, with similar spectacular results. Four months later he was promoted two levels to deputy head of the IT department, where he is now running one of the biggest business process re-engineering projects in the world.

Institute a small cost-monitoring unit

Role of the cost-monitoring unit

'Review the cost benefit' is basic business management in one sense, but can be very hard to do in practice. What tends to happen in any review of IT cost benefits is that some reasonably obvious changes in investment priorities or project terminations are identified, primarily because either economic and market conditions have changed or because projects that once looked promising have for whatever reason run into problems. Similarly, there are likely to be a few stellar projects that everyone agrees it would be foolish to curtail, and that might even merit further investment beyond that already planned. However, the majority of IT spend falls into neither category, because the cost benefits are unclear, particularly the costs. This is where a cost-monitoring unit comes in.

At the start of the chapter we looked at the distinction between the tactical cost reduction initiatives and the work of the cost monitoring unit, and found that the difference is one of management structure, but the work done can overlap. It is not worth getting too distracted by the differences between the two, and we see it more as a progression from the time when a firm needs to get something going (tactical cost reduction initiatives) to the next stage, when the firm is able to begin to put more structure in place around the initiatives. Any management structure set up to administer the tactical cost reduction initiatives, such as a cost reduction task force, might well become the basis of the cost-monitoring unit. Such things will depend on the circumstances of the organization concerned, and are not of great interest here.

Analytical role of the cost-monitoring unit

Although the subject matter of the tactical IT cost reduction initiatives and the cost monitoring unit may overlap, there is a difference in the kind of analysis undertaken, and this is worth briefly explaining here. The cost-monitoring unit has two purposes, which are not met in any systematic way by the cost reduction initiative. These are:

- to analyze and understand the key cost drivers in the firm's use of IT; and
- to take a firm-wide view of opportunities for cost reduction.

Key cost drivers of a firm's use of IT

The cost-monitoring unit should identify those factors that determine or drive IT costs, and analyze them to decompose them as far as possible into their elements. For instance, property rents are usually a major driver of IT costs. The elements of property costs are location and density of staff. Central locations incur higher rents than out of town or offshore sites, and increasing the density of staff will reduce costs. This breakdown could go further, and within density, for example, look at desk occupancy rates, which will be lower where individuals have their own desks than where 'hot-desking' is practised. Some typical key cost drivers are shown in Table 4.9. The cost-monitoring unit should understand these and know to what extent each can be controlled, and how. Having done so, it should have gained some insight into how the firm's overall IT costs can be managed better and efficiency gains achieved. For instance, if the location of IT development staff is likely to be the single most important IT cost driver over the next five years, then it is probably worth investigating the opportunity to increase efficiency by moving developers offshore. On the other hand, if legacy systems are identified as being the main source of controllable cost, then the cost-monitoring unit should investigate options for migrating away from legacy systems.

The cost-monitoring unit should be set up within a month to six weeks of the cost reduction initiative. Part of its work is to perform more detailed analysis for the cost reduction initiative, primarily in determining exactly what the specific IT costs under examination are, in cash terms. Some managers feel that this role should be performed by the financial controller's department. In practice the complexities of IT expenses have meant that most successful attempts at IT cost-monitoring have been performed by staff under operational control of the IT department. This may be financial controllers staff seconded to the head of IT, or a joint controllers/IT working group, or a special unit within controllers: the point is that one should not just expect the existing financial controllers' organization to start producing quite different cost data and cost analyzes from those produced to date without any organizational changes. Further, it seems that the simplest organizational change is to have a few people, typically four to eight in a large organization, working closely with IT and reporting directly to the head of IT, to monitor IT costs and perform detailed cost analysis as necessary in support of the cost reduction programme.

Table 4.9 Some typical key IT cost drivers

Driver	Elements
1 Compensation costs	Attrition rate Temporary to permanent ratio Management to staff ratio
2 Rent & property costs	Location Density – sq. ft m ft/desk Density – people/desk
3 User competence	User training Availability of helpdesk Changes to GUIs
4 Architectural complexity	Variety of different core systems Average age of systems (weighted)
5 Management reporting requirements	Cost transparency Number of change controls Systems documentation

A firm-wide view of opportunities for cost reduction

Many firms claim to be global organizations, because they understand that their customers are increasingly global and want suppliers and service partners who are also global. It is the nature of things that firms tend to be considerably more global in the customer-facing activities than in their internal administration and management, and herein lies a significant opportunity for cost reduction. The cost-monitoring unit should establish who buys what kinds of IT equipment and services, and look out especially for opportunities to achieve better deals with suppliers by negotiating on a global basis through a single point of contact. There are great economies to be made in most firms by negotiating for the supply of IT goods and services through a single function with global responsibility, rather than leaving all regions or countries to make their own arrangements.

Some goods and services inevitably have a strong local dimension, for instance temporary staff agencies or payroll agencies. Others, such as telecommunications and office desktop software are increasingly globalized commodities, where one supplier or a handful of suppliers can provide all a firm's needs globally. In many firms there is a global supplier, or a few global suppliers for particular IT goods and services, but your firm might have several supply contracts, each negotiated locally. It is the job of the cost-monitoring unit to identify all such duplication and evaluate the scope for increasing efficiency in negotiating with suppliers. Most often, several contracts are in place because the organization is in the process of moving from a regional struc-ture to a global structure, and a natural tendency of local managers to keep their own empires has discouraged moves to global sourcing.

Even if global arrangements with suppliers are in place, the cost-monitoring unit can usually do useful work in monitoring how well these are being used. There are many cases where global agreements exist with suppliers, but local management is either unaware of the agreements or is able to circumvent the agreements.

Staffing the cost-monitoring unit

Who should these people be? Aside from a competent and experienced manager, the workers on the team should be trained in accounting techniques, and have some experience of IT cost management. In a team of eight, the following approximate mix has worked well in a number of organizations: one manager, four trained accountants with experience of IT cost management, one or two trainee IT cost controllers (who can be trainee financial controllers or accountants under training), and one or two IT specialists who are keen to broaden their skill set by learning about accounting and finance. Many organizations staff half or more of such a team with contractors or other short-term workers, although many of these tend to end up as permanent employees, and we recommend against staffing more than half the team in this way. The demands of the work are usually intense for several months after initiating the cost-monitoring unit, which in many organizations will render the job unsuitable for part-time workers, although organizations with a strong ethical commitment to work sharing or part-time working may surmount this obstacle easily.

Endnotes

1 For a more detailed discussion of winners' games and losers' games in the context of financial management and particularly investment decision making, see Ellis (1975) or Ellis (1998).
2 For a description of a typical structure of an IT department and what each element does, see Appendix.
3 *Financial Times* (1999).
4 Lock (1992).
5 IBM's view. IBM is one of many organisations that have invested heavily in developing special-ized project management tools.
6 Turner (1992) quoted in Chapman (1997).
7 Crainer (1995).
8 There is at least one organisation whose Year 2000 project is due to end sometime in 2001.
9 E.g. projects for electronic retail commerce using proprietary systems rather than Internet are still alive and destroying shareholder value in at least two UK retail banks as at March 1999. Most of the rest of the world knows that Internet is at least ten times cheaper and hundreds of times easier to use, and can be made as secure as the users want.

10 This is no exaggeration. The author knows three people, two in London and one in New York, who worked in coffee bars one day and had jobs on Year 2000 projects the next. None had previously worked in IT. But then how much difference is there between being good at running a team shift in a coffee bar and running a team anywhere else? In October 1999 a managing director in the Fixed Income department one of the biggest US bond houses said, 'At least half of our Year 2000 project is a complete waste of money because the work is basically unnecessary – but I guess it's the firm's contribution to social welfare.'

5 Key performance indicators and benchmarking

You can't manage what you don't measure.

Anon

Ever since the new data processing tools first emerged 30 or 40 years ago, businesspeople have both overrated and underrated the importance of information in the organization.

Peter F. Drucker[1]

Key performance indicators (KPIs)

A KPI is a metric or systematic estimate of the performance of an individual business function or activity that is critical to the performance of the overall business unit or firm. KPIs can be used by management to run their businesses optimally. Why use a KPI rather than just measuring the output of the business unit directly? KPIs are most useful when it is either impossible or impractical to measure the output or a critical aspect of the output of the business unit directly, or when there are so many aspects of the output that could be measured that to measure all of them would yield more data than is manageable. Grove's 'breakfast factory' described below illustrates the problem that KPIs are used to overcome. Good KPIs will enable managers to link business activities to business performance. We are interested in using them to link IT activity and expenditure to business performance.

Benchmarking will be discussed later in the chapter, but at this point it is worth clarifying our terminology and pointing out the conceptual link between KPIs and benchmarking that often has considerable practical value for managers wanting to improve their understanding and control over IT costs in their organization. In some ways a KPIs is a benchmark. In this sense, benchmarks or KPIs measure the efficiency or effectiveness of some aspect of an organization's IT. For our purposes, however, benchmarking is the activity by which the KPI is obtained; we use the term 'KPI' rather than 'benchmark' for the metric, and the verb 'to benchmark' to refer to the activity of obtaining comparative data including KPIs from other organizations.

An example of a good KPI is the output of the IT helpdesk in an organization. Let us assume that the purpose of this organization's helpdesk is to help staff use their IT equipment effectively by managing the maintenance and repair of defective hardware and software, and to answer basic questions about how to use the organization's most common software packages. Given this statement of the helpdesk's purpose, it is not too clear what a measure of the helpdesk's output would be. To measure the number of repairs carried out would ignore the preventative maintenance and 'questions answered' roles of the helpdesk, besides failing to reflect that some problems are more severe or just take much longer to fix than others. To measure the number of hours worked does not measure the productivity achieved in those hours. Yet the firm as a whole will tend to have a view on whether its helpdesk is good or not so good and whether its service has improved or worsened over the last year. The helpdesk manager would like to be able to measure something that he can manage in order to ensure that the helpdesk keeps improving the service provided to users. KPIs and benchmarking are about measuring things so that you can manage them. Andy Grove of Intel gives a simple example of KPIs (which are called 'indicators' at Intel) in the example of the breakfast factory reproduced below.

So KPIs are indirect measures of output. They are used in managing business units (including business support units) where direct output metrics are difficult to obtain or use. As such, they are valuable to any management team committed to understanding and managing IT costs. A good set of KPIs is rated very highly as a tool to improve the efficiency of IT management, but are KPIs in fact widely used? A recent survey[2] found that only 50% of companies claim to use metrics actively in the management of IT, and, of these, only 15% use them on at least a monthly basis. The use of KPIs is increasing and within five years most medium to large firms will be using KPIs to manage IT and IT-dependent functions because of their great value as management tools.

Andy Grove, President of Intel: 'Indicators as a Key Tool'[3]

[Grove imagines a 'breakfast factory', which serves to illustrate the use of performance indicators. The breakfast factory is a factory dedicated to manufacturing or cooking breakfasts of fried eggs, bacon, sausages, coffee and so on.] . . . *As a manager of the factory, you have a substantial staff and a lot of automated equipment. But to run your operation well, you will need a set of good indicators, or measurements. Your output, of course, is no longer the breakfasts that you deliver personally but rather all the breakfasts your factory delivers, the profits generated, and the satisfaction of your customers. Just to get a fix on your output, you need a number of indicators; to get efficiency and high output, you need even more of them. The number of possible indicators you can choose is virtually limitless, but for any set of them to be useful, you have to focus each indicator on a specific operational goal.*

The term 'KPI' is in widespread usage, but there are several other terms which are sometimes used to mean the same as we mean by KPI. These include:

- performance indicators;
- performance measurement indicators;
- operational metrics;
- strategic management metrics;
- indicators;
- indicators and warnings;
- vital statistics;
- leading indicators.

The three main kinds of KPIs have to do with performance, cost and macro KPIs.

Performance related KPIs

These are KPIs which measure the rate at which an input or resource is used, or what service level is achieved. Examples of inputs or resources used include:

- proportion of memory used;
- proportion of bandwidth used;
- number of programmers or developers used;
- man-hours used;
- minutes of calls to third line technical support (if this is charged by the minute).

Examples of service levels against which achievement can be measured include:

- average time for helpdesk to answer calls;
- proportion of email traffic delivered internally within five minutes;
- proportion of non-trivial errors in database (be sure to define what counts as trivial);
- web availability to clients;
- mean time between failures (mainframes especially);
- wait times between device usage;
- network availability (client/server systems).

Cost-related KPIs

Many costs can be tracked in IT, the key for KPIs is to keep to those which are relevant to business performance. Cheap web access is not the same as cost effective web access, for instance. Examples of cost-related KPIs include:

- ■ $ per millions of instructions per second (MIP). Often used for mainframes or datacentres.

- ■ $ per user per year – meaning the fully loaded IT cost of supporting and providing for a user's computing needs (usually a desktop PC) for a year.

- ■ $ per line of code. This metric is discredited, as, unsurprisingly, it encouraged verbosity in programmers who were rewarded on this metric.

- ■ $ per gigabyte. This can be used to measure memory capacity, or as gigabytes per week to measure Internet or other network traffic.

- ■ $ per project. An interesting one, used more to help managers understand the average size, and by implication complexity, of projects than as an indication that particular projects are too large or too small.

- ■ $ per web hit. This measures how much you are spending for each hit on a website.

Macro KPIs

These are also known as 'structural KPIs'. Macro KPIs are a slightly different kind of KPI to cost and performance-level KPIs, and in a sense are sometimes KPIs about KPIs. Examples include:

- ■ number of levels in the hierarchy of an IT department;

- ■ number of points at which a service-level KPI is measured. This can be important when the accuracy or complexity of a KPI is an issue;

- ■ rate of change of KPIs. This can indicate organizational readiness or ability to change, or the uptake of a re-engineered process.

KPIs are context-dependent. That is, the right set of KPIs to use will depend on the context of your business unit. Lower-level business managers will need lower-level KPIs than higher-level managers. The case study below of examples of benchmarking in use in IT management, shows an example of such a hierarchy of KPIs. The structure and availability of management information and the culture of an organization will also influence what is the most appropriate KPI for you and your organization. KPIs should support the organizational structure, which means that managers should manage by KPIs over which they have control or influence. It may be that in the course of designing a set of KPIs, deficiencies in the structure of the organization are revealed, but this circumstance falls more properly under the heading of IT strategy, which is addressed in Chapter 6. The culture of an organization affects everything about the organization, and KPIs are no exception. We will not spend more time addressing cultural issues here.

Benchmarking

Perhaps the most obvious traditional approach to identifying aspects of information strategy is benchmarking.

Thomas H. Davenport[4]

Benchmarking means making a comparison between a process and a type of resource or an organizational structure in different organizations. Benchmarking will be familiar to most managers, at least through indirect experience. The rationale of benchmarking is simply to avoid re-inventing the wheel. Is someone else more efficient than you are? If you can find another organization that manages to run the same business process that you run but at lower cost, it's probably better to copy what they do in this area than to start from scratch in trying to improve your process. Benchmarking means comparing how your organization does things to how those things are done elsewhere so that you can improve. Benchmarking is about measuring so that you can manage better.

The most widely experienced instance of benchmarking is in the marketplace: your customers benchmark your price and quality against your competition's almost every time they make a buying decision. Monopolies tend to be inefficient, and often this is because customers have no choice. However, it can also be because customers have no comparisons to make, or it is not possible to benchmark. Benchmarking is a way to increase the range of comparisons that management can make concerning the processes and resources they manage. The marketplace may be the most widely experienced form of benchmarking, but the term 'benchmarking' is usually reserved for application to processes, resources or organizational structures that are hidden from the end customer, and most of what goes on in an organization is entirely hidden from the customer. The case study shows four different examples of benchmarking in use in IT management.

Peter Drucker makes the point memorably: 'Inside an organization, there are only cost centers. The only profit center is a customer whose check has not bounced'.[5] The customer is the most important benchmarker, but the score he gives to your product or service depends on a myriad of processes that go on out of sight of the customer but within your firm's control, inside your firm. To control your end-product and so ultimately induce changes in your customer's behaviour, you need to optimize this myriad of hidden processes. Benchmarking can help you to do this. Benchmarking is about optimizing your firm's processes and resources and structure so that ultimately your potential customers spend more with you than they would otherwise.

Examples of benchmarking in use in IT management

IBM and Barclays

Barclays Bank, the UK retail banking group, appears to have nothing in common with IBM, but IBM had a reputation for managing its laser printing and photocopying efficiently. IBM was a major supplier to Barclays, and when Barclays was moving a division to new offices in London, IBM was happy to allow Barclays to investigate its structure, processes and management of printing and copying. IBM was able to equip its offices with significantly fewer printers and copiers than Barclays, despite having a comparable amount of clerical work per worker according to offices studies. For example, IBM had a hierarchy of printers of different capacities, with lower-capacity printers for small jobs closer to workers and larger-capacity machines in separate print rooms. The studies enabled Barclays to reduce the cost of printing and copying when it moved to its new offices.

PolyGram

PolyGram is a global entertainments company with revenues of over $5bn. PolyGram's market research department uses KPIs to improve efficiency in analysis, modelling and distribution of research information. According to PolyGram's international systems manager, PolyGram needed to replace its existing market research system quickly and move that function to a new location. Benefits include more effective market research and a reduction of paper reports. More effective market research meant that PolyGram had better insights into its market, which is how KPIs helped PolyGram become more effective.

British Airways

British Airways is the world's most successful ex-state-owned airline. It is passionate about two things in particular, customer service and IT. British Airways uses KPIs as one of the links between the two, as a way of ensuring that investment in IT actually results in an improved and cost-effective customer service. KPIs are integral to the way that British Airways is managed, in IT as well as in other areas. We believe that British Airways has been especially successful in developing KPIs that ensure technology is managed to give the best possible business results, such as the best possible level of customer satisfaction at a given cost. Sir Colin Marshall, the chairman of British Airways, often acknowledges the role that good use of IT has played in BA's success. For instance, he said 'We also are working on a joint approach to information technology, which should provide the underpinning for a greater uniformity of customer service . . . This technology integration will allow us to share information on customers and costs, which will then allow partners in the network to take a network perspective when they make decisions about investments ranging from aircraft purchases to catering.'[6]

Charles Schwab

Charles Schwab has terrified the traditional investment bankers – a rare feat! By understanding the potential of technology, especially the Internet, Schwab has grown from being a minor brokerage house to a greater market capitalization than Merrill Lynch. It seems that Charles Schwab's ability to implement technology is what actually enabled him to have such a good vision of the way forward, the vision did not just happen in a vacuum. Benchmarking and KPIs are essential to Schwab's ability to implement technology efficiently. Schwab is thought to spend more than $250m each year on IT, so managing IT is no trivial issue for Schwab. Schwab is unusual in using KPIs that focus on the risk of not investing in particular new technologies, and some of these KPIs work by using options pricing theory. Customer satisfaction is among the more traditional KPIs used by Schwab.[7]

In the context of understanding and managing IT costs, benchmarking can be used to answer questions of several kinds.

Operational level – business unit/support unit management

1. Am I paying too much for particular IT services?
2. Are we at a competitive advantage/disadvantage with respect to the responsiveness of our IT?
3. How well does IT meet our business needs compared to key competitors?

Corporate management

4. Is the firm investing the right amount in IT compared to key competitors?
5. How does the firm's return on its investment in IT compare to key competitors?
6. What strategic options have we got through our investment in IT?
7. How does the skill level of our IT people compare with key competitors?

Naturally the corporate management questions are at a more abstract level than the operational-level questions. If you are new to using KPIs to manage IT efficiency, it is probably worth thinking in some depth about what sort of questions you should be answering given the level at which you manage in your organization. This point is similar to the point about Barclays using IBM's laser printing and photocopying or benchmarks (see case study above).

Practical steps to implementing KPIs and benchmarking

We started this chapter by looking at what KPIs and benchmarking are and then at how they are used. KPIs have been used to achieve large increases in IT efficiency in many organizations, often accompanied by overall cost reduction at the same time. However, there are some practical issues to consider in implementing KPIs. The aim of this chapter is to enable a business manager to design and use KPIs and see results. Next we will look at practical steps to implementing KPIs.

How to implement KPIs

There are three main practical issues in selecting, implementing and managing KPIs. These are:

- data availability and cost
- balance versus directed action
- organizational and behavioural evolution.

The first two issues have been identified at the start of the chapter, but are worth exploring in more detail here. No less important from the practitioner's point of view is the impact of the evolution of organizations and human behaviour, which we will also look at here in more detail.

Data availability and cost

The availability of management information sets the boundaries to what KPIs can be used. A manager never has complete information, and formulating KPIs is no exception to this rule. The key to formulating KPIs when working with information that has obvious gaps is to distinguish between when data are definitely not available and where they might perhaps be available but appear not to be. If it seems that the data you need to make a KPI useful don't exist, it's worth thinking what substitutes there might be. Data availability is a major problem in implementing KPIs, and some lateral thinking can save millions of dollars.

For example, suppose that a KPI requires data about the rate at which a new systems is being used by employees. Perhaps the new systems will do something at much lower cost than the old system, or will lower the company's exposure to litigation. So you've designed a KPI to measure the migration of employees away from the old system to the new system. Unfortunately for some reason you can't measure the number of users of each system directly. No-one keeps records, and to set up a record-keeping system would be expensive but also would just take too long. You could survey a sample of users at regular intervals, but again this would be expensive, and would convey the wrong impression about your company's IT capabilities. So how can you get the data for this vital KPI? It could be that the helpdesk logs calls by type of system used. Without knowing the ratio of calls to the helpdesk to users, you could still readily obtain the change in the ratio of calls to the helpdesk about the old system to calls about the new system. This would indicate the rate of conversion, and may well meet the needs of the KPI, all at no cost because the data is already there. This is the kind of thinking required if lack of data is not to hamper an initiative to put KPIs in place.

Balance versus directed action

The corollary to the dictum 'You can't manage what you don't measure' is 'you end up managing what you do measure'. In other words, once something has become a KPI, it becomes a focus of management attention. Management attention is a limited resource, and so other things on which management previously focused now get slightly less attention.

Suppose there is a company that is doing reasonably well but that somehow has no system of regular management reports, let alone KPIs. Now, if a single KPI is introduced throughout this imaginary company, say, a KPI that measures the cost of inputs, the management attention shifts to costs of inputs. These probably could be improved, and for a few months excess costs of inputs are eliminated, resulting in greater efficiency to the organization overall. However, at some point input costs become well-managed, and diminishing marginal returns set in, and there are more productive uses of management's time than to keep focusing on input costs. The problem is that KPIs shift management focus, and the shift in focus is valuable for a limited time only. So the question is how to know when to reduce the focus induced by the KPI.

One answer is to pair KPIs, each primary KPI being paired with a secondary KPI. The purpose of the secondary KPI is to limit the management action suggested by the first KPI to what is reasonable. Think of being given directions to a hotel late at night when it's dark. You might be told 'Go over the bridge over the river, then turn left and drive along a road with a forest on your right. It's about five miles, but if you come to a lake you've gone a mile too far.' With respect to finding the hotel, the forest on the right is a KPI (indeed as is the bridge over the river), in that it tells you that you are going in the right direction, at least for the first five miles. The lake is the secondary KPI, because it indicates that you have been acting on the first KPI for a little too long and need to stop or turn round. The primary KPI tells you how well the key activity or resource or structure is performing. The secondary KPI tells you when you should shift your management focus away from this primary KPI on to some other KPI. Secondary KPIs are useful but not always essential, which is why they are called 'secondary'.

In practice there may be occasions when time does not permit you to design a secondary KPI, or where there simply isn't one. You may also feel it more efficient to implement the primary KPI first, and the secondary KPI some time later. In practice you should expect it to take some time to get the right KPIs for your organization. Finally, if you are not happy with your understanding of how your IT costs work and how they can best be managed, a well-designed set of KPIs will greatly improve things.

Let's now design a pair of KPIs. Suppose that some of your staff are unhappy with the service provided by the IT helpdesk, and you have noticed that your department is allocated substantial costs for the provision of helpdesk services, but you have no feel at all for whether your department is getting value for money from the helpdesk. What you want is a pair of KPIs to measure the value for money you are getting from the IT helpdesk. We will describe a simple four-step process to achieve this:

■ problem analysis and data gathering

■ identify team to design KPIs

■ design and test KPIs

■ implement and monitor.

However, do first ask yourself whether instituting KPIs for the problem under consideration is the best option. Just because you've got a tool doesn't mean you have to use it, and there are other ways to manage IT costs that may be better. In particular, note that in the very process of instituting KPIs you may discover solutions better than KPIs to some of your IT cost and management issues, thus leaving a better potential set of KPIs remaining. One manager in Texas was halfway through implementing KPIs to improve the utilization of spare parts for workstation computers. She noticed in the data-gathering phase of the project that every spare part except for modems were carried in the inventory, and this led her to discover that remote diagnostics by modem would eliminate the entire need for repair and maintenance stocks. The service engineers had been keeping quiet about this possibility in order to preserve their jobs, understandably enough.

Problem analysis and data gathering

The aim of this step is to define as clearly and completely as possible the problem for which KPIs are needed. We have just supposed that as a manager your subordinates have expressed unhappiness with the helpdesk service. The aim is to determine in as much detail as possible what this means. Is the issue that the helpdesk is slow to answer telephone calls, or that its staff are ineffective through poor skills or through poor motivation, or that after logging a call there is an unacceptable delay? Or some combination of these? When is the problem most severe and least severe – what time of day, what day of the week, when in the month, after what other kind of event? These are the sorts of questions to ask in defining the problem. See what data are available to answer the questions; for example, if the concern is that the average time for the helpdesk to answer a user's telephone call is too long, how long is the average wait? Is the average waiting time recorded anywhere? If not, has it ever been? If is was once recorded and is no longer, why not, and who changed it – they might be worth talking to? If no data is available from elsewhere, then one of your staff perhaps should make sample calls and keep a record of the waiting time.

This example of calls to a helpdesk is deliberately simple and probably would not be the subject of any KPI at a senior level in an organization, but the purpose of choosing a simple example is to show how you can go about implementing KPIs in your own organization tomorrow. Later we will look at more complex cases, but the best implementation of the same KPI will vary between different organizations.

Once you are happy that you have the best possible description of the problem for which you want a KPI and any available data, consider whether a KPI is the best approach to this problem. For instance, if the proposal is to monitor the average time taken by the helpdesk to answer calls, first of all check that the delays are a material cause of problems to your department. Is the length of delays merely irritating, or is business performance being degraded? It may seem slightly unnecessary to make this point, or to make the point that managers should aim to implement first those KPIs that will have the greatest business impact. However, experience suggests that often the KPIs that get discussed and implemented first are those that are either most familiar to staff involved from previous work with KPIs, or are those KPIs that are easiest to implement. In managing IT costs getting the right KPI is often hard work, but yields proportionately high dividends to the easiest KPIs. So at the end of the problem analysis stage, ask three questions:

■ From the analysis done, is there a real problem here, or are we focusing on an irritation rather than something critical?

■ From the analysis done, is there likely to be a better solution than implementing a KPI?

■ Are we focusing on the greatest KPI opportunity, or have we picked something too easy but relatively minor compared to some of the other IT cost or efficiency areas of concern where KPIs would help?

In the example of the delay in answering users' calls to the helpdesk, it could be that the IT department is well aware of the problem. Perhaps the cause is an unexpected epidemic of flu, which has left the helpdesk short staffed for six weeks, but the helpdesk management has a plan that should remedy the problem soon. In such a case it is probably not worth pursuing KPIs for time to answer calls.

Identify team to design KPIs

Suppose that the problem to be measured by KPIs is significant, is not temporary, and is a legitimate top management priority in your area of the firm. You have defined the

Memo
From: Margaret Hildegarde, President, Global Web Marketing
To: Dennis Downing, Divisional IT Mgr

Bill,

Last week's management committee discussed the company's web marketing pilot, and agreed that we should plan to roll this out as a major marketing initiative as soon as possible. This is a major increase in scale for the project, which had started as an informal and very small project. Your assistance will be vital to ensuring the success of this scaled-up initiative.

One of the first things we need to do is to set up some KPIs to help us ensure that the transition of this project from small pilot to major initiative is managed as efficiently as possible from the IT perspective. Over the last two weeks Nigel Carrington has been leading a project to gather data for this, summarized below:

1. There is strong consensus at all levels in our company and among a sample of customers that web-based marketing is vital to our future.
70% of our competitors already have similar initiatives, and we believe all the rest plan to do so within the next year.
2. The rationale for web-based marketing in our industry is threefold: to increase the number and types of potential that we can reach; to improve our quality of service by delivering solutions to customers faster and making sure those solutions are better aligned to customer needs; and to reduce our sales-related expenses.
3. Our market is primarily English speakers, and so far we have served English speakers in the US and UK. However, another 40% of potential customers are outside the UK and US, and the web-based marketing initiative should cater for this.
4. Our existing website is receiving an average of 3,500 hits per day, increasing at a rate of 6% per month, as of last week. With our existing site, only 6% of sales orders received through the site are processed into shipments with no further manual intervention. Benchmarking data from the recent Vain Consulting survey suggests that a figure of over 80% is achievable, although interviews with senior managers here indicate that for us 50% is a more realistic target and would anyway reduce our cost of sales significantly (30% or more at a ballpark estimate).

5. Customer satisfaction with our site is poor. An independent survey shows our existing website as being rated seventh out of 11 among the major firms operating in our sector on the web. Similarly, the site scores only 3/10 in the Rouge, Robert & House survey of website user-friendliness, against 8/10 for the top quartile.

As a small pilot our IT spending to date on the web initiative has been minimal, and we have used redundant hardware and third-party access to keep costs low. It is likely that a budget of several million dollars will be allocated for transforming this from a pilot to a marketing initiative. As will all our IT, the Chairman is very concerned that any budget for this initiative, once approved, will run the risk he sees in all IT projects of money being spent to no visible effect. I'd like us to come up with a few KPIs to help us make the best investment decisions as we make the transformation and so that everyone else can see that too. We're certainly going to have to spend something on increasing our capacity, we just need to make sure we spend it in the best places.

Let's talk about this in the next day or so.

problem and gathered as much data as is feasible. The above example is a memo that details the sort of data you are looking for. The next step is to put together a team to design the KPI pair or pairs. Who should be in this team depends very much on where you sit as a manager in your organization, and at what level a KPI is required. Typically, you will find that your needs fall into one of three kinds of situation:

- **Tactical:** where a business unit manager wants KPIs primarily as a tool to exert greater control over the business unit's IT cost allocations. The two key features of this situation are that, first, your needs are to work with another part of your organization, typically the IT department, to develop KPIs, and secondly, you might be doing this without the support of a high-level mandate from corporate headquarters.

- **Strategic:** where a corporate headquarters or other firm-wide group of managers, such as a group of business unit managers, have decided to implement KPIs to improve the firm's overall understanding of its IT cost drivers and its managers' ability to maximize the effectiveness of IT in many business units. The two key features of this situation are, first, that there will very likely be a stronger mandate in the previous, tactical, situation, and secondly, the whole firm is involved, which will mean that many of the KPIs are likely to be higher-level KPIs than those in the tactical case.

■ **Intra-divisional**: where one department wants to institute KPIs in order to manage itself better. Typically in the case of KPIs for IT this will be the IT department itself. The two key features of this situation are, first, that no other part of the firm needs to be involved, and secondly, that many of the KPIs will have a more technical emphasis than in the strategic and tactical situations. As this book is designed for the ordinary business manager, this fascinating area is outside its scope. However, in contrast to the situation facing ordinary managers attempting to understand and manage IT costs, there is a substantial body of literature for IT professionals who need KPIs and other performance metrics for the IT organization.[8]

One reason for having a team to design the KPIs is that for all but the simplest problems, to design good KPIs for IT cost and IT management will require input from the IT function and probably some other functions, such as finance. Another reason for having a team to design the KPIs is to be able to include individuals who will be key to implementing KPIs later on. The best implementations begin before the implementation phase. The following list shows the interests that are typically represented in a successful KPI design team, although much depends on the particular structure and nature of your own organization:

Tactical situation	Strategic situation
■ Business unit management	■ Firm management
■ Business unit users	■ Divisional management
■ IT	■ IT – main IT sub-departments
■ Finance/allocations	■ Support unit management

Once the team is in place, then start designing your KPIs.

Design and test KPIs

The first thing to do in the design and test phase is to review the analysis you conducted in the first phase, 'Problem analysis and data gathering'. There are two reasons for this. First, the team brings new expertise and information, and it is valuable to have your findings reviewed to identify any gaps or errors. Secondly, as at the start of any project, it is important to get the buy-in of all participants, and to ensure a shared understanding of the task ahead.

Next, design some KPIs. There are a number of ways to do this depending on the actual data available and your experience. Sometimes the KPIs can be designed by a virtual group, which never meets physically but communicates ideas and makes decision by email and the occasional conference call. Sometimes a series of meetings will be the most effective way to design KPIs. And in some organizations there will be a preference to call in external consultants to undertake this work, and most of the major consulting firms and many of the minor firms working in the field of IT management have some expertise in designing and implementing KPIs. Choose whichever approach you feel most comfortable with, they all work.

Table 5.1 shows the information to include in a design specification for KPIs.

Table 5.1   Information to include in a design specification for KPIs

	Information	Comments
1	Rationale for the KPI	A statement of the problem that the KPI is being designed to help solve, and a brief explanation of how the KPI is intended to be used to solve the problem
2	Size of the problem addressed by the KPI	The approximate dollar cost of the problem, if possible, or the specific law or regulation that requires the KPI. (This latter piece of information is useful in helping to ensure that if regulations change, redundant KPIs can be eliminated.)
3	Description of the KPI pair chosen	The description should show how the KPIs should be calculated and explaining any special terms used.
4	Data sources	A list of data sources required for calculating the KPIs, together with the owner of each data source. The data source owner means the part of the organization responsible for providing the data, not the individual, who may move on to a different role.
5	KPI frequency	The frequency with which the KPI should be reported
6	Who should receive the KPI?	The recipients are likely to be reasonably obvious, but it may be worth considering who should also see the report for information. Are there political allies you need in the organization who have an interest?
7	Who was involved in deciding the KPI?	So that if the KPI needs to be redesigned at a later date, the corporate memory exists to identify efficiently who may be able to help or explain decision in more detail
8	Key issues and risks	Note briefly any risks or issues identified. It may well be that in the analysis or design phases factors were identified that may invalidate or increase the importance of the KPI at a later date.

See the example above of the memo which contained information to be included in a new KPI. From that memo the sort of design specification shown in Table 5.2 could be written.

Table 5.2 Design specification

	Information	Comments
1	Rationale for the KPI	To ensure that the $3.5m IT investment in transforming the pilot project into the full-scale global web marketing initiative is as efficient as possible, and seen to be so
2	Size of the problem addressed by the KPI	1) $3.5m spend over two years on technology; 2) Estimated $10m of existing sales related costs that could be eliminated by a good web-driven sales process
3A	Description of the first KPI pair chosen	*Primary KPI A:* Percentage of 'end-to-end' sales transaction through the site. This is the number of sales which are initiated on the website and progress to fulfilment without any further manual intervention, which means no further telephone calls, none of our staff access any paper records, no manual checking of data. *Secondary KPI A:* Expected cost per transaction at full scale of operation. This is the cost per transaction, after adjusting actual costs incurred to (a) amortize investment over five years, and (b) allow for our marketing effort being in only a limited part of our overall market initially. The net effect is that this KPI should show what our costs per sale would be if we were operating at full scale.
3B	Description of the second KPI pair chosen	*Primary KPI B:* User-friendliness score in the consultants' (Rouge, Robert & House) survey, provided that we can get them to update this score monthly. If not, then we will execute our own customer satisfaction survey every month for the first 12 months, and then review moving to a quarterly measure. *Secondary KPI B:* Standard deviation of user-friendliness scores (or survey scores) for top ten competitors

Table 5.2 (cont.)

	Information	Comments
4	Data sources	*Primary KPI A:* ■ Sales data from shipping department ■ New database of 'end-to-end' sales – IT department to build? *Secondary KPI A:* ■ Financial control department *Primary KPI B:* ■ If they can provide monthly data, Rouge, Robert & House ■ If not, marketing department as an in-house project *Secondary KPI B:* ■ Marketing department
5	KPI frequency	Review regularly, but for the moment plan on monthly KPI reporting. In any case, review after one year.
6	Who should receive the KPI?	*For action:* Executive management of global web marketing initiative *For information:* All senior management
	Who was involved in deciding the KPI?	Global web marketing team, finance department, IT department
7	Key issues and risks	■ Monthly data may not be sufficiently frequent ■ Adjustments for secondary KPI A may be so inaccurate as to be meaningless ■ User-friendliness score may not be well correlated to probability of a sale

If you have not been involved yourself in creating the KPI, do not be afraid to ask where the data for the KPI will come from, or why the proposed KPI is relevant to the agreed definition of the problem. There are many cases where much effort has gone into designing KPIs that do not achieve their intended purpose.

Implement and monitor

As discussed earlier, it helps in implementing KPIs if the key managers involved in implementation have been involved in the process of designing the KPIs, and they certainly should have been involved in testing the KPIs. Usually the key individuals will include at least one manager from the IT department, and may include a manager from the financial controller's department. The need for input to implementation from the financial controller's department will depend on the functionality of your organization's management information systems. If you have a comprehensive activity-based costing system, then it might be the case that any cost data necessary for the KPI can be extracted without specialist help from financial controllers. Or perhaps only a minimal amount of programming by their department is needed and can be obtained by a routine request for setting up new management reports. However, if management accounting data is not readily available, then managerial-level support from the financial controller's department may be necessary for implementing the KPI.

Implementation should mark the transition from the project stage to the business as usual stage of the initiative to set up KPIs. That is, all specially convened structures and processes such as the KPI design team can be wound up, and from now on KPIs should be produced regularly as part of the normal business routine. This is accomplished in the normal way, and an individual is nominated to be responsible for ensuring that the KPIs are reported regularly.

Who should design KPIs?

KPIs are best designed by teams including the business unit manager who bears the IT costs.

Organizational and behavioural evolution

One of the world's largest software companies faced a serious earnings quality problem about ten years ago. One of the main causes was identified by management as being a decline in the level of customer satisfaction. The company had once been a byword for reliability, value for money, innovation and customer focus. But a large increase in sales seemed to have caused an attitude of complacency and arrogance to pervade not just the clerical workers but also the sales force and researchers of the company. One of the steps taken to turn things around was to institute a set of KPIs, which included a customer satisfaction KPI. The KPIs helped the company to turn itself. The KPIs worked very well for many years, and were acknowledged as a key part of the new corporate culture.

However, ten years later the company was in trouble again and senior managers were beginning to doubt the accuracy of the customer satisfaction KPIs. They were still calculated in the same way, but the results seemed intuitively wrong. The company hired an independent firm to audit the results given by this KPI. The audit found that the software company's organization had gradually evolved a mechanism to massage the customer satisfaction upwards. It identified 30 individual patterns of

Table 5.3 Some common KPIs

	Purpose of KPI pair	Primary KPI	Secondary KPI
1	To indicate efficiency of applications development management	$ value of days by which projects are behind schedule	Ratio of – % delay in top priority projects : % delay in rest of projects
2a	To measure IT helpdesk efficiency	$ per call	% problems resolved
2b	To measure IT helpdesk efficiency	% problems resolved	Customer satisfaction with helpdesk
3	To indicate the degree of flexibility in hardware utilization and standardization of support required	Number of applications supported per type of hardware platform	Customer satisfaction with range of applications available
4a	To indicate over-/under-staffing of the IT function	Ratio of number of IT support staff to number of other staff	IT staff turnover rate
4b	To indicate over-/under-staffing of the IT function	IT cost/head (over whole organization)	IT staff turnover rate
5	To indicate quality of IT staff	(1) Educational and professional qualification level of IT developers, and (2) years of work experience of developers	Customer satisfaction with (1) functionality of systems developed in-house, and (2) timeliness of development

behaviour, such as taking the customer to lunch immediately before asking them to fill in the customer satisfaction form. Apparently this had not been a common practice in the company ten years ago. On their own none of these 30 individual behaviour patterns would affect the survey results significantly, but the audit estimated that the combined effect was to overestimate customer satisfaction by at least 10%. This kind of evolution in corporate behaviour is of course inevitable, and you should be aware of the risks over time to the effectiveness of KPIs posed thereby. The remedy is simple, just change KPIs every few years. Indeed, if you take over a new department or function that has KPIs, one of the first things to do is to review them for signs that organizational evolution has limited their effectiveness. There are usually several potential KPIs that can all meet the same management requirement.

Benchmarking

The single hardest thing in benchmarking key aspects of your IT organization is likely to be in obtaining reliable data. The problem is not so much that other organizations are secretive about information relating to their own IT organization; the problem is that many organizations don't even have much reliable data on their own IT organization. There are three main problems. First, few firms know what they really spend on IT. Secondly, in areas where firms do know, they may define key terms differently from how your organization defines them, so you might think you are comparing like with like when it is not in fact the case. The third problem is a more subtle one: much of IT spend depends on how the non-IT parts of the firm are structured and managed. For instance, firms that have adopted a highly centralized management structure also have a highly centralized IT function, while firms that have adopted a more devolved management structure also have separate IT functions within each of the operating divisions. It may well be feasible to perform a benchmarking study between various IT services of the two organizations, but the findings need to be treated with caution.

Implementing benchmarking

Figure 5.1 sets out the main steps in implementing a benchmarking project for the purposes of understanding or managing your IT costs are as follows.

1. Will benchmarking add value to your organization?

The first thing to decide is whether benchmarking will add value to your organization; that is, will it help you right now? Before answering this question, it is best that you should have some practical experience of benchmarking, or if not, find someone in your organization or a reasonably close friend in another organization or alumni network and talk through their benchmarking experience. There are two key questions to answer in order to decide whether benchmarking can help your organization. Affirmative answers to either are likely to be sufficient indicators that benchmarking can add value to your organization:

1. Are there the same KPIs both in your own organization and in other organizations, and are these appropriate for comparison?
2. Is it probable that another organization would share comparative data with you?

The first question will be straightforward to answer where several firms in one industry use the same KPIs. More thought will be required where the only other companies using KPIs similar to yours are in different industries. In this case, there is an issue of credibility as well as absolute usefulness. Even if you know that a comparison

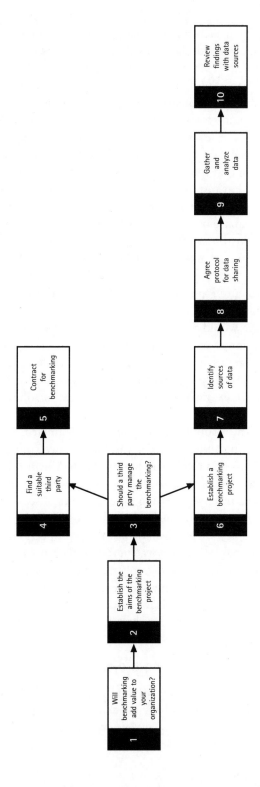

Fig. 5.1 Decision chain for benchmarking

would be useful, is there a risk from the internal politics of your organization that the benchmarking will be declared invalid, or worse, used to discredit your judgement or your department's reputation? Such political risk can be minimized by thinking carefully through the other major issue to be considered when benchmarking against a firm from a different industry, namely how valid is the comparison?

A starting point for such a consideration is to list for each area of proposed benchmarking all the issues that benchmarking is supposed to address, their similarities, differences, any interesting points, and remaining areas of uncertainty. It is worth checking that the problem to be solved by benchmarking is well defined and not too vague. For instance, 'our database technology may not be up-to-date' is too vague and any KPI derived from this will be of little value. Whereas 'Can we search our database of service calls by customer location, customer name and date as well as by customer reference number?' is a more tightly defined question, and could be used in formulating a KPI that would be the basis for valuable benchmarking.

The second question is whether other organizations would share data with you for benchmarking purposes. The answer to this usually depends on how much competitive advantage would result. If benchmarking would reveal information that would reduce a company's competitive advantage, then it is unlikely to be shared. Most likely to be shared is information that would reduce an entire industry's cost base without altering the competitive advantage of each firm. Industry-wide standards or best practice are examples of where the value of a solution to one user depends on how many others adopt it, and thus do not necessarily alter competitive advantage in an industry. The adoption of near-industry-standard desktop platforms based on Unix (engineering industries, derivatives and investment banking), Windows NT (general business and retail banking) or Apple Macintosh (graphics, printing industry) operating systems have lowered costs for everyone in their respective industries. They have done this by increasing the economies of scale obtainable through encouraging a larger pool of trained talent, standardized training courses and re-usable processes and software tools, all on a scale disproportionately greater than any single industry participant could have achieved on their own.[9]

Where competitive advantage restricts the opportunity for benchmarking, there may be value in benchmarking with firms outside your own industry. Suppliers may feel particularly well-disposed to invitations to exchange data on benchmarking, as this is a way for them to become better-acquainted with your organization.

2. Establish the aims of the benchmarking project

If it seems that benchmarking will add value to your organization, the next thing to do is to establish the aims of the benchmarking project in more detail. It cannot be repeated too often in business, and elsewhere, that without clear aims any endeavour is less likely to succeed. Where there are no clear aims that can be acted on, it makes sense to undertake an evaluation exercise or a project definition or feasibility exercise, in other words to have a project to identify some aims that can be acted on. But by the time you decide to commit resources to benchmarking, you should have sufficient knowledge of your organization's capabilities and needs to define reasonably clear aims for the benchmarking project.

Some examples of aims are:

■ to benchmark the IT Value Added (ITVA) of the firm against the top five firms in the industry globally;

■ to determine how the firm compares to best practice at its peers in software development;

■ to identify options for process improvement in database administration;

■ to benchmark new product turnaround time in areas where IT's input is the limiting or critical factor;

■ to identify best practice in IT human resources policy and measure the firm against best practice.

In formulating your aims for the benchmarking exercise, the following four questions may be useful:

1. What questions is benchmarking supposed to answer?

2. Why are these the right questions? Or – do these questions address the real issues?

3. What would examples be of ideal answers? (Write them down.)

4. What level of detail is required? Is this a tactical or strategic project?

It can take you several hours to formulate your initial draft set of aims and up to three weeks' elapsed time to obtain a final set of aims. Benchmarking is not a trivial process and it is important to set off with the right aim. The two to three weeks' elapsed time should enable input from all those likely to be involved or likely to have a useful contribution to make. It will be politically sensible to ensure there is buy-in from management peers to the benchmarking process. Once the aims are clear and agreed, the next step is to decide whether to use a third party to run the benchmarking, or whether to do it in-house.

3. Should a third party manage the benchmarking process?

There are five key questions to consider in answering the overall question of whether to use an outsider to run the benchmarking exercise:

1. **Skill** – what is your firm's skill level at benchmarking?

2. **Management availability** – will sufficient management time be available to run a benchmarking project?

3. **Commitment** – even if management time is available, how committed will the individual managers be to running a benchmarking project? What's in it for them?

4. **Confidentiality** – is the sensitivity of the data to be obtained by benchmarking such that a neutral third party is more likely to obtain accurate or complete data than your own organization?

5. **Quality of interpretation** – does your organization have the analytical capability to get full value out of the raw benchmarking data, or is a specialist benchmarking consultancy better equipped for the task?

In general we have found that more junior managers, who tend to be less experienced in benchmarking, tend to overestimate the quality of results likely to be obtained by running benchmarking in-house, and tend to underestimate the management effort (and, indirectly therefore, the cost) of so doing.

Many consultancies undertake benchmarking that they know is likely to interest existing and potential clients, without having a specific brief to do so. Often such exercises are called 'multi-client studies'. Whatever they are called, such consulting-initiated benchmarking exercises can be very useful sources of data. While the data thus obtained might not be exactly as you would have specified had you commissioned a benchmarking study, it tends to be cheaper and can be free, and it tends to be more detailed and perhaps more accurate. This is because more effort and expense is often put into such studies than a single client or small group of industry clients can afford.

4. Finding a suitable third party

This should be a relatively easy task, as almost all management consultants and IT consultants profess experience in benchmarking and many will undoubtedly be willing to help you. There are no special rules for finding a suitable benchmarking consultant. As with any consultant, look most of all for evidence that the consultants have the skill and experience relevant to the benchmarking task, and ask to speak to references they produce. A 15-minute telephone conversation with a few references will usually help in selecting the consultants.

5. Contract for benchmarking

As in any other commercial agreement, a contract should set out the obligations and rewards both sides. Be as clear and specific as possible in what you want, and ensure that the contract sets out what should happen if the quality of the benchmarking data obtained is unsatisfactory for your purposes and who decides what 'satisfactory' means. Ensure that any confidentiality considerations are adequately addressed. You may also wish to consider ownership of the resultant data. Should the consultant end up owning the data and have the right to sell it on to anyone they wish? This is normal, and to restrict their right to do this would probably only raise the cost of the exercise. However, you could consider asking for a list of all parties to whom the results of the benchmarking are sold on. This should not raise the cost but will let you track who else in your industry is taking benchmarking seriously and know with whom your consultants are also working.

6. Do-it-yourself – establish an in-house benchmarking project

On the other hand, if you decide that it is best to run your own benchmarking exercise, the key steps are:

- identify sources of data
- agree protocol for data sharing
- gather and analyze data
- review findings with data sources.

These steps are each self-explanatory. The three key requirements in a do-it-yourself benchmarking project are, first, to keep the aim clearly in mind, secondly, to check the benchmarking project's progress against that aim every day, and thirdly to allocate enough time to those involved.

Case study | **Tactical benchmarking for the business unit manager**

In May 1997 James D. had been promoted to manage the invoice processing office of an American regional airline. James' background was not in finance, but in IT, and although he did not know it at the time the promotion was intended by the airline's senior management to serve two purposes. First, to broaden James' management experience by including a significant non-IT responsibility. Secondly, to see if through his experience of IT, James could identify any efficiency improvements for invoice processing, which senior management felt was inefficient and had caused a few problems with suppliers recently.

James D. understood the basics of invoice processing, and from indirect experience of his firm's procurement systems knew that there were problems in invoice processing. His first few days on the job confirmed many of his suspicions in his own mind. The staff worked very hard indeed, but everywhere he looked there were mountains of paper. Invoice processing made use of no fewer than five IT systems. James' hunch was that invoice processing should be a priority issue for the project to consider a new accounting system for the firm. While a new system was the long-term solution, James felt that if he could focus some analysis on to accounts payable, there were likely to be immediate improvements possible in two key areas. First, James felt that small invoices should be paid in full with a small random sample processed in full. Secondly, he felt that one of the systems should be eliminated immediately. The objection to doing this came from the engineering department of the airline, who had grown used to it and were politically powerful in the airline.

But these were feelings only. James needed some hard facts, and quickly, to back them up before he made a presentation and request to the Operations Committee of the airline for the accounting system replacement study project to look at his area of concern. He wanted to show a few quick wins and ensure that his department would be one of the first to benefit from a new package.

First James called eight acquaintances in the industry and talked through his invoice payments problem. Seven of his industry colleagues were experiencing similar problems, and soon James had agreed an informal information-sharing agreement. All data was to be confidential among the eight airlines, only data directly related to invoice processing would be exchanged, and James would provide the project staffing and administration. The other seven airlines were to have access to the project staff by telephone to answer any questions, if they wished. Next James found two bright graduate trainees, one with some experience of finance, and the other with IT systems experience. He formed a project team around these two individuals working part time while they were also engaged on other projects.

James wanted the following questions answered:

■ Are all invoices processed fully, or is there immediate payment with random sampling for small invoices? If so, what is the dollar definition of small? How has sampling reduced costs?

■ How many systems were other airlines using for invoice processing? What systems? What were the trends in variety of systems used?

■ How many staff/invoice, and how many staff/dollar-processed? Were there any correlations to systems variety?

Within two months James had answers to all these questions, although in some cases fewer than all seven of the other airlines had participated. The answers suggested strongly that James' employer was considerably below average in invoice-processing efficiency, although not the worst, and that the greatest scope for improving efficiency was to reduce the number of invoices processed fully. This would be done by (1) aggregating invoices wherever possible, and (2) paying small invoices in full with statistical checks to ensure the same level of fraud and error protection as full processing. Other findings indicated that a full re-engineering project would reduce the cost of invoice processing by at least 35%, but that this should be incorporated into the study for the new accounting system. James achieved his objective.

Note that James knew intuitively all along the major issues in reducing costs, including IT systems costs, in invoice processing. But benchmarking enabled James to prove what he knew intuitively by quickly assembling facts from key competitors.

Strategic benchmarking – organizational structure and shareholder value

Nicola H. faced a tough problem. As a divisional manager with a reputation for sound financial decision making and some knowledge of IT, she had been asked by the Chief Executive of her employer, a multinational oil company, to lead a taskforce to decide on the shape of the future IT organization. The IT managers felt that a more decentralized model of IT was essential if the firm was to be able to respond to changes in the marketplace, both upstream and downstream. The finance director argued that a centralized IT department was key to maximizing shareholder value, and had recently produced some impressive-looking quantitative research from a well-known management consulting firm to back up his assertions. In response, the IT managers had commissioned their own research, using another firm of consultants that claimed to specialize in the field of residual cashflow, otherwise known as economic value added. Relations between the finance and IT functions had been cooling for some time, and frankly Nicola did not look forward to this task.

The CEO had asked to brief Nicola on the problem. As she prepared for the meeting her heart sank; both sides had well-prepared cases, with no obvious defects. The CEO confirmed her assessment, but looked at it another way.

'Nicola,' he said, 'This one's politics pure and simple, and that's why I chose you. Frankly I don't know and I don't care which side is right, and I suspect that some of the IT managers see a chance to build their own empires under a decentralized model, while I guess that the finance people have never really got over taking IT away from their organization and making it separate. But instead of going into those issues too deeply, I want to use this conflict for something else. We're getting behind our competitors on some key things like return on capital employed [ROCE] and earnings per share [EPS]. I don't care how our IT is structured, but I'm sure that if those two departments go on arguing over it and losing focus on their own jobs, then our ROCE and EPS will get worse and we'll all be in deep dooh-dah.'

The CEO outlined his plan. He wanted a benchmarking exercise as a way of forcing management to focus on some key issues, and to show both sides where they should improve. The dispute about the structure of the IT department would be a pretext only. The key deputies that the heads of the department normally relied on to do much of their day-to-day checks were to be occupied as fully as possible by the benchmarking exercise so forcing the department heads into doing more routine work. Any finding showing the firm doing badly in finance or IT compared to key competitors was to be fed back to the appropriate department for comment. The key finding should be about ROCE, and should require both finance and IT to improve their ROCEs immediately.

Nicola left the meeting with her CEO with a much clearer insight into top company politics, but also with a strong conviction that a strategic-level benchmarking exercise could be very valuable. She spent the next three days planning the project in outline, and then involved her project group. Outside strategy consultants were used, but much of the data required from within the firm was hard to get. The senior managers who occupied themselves most with internal politics were the ones who had to give up most time to help in obtaining the necessary data. This amused Nicola because such data really should have been in their regular management reports.

The project proceeded well, and the key drivers of ROCE and EPS in the firm were much better understood by senior managers as a result. However, as intended, another consequence was that several serious shortcomings with existing management systems, both in IT and in finance, were highlighted. As management attention shifted more on to these issues, the more emotional concerns about the exact structure of the IT department faded slightly, allowing a fact-based discussion and eventually a consensus to emerge, albeit 18 months later.

Nicola now sits on the main board of the oil company, and has the ear of the CEO.

A word of caution: Baldrige syndrome

Having set out what KPIs are and how to use them, it is worth emphasizing again that KPIs are a means to an end, and should never become an end in themselves. This seems to be the greatest risk to a poorly run organization which implements KPIs, and therefore it is worth saying a few words about this risk. It is only good practice that a firm should have KPIs to improve business efficiency or effectiveness. However, should managers start to behave as if quality metrics are ends in themselves, then quality metrics will be much less useful. Some managers are occasionally seduced into placing too much emphasis on quality metrics as ends in themselves.

Throughout the early 1990s IBM's business declined and it headed for one of the largest corporate losses ever in US corporate history, $8bn in 1993. During this descent into unprecedented losses, IBM's senior management was devoting ever-increasing effort on winning a Baldrige award. The Baldrige awards are administered under a US law by a board of examiners. Members of the board are drawn from not-for-profit groups, health care, academia, professional and trade organizations, government agencies, and business. Peer recognition is a key criterion. Baldrige awards are offered in three categories: manufacturing, services, and small businesses.[10] In fact the Baldrige programme sets out very well almost everything a business needs to know about quality-related KPIs. Problems arise when a business overemphasizes the processes in Baldrige awards at the expense of substance, as IBM may have done.

It was not until new management under Lou Gerstner arrived to turn around IBM that IBM ceased to focus on the Baldrige award as an end in itself. One of the first changes under Lou Gerstner was for management to stop focusing so much on winning Baldrige awards, and instead to shift focus back on to making and selling technology. This was just one of many changes that were made in IBM at the time, and no single change alone was responsible for IBM's change in fortunes. However, the memory of prosperous but unimaginative middle management at IBM regurgitating the Baldrige mantra while obviously having no idea how it was supposed to help IBM serve the customer better is a Kafkaesque piece of surrealism that will be remembered by all who saw good profits lost because of it. Fire any manager stupid enough to think of KPIs as ends in themselves, or watch your business die a bureaucratic death in front of your eyes.

IBM was lucky. Lou Gerstner and his team helped IBM turn itself around. The Wallace Company was not so lucky. The Wallace Company won the Baldrige award in 1990, then suffered huge losses and became insolvent in 1991, proving that you can get all the metrics right, but these metrics are only a means to an end, and it is the end, the ultimate purpose of the business that matters. The Wallace case illustrates the extreme in using KPIs badly, and it is unlikely that its problems are attributable to KPIs more than to general weakness of management. However, even in well-run companies it is important that if KPIs are used, they should be used efficiently. However, in this chapter we've concentrated on the practical issues in implementing KPIs and benchmarking, to enable you to implement KPIs and benchmarking effectively in your organization.

Conclusion: key points of KPIs and benchmarking

KPIs and benchmarking are related. KPIs are measures, metrics or indicators of those things critical to managing an organization or part of an organization effectively and efficiently. KPIs change from more detailed and concrete to more general and abstract the higher one goes in an organization; the idea of a pyramid of KPIs may be helpful here. A good set of KPIs invariably improves a manager's ability and efficiency in managing. The corollary of this is that designing a good set of KPIs is not a trivial task, and requires careful thought and experience. KPIs inevitably shift management focus to the subject of the KPI and away from all other matters, if only to some extent. This raises the issue of balance, and KPIs must be designed so as to ensure the right balance of management attention. One way of doing this is to pair KPIs, so that for each primary KPI a secondary KPI informs management when enough attention has been focused on the primary KPI and it's time to concentrate on other things for a while.

'Benchmarking' means measuring something, and in the sense most commonly used in management, means measuring a part of your organization's processes, technology, assets or people against the equivalent elements of other firms, especially key competitors, complementers or suppliers. Benchmarking is most convenient and effective when the other party uses the same KPIs as you. This will not often be the case, and when it is, the other party may not be willing to share information.

However, in cases where there is more benefit to be achieved by sharing data than by not sharing, many companies are willing to engage in benchmarking activities, which can be of a more or less formal nature, and executed at tactical or strategic or intermediate levels.

Managers wishing to understand and influence their IT costs and IT effectiveness should probably make use of benchmarking and KPIs, and should certainly know how their key competitors are using these tools.

Endnotes

1 Drucker (1995), p.54.
2 Rubin (1999).
3 Grove (1995) p.15.
4 Davenport (1997). (On 6 October 1999, the market capitalizations of Schwab and Merril Lynch were $28.5 and $26.3 respectively.)
5 Drucker (1995), p.61.
6 British Airways is well-known in Europe for being an especially effective user of IT. This quote is from Prokesh (1995).
7 O'Brien (1999).
8 See, for example, Schulmeyer (1990).
9 This claim is essentially about economies of scale and scope. The classic work in this field is Chandler (1990).
10 National Inst. of Standards and Technology (1999).

6 IT strategy

The overall aim of this book is to help managers understand their IT costs so that they can get better returns from investment in IT. IT managers should be able to avoid on the one hand hugely disastrous IT projects that consume great quantities of money, time and reputation while never delivering any business benefits, while identifying on the other hand those lucrative opportunities where a well-judged investment in IT will deliver enormous business benefit. Chapters 2 to 5 of the book focused more on controlling costs and on suggesting short-term tactical actions that managers can take to control costs. However, once those things have been done, there is a need to look at the bigger picture and consider strategic issues in an organization's use of IT. For example, sorting out a few poorly run IT projects is not the same thing as putting in place an IT management framework to raise the average standard of IT project management throughout the organization: the first is a tactical action, the second is strategic. Should you spend time on an IT strategy? It depends on two things – what your organization does and where you sit in your organization. If IT does not affect your organization significantly, there may be many better things for a manager to spend their time on than an IT strategy; similarly, if you are below board level and a well-thought out IT strategy is already being implemented in your department, then it may not be appropriate to spend much time thinking of an IT strategy. However, if you work in an industry where IT is a significant factor, and if there is no clear IT strategy for your department, there may be significant value in at least being aware of some of the main issues in IT strategy.

Introduction

There are many different approaches to IT strategy[1] as there are to business strategy. We believe that the right approach to IT strategy depends on the organization in question. Furthermore, we believe that the particular methodology used to implement an IT strategy is less important than first, having a good understanding of the strategic IT issues faced by your organization, and secondly, having good teamwork between the people tasked to come up with a solution. So rather than present one set approach for how to formulate and IT strategy, we instead will start by setting out four main issues that should be addressed or at least considered by an overall IT strategy. For each element we first explain it, then show how it can add value to an organization, and finish by showing how to implement this element of an IT strategy. This 'menu' approach means that you can decide which elements are relevant to your organization and then formulate an IT strategy around only those, rather than pursuing a 'one size fits all' approach. The four elements of IT strategy are:

- end-user computing;
- information security;
- software asset management;
- intellectual capital management.

Many successful managers believe that IT strategy is an area where external consultants can be particularly valuable, because external consultants have greater experience of the variety of approaches to IT strategy. If external consultants are used, then as always in such situations, the client should ensure that while taking advice on IT strategy from the consultants, the client's organization does not abdicate management responsibility to the consultants. As an example of what this distinction means in practice, consider a recent case in IT strategy where consultants had recommended to their client, an investment bank, that central IT management should have a high degree of control over what application each employee would be allowed to use. In fact this was not appropriate to one-third of the workforce of the investment bank concerned. The consultants proposed the idea because it was pushed strongly by the IT department. The general management of the investment bank concerned were in the best position to understand that the degree of centralized control being proposed was unworkable, but as they never attended the monthly IT strategy meetings, they were unaware of this key part of the proposed IT strategy until towards the end of the IT strategy project. One way that the senior management of this bank could have avoided the resulting waste of much of five months of work would have been to have a senior management representative who understood IT, or at least was not afraid to ask obvious questions, to attend all key IT strategy meetings. Several individuals were in fact selected to do this, but none of them attended after the first two meetings. It is true that the meetings were poorly run by the in-house IT department, but senior management could also have assisted with that problem. The moral of this example is simply that IT strategy consultants can help you with good ideas, but your organization's management must play a full part in creating and planning any IT strategy.

After setting out the four key elements of IT strategy, we finish the chapter with a case study of how a large insurance firm successfully used an IT strategy to increase shareholder value. The case study is not meant to suggest any particular approach to

IT strategy, but rather its purpose is to document in detail how one organization went about creating and implementing some of the elements of IT strategy set out in this chapter, and to show how these were integrated into an overall business strategy.

The four main elements of contemporary IT strategy

End-user computing

What is end-user computing?

The term 'end-user' in 'end-user computing' means someone who uses computing directly for business purposes as opposed to someone who uses computing to enable others to perform business functions. A salesman is an example of an end-user, whereas an application developer in the IT department is not an end-user. The salesman uses computing to sell more goods or services of his employer, whereas the programmer is writing applications to help others in the organization.

A common perception of the history of end-user computing is as follows: traditionally the IT department created or purchased applications and the end-users used them. For example, the IT department would develop the corporate payroll system, and the payroll department would then use it, where 'using it' means entering data, running reports and downloading the processed data. The IT department had responsibility for maintenance and changes to the payroll system. Even if reality was never quite this tidy, ten years ago as far as most end-users of computing in commercial organizations were concerned, this picture of computing was broadly correct: end-users used, the IT department designed, built or purchased computing. This has been changing for a while, and for many end-users the invention of the spreadsheet marks the beginning of the change. The spreadsheet enabled the mass of end-users for the first time to create their own applications, and the spreadsheet started to be widely used in the early 1980s. Since then database applications have become almost as widely used as spreadsheets. The result has been that many decisions about how an organization uses its IT assets are now in the hands of the end-users, the business people, rather than being controlled centrally by the IT function or the finance department. For instance, a small Microsoft Access database that was first written by a sales manager to track the salesforce may have become the marketing department's global standard for mailing list management; in effect the sales manager took a decision that shaped the software standards and data architectures of the organization in ways that may have profound consequences. If the sales manager's database has no provision for cross-referencing subsidiaries of a company to each other, then it can be very expensive later on to modify the database structure to give an overall view of the organization's relationships with its biggest customers, because by then the database may be in use as a business critical system in hundreds of offices around the world and will require much effort to change. There is also the risk that the employee who built the database may leave, and if they leave without having documented how the database works, it may need to be rebuilt from scratch at great expense and inconvenience if it crashes or needs updating.

IT strategy should address the issue of end-user computing where end-users have the potential to make decisions that have such far reaching effects. In this respect IT strategy should not try to control end-user computing absolutely, as if attempting to force the world back to the 1970s when the IT department could impose rules about computer usage from the centre. Instead, with regard to end-user computing IT strategy is about first, assessing the risks, opportunities and issues faced in a particular organization from the existence of end-user computing, and then putting in place measures to exploit the opportunities to the fullest while mitigating the risks to an acceptable level. To take our earlier example of the sales manager and the Microsoft Access database, a good IT strategy would help the sales manager build the database quickly and efficiently, by ensuring that any necessary training, standards and development guidelines are available, and by encouraging the IT department to work with such an initiative or at least not to be too hostile to it.

Why have an end-user computing strategy?

Almost every organization now has end-user computing. The benefits of having an IT strategy for end-user computing is that this maximizes the benefits of end-user computing, and minimizes the risks and costs. It's not about deliberately deciding whether to have end-user computing or not, although there may be some choice in encouraging or discouraging it.

There are three main business benefits of having a strategy for end-user computing:

- **Effectiveness of applications**. Users are more likely to get the applications they need, because they themselves effectively build the applications.

- **Development efficiency**. Users have more incentive to get their systems delivered on time, and the bureaucracy of the traditional application development channels is reduced.

- **Short-term costs**. Often the cost of developing and running an application appears to be lower if these activities are done in a business unit rather than a datacentre. However, it may be that the cost allocated to the business units is lower for end-user computing but the overall cost to the organization is the same.

And there are two main costs and risks:

- **Long-term costs**. Applications developed by end-users can be fragile, poorly documented and have poor data integrity. These issues can lead to increased costs and risks, especially in the long term. More visibly, fragile or poorly documented applications can cause great frustration to users.

■ **Inefficiency**. When users are spending time on application development, they are not spending time on their own work. This is probably not always going to be a worthwhile trade-off.

As new tools and systems are developed to meet the increasing demand for end-user computing, so the main risks associated with end-user computing are being reduced. For instance, new tools are becoming available that help users to apply some of the key application development disciplines of clarity, documentation and data integrity when developing applications.

Case study   ## End-user computing

There are probably many examples of end-user computing in your own department; these will be the best case studies from which to understand the advantages and limitations of end-user computing. However, we will also give the case of end-user computing in a lumber yard in the northeastern USA. In this yard a saleswoman felt that the existing customer database lacked functionality and data elements vital to selling lumber. She therefore built her own database in Microsoft Access, spending time at weekends on this project. The old database had a poor user interface, and no provision for storing the pieces of information that the saleswoman regarded as critical to effective selling. The missing pieces of information included: each prospect's email address, a short qualitative description of the mood of the prospect during the last sales call, and the 'hot button' of the prospect (a 'hot button' is the business issue that interests a prospect most, their key issue). The saleswoman added these three data fields, and wrote the user interface that allowed the user to determine how the data fields were displayed on screen. The benefit was that she could have all the data that she needed on the screen at once when speaking to a sales prospect, and so could concentrate more fully on the conversation with the sales prospects. The firm's previous standard database for managing prospects was so slow and cumbersome to use that most people either used paper-based sales lead management systems or their own individually purchased software. However, the saleswoman's new database was soon in use with two-thirds of the sales force and had become in effect the standard application throughout the firm.

In this case there were two main benefits. First, the saleswoman's application did what the old system was supposed to have done but hadn't, and made the sales force more productive in terms of sales leads handled, calls made and sales closed. Secondly, for the first time up-to-date information on the status of most sales prospects was in one place. This enabled the lumber firm to analyze the data to see industry trends more clearly. Previously salespeople had entered data into the system only after successfully completing the sale. This had meant there was little fact-based information about prospective orders available to the lumber yard's management; management would also have appreciated more information on sales lost and recent industry trends, neither of which were easily obtainable from the old database but which the new database could provide. Once the sales force were using the new database, senior management had up-to-date information on their sales and were able to analyze it to obtain industry trends, summaries of prospective orders one month, three months and six months out, and reports on lost sales and reasons for the losses. For instance, some basic data mining revealed that successful sales were correlated with and lagged unsuccessful sales calls to architects. In other words, the new database suggested that sales calls to architects resulted in indirect sales even though there were no direct sales to architects themselves. As a result of this particular analysis, the lumber firm set up a trial project to target architects specifically. This trial also used other data from the new database to focus the marketing effort, for instance by identifying which products architects had expressed most interest in so far. The refocused marketing effort was successful, and led to substantial additional sales.

Of course the original system was meant to achieve exactly these results, but it just didn't. And this is precisely the reason that there is an increasing amount of a end-user computing: it often delivers results.

How to formulate IT strategy for end-user computing

The key steps to formulate IT strategy for end-user computing are shown in Table 6.1.

Table 6.1   Formulating IT strategy for end-user computing: key steps

1. Determine the current state of end-user computing in your organization.	
Key questions:	▪ How much end-user computing is there? ▪ What kind of end-user computing is being done well at present, and what done badly? ▪ How is it managed and measured?
Where to find answers:	▪ The I T department – they are likely to be able to help answer these questions, if only because of the problems end-user computing creates for them. ▪ End-user.
Examples of possible answers:	▪ There is widespread end-user computing, but significant opportunities to create value by increasing end-user computing exist, particularly in marketing and expense analysis. ▪ There is some end-user computing in R&D and the finance department, elsewhere end-user computing is often of poor quality and has cost much in staff time.

Table 6.1   (cont.)

2. Determine how much end-user computing there should be in your organization.

Key questions:	■ What amount of end-user computing should there be in your organization? ■ How much need is there for end-user computing?
Where to find answers:	■ One rough indicator on the degree of need is the amount of re-keying of the same data currently undertaken in your organization. ■ End-users.
Examples of possible answers:	■ A significant increase in end-user computing in the Wholesale Division should be encouraged, because IT requirements change all the time and the business users are better placed to understand the requirements and lead the development efforts, which are not overly complex. In the Retail Division there should not be a significant increase in end-user computing, because of the greater complexity and greater regulatory risk compared to the Wholesale Division.

3. Encourage or discourage end-user computing accordingly.

Key question:	■ Is there excessive end-user computing already, or should more end-user computing be encouraged?
Where to find answers:	■ CIO. ■ Business unit heads. ■ External advisers – consultants, industry bodies, suppliers, competitors.
Examples of possible answers:	■ Management should aim to increase the number of end-user computing projects by 15% over the next year in the Wholesale Division and the Finance Department. ■ The Export Division needs a new application for foreign pricing which the IT department cannot develop for six months. A pilot end-user computing project should be set up in the Export Division, composed of six people, with one day of basic training in application development given by the IT department. ■ The HR Department should change the recruitment policy to increase the minimum level of IT proficiency in all management trainee hires, and to monitor the IT project management experience of senior hires. Management trainees should have had some formal training in database or spreadsheet development, including the use of macros.

Table 6.1　(cont.)

4. Formulate and implement a plan to increase benefits and reduce costs and risks of end-user computing.

Key questions:	▪ What kinds of systems can users be expected to develop well, and what kinds are likely to be high risk?
	▪ What policy should there be on the kinds of end-user computing to be encouraged or discouraged? What policy should there be for documentation – standards, monitoring?
	▪ What should be the policy on standards for formatting, readability, and naming conventions. (These three areas are critical in efficient application development, whether performed by end-users or others).
	▪ Who should be able to develop end-user applications?
	▪ How can end-users be better supported in their computing efforts?
	▪ How should user-developed applications be tested? Testing needs to be objective. Should testing be performed internally or by external software testing consultants?
	▪ (The above are also the key policy areas if the aim is to reduce the amount of a end-user computing, although the actual policy chosen will be rather different to when the aim is to encourage more end-user computing.)
Where to find answers:	▪ Business management.
	▪ End-users, especially veterans of successful end-user computing projects.
	▪ CIO, IT department.
	▪ External advisers – consultants, industry bodies, suppliers, competitors.
Examples of possible answers:	▪ R&D, Finance and Special Projects departments have so far had the most success with end-user computing. It seems that only in the retail division is there likely to be significant risk to the business from increased end-user computing, and this is because of the tough regulatory environment in which our retail division operates.

Table 6.1   (cont.)

- Our IT department has worked closely with our management consultants to develop a simple set of standards and naming conventions for end-user computing applications. These have been tested on a sample project from the Finance Department and do not appear to impose too much bureaucracy on user development. It is recommended that these standards are posted on the corporate intranet, and business managers are encouraged to see that they are used. At this stage they should not be mandatory, but this should be reviewed in a year's time.
- The IT department should identify a short course (say two days) to be made available as part of the company's normal training portfolio.

5. Set up a formal evaluation process for end-user applications.

Key questions:	- How will end-users' applications be evaluated on functionality, documentation, risk management and controls over usage, development and data integrity? (The main choice is between a system of peer review or internal review.) - Is there a size cut-off below which applications need not be evaluated? - How can you ensure that small applications that could expose the organization to major risk are evaluated?
Where to find answers:	- Business management. - IT, CIO. - Key end-users.
Examples of possible answers:	- A random sample of 25% of end-user developed applications should be evaluated three months and six months after completion. The IT department should conduct a risk review of the application, focusing particularly on the risk of client-confidential data leakage and regulatory risk. Senior business management of the department should review the functionality of the application, and estimate a net present value of the project. Neither review should take more than two days, and all costs should be born by the business department in which the application was developed. The aim of this exercise is to check that the company is getting good value for money from its end-user computing, and to identify managers with the most talent in this kind of work so that they can lead the company's thinking in end-user computing.

Information security

What is information security?

Effective information security means that information is readily available when needed to those who should have access to it, and is not available to those who shouldn't. In practice there are two common failures of information security. Either security is so complex that if used it would restrict the availability of information excessively, or security procedures are ineffective and hackers or other unauthorized users are able to obtain confidential data. Perhaps the most prevalent example of overly complex security procedures is in password security; despite strict rules in many organizations to the effect that individuals must never disclose their passwords nor write them down, most offices seem to ignore this rule and either individuals have access to each other's passwords or a secretary will keep a book in which all passwords are written down. This is not because most people are determined to break the rules, but rather because the rules do not take account of practical necessities in how IT support departments and network managers actually force employees to work. For instance, when IT systems do not provide adequately for teams to share data and email, staff may decide to share passwords in order to achieve the necessary degree of information sharing and teamworking to achieve the tasks required of the team. This at a stroke negates any IT security plan that assumes that passwords will be kept strictly confidential by individual users. In an informal survey in 1999 among ten multinational organizations in the IT and finance industries, we found that more than 50% of staff surveyed said that they shared passwords on a regular basis, despite explicit rules stating that to do so was a dismissable offence in most of these organizations.[2]

Key aspects of information security are:

- **Availability** of data, including the backing-up of data and availability of alternative systems and networks.

- **Data integrity**, which means ensuring that recent data replaces older data, and that inconsistencies among data are resolved.

- **Access control**. Who can access the data? Should a user have full or partial access? What can users do with data – read only or update also?

- **Confidentiality**. Confidentiality is about protecting data, in transit as well as in the database.

- **Authentication**. Authentication is about proving that data users are who they claim to be.

Why have an information security strategy?

The main benefit of having an element of IT strategy that addresses information security is a better balance between resources expended on information security and the real information needs of the organization. Less money will be spent on needless security measures, but critical needs (such as backing up key data) will be met. Further cost savings will result from rationalizing the systems used to archive information security – why pay to run two sets of data back-up systems when one will do?

Breaches of data security are a major problem for the modern corporation. This may not seem to be the case because few breaches are reported. It is estimated that 5% or less of IT security breaches appear in the press.[3]

A good information security strategy goes beyond relying on systems providers. For instance, the widely used Microsoft NT operating system has had security weaknesses exposed,[4] so it is probably unwise to rely entirely on the security features built-in to an operating system. Every organization should to review its own security needs against security provided by its existing systems, determine what gaps exist, assess the risks, and then decide what, if any, of action should be taken.

Examples of information security problems

The Pentagon suffers 250 000 attacks against its information security annually.[5] And according to a recent report, hackers in Moscow attacked a US military system at the Space and Naval Warfare Systems Command in San Diego, California, by effectively tapping into the print files as they went from a PC to a laser printer.[6] Security issues in the public sector tend to be better reported than their private sector equivalents because there is a higher requirement for public accountability and greater general interest. Numerous private sector information security breaches are in fact reported in a verifiable way, and the scale of the problem disclosed in the public sector indicates that the private sector most probably suffers a similar scale of problem. Just one private sector example is that in January 1999 the Air Miles website in Canada exposed data on 30 000 Air Miles members to hackers. Information revealed included names, home telephone numbers and credit card numbers.[7] This kind of breach potentially enables backers to create false electronic identities and use credit cards fraudulently, and could expose an organization to substantial litigation risk from citizens whose rights have been infringed.

How to formulate IT strategy for information security

Risk management should be the backbone of an information security strategy. It is easy to spend too much money and create unnecessary bureaucracy and administration by spending time addressing risks that would do little damage if they materialized, and addressing risks which could do much damage but which are very unlikely to materialize. For example, in the late 1980s the senior management of many firms spent much time worrying about credit card fraud on the Internet, and almost no time worrying about the risk to their IT systems from macro viruses. In fact the risk from Internet-based credit card fraud was the same risk as from non-Internet-based credit card fraud, which management had lived with quite happily, but the risk from macro viruses was both probable and likely to have serious consequences. It is still not clear why in so many organizations management preferred to concentrate on the one, irrelevant risk while ignoring a major source of unnecessary cost in the other risk. One of the difficulties seems to be that this is more an issue of human nature than a technology issue, and consequently attempts at solutions that assume the right solution is based only on technology are likely to be inadequate. It is also easy for management to overlook inexpensive or even free precautions that

Table 6.2 Example of IT risk assessment

	Risk	Probability	Consequences	Recommendations
1	Virus infection of network and data via email	High	1. Moderate, except for 2. Client service and sales by email, which are business critical. (Estimated cost in Melissa type attack, excluding remedial effort by IT department: $ 250 000 per day for an expected three days' disruption.)	A. Contract for daily updates to virus filters (cost $50 000). B. Implement backup email network for business-critical systems (cost $300 000).
2	Client proprietary data leaks from our databases into public domain Internet	Medium	1. Severe damage to our reputation, would take a long time to fix. 2. Statutory sanctions if proved that we were negligent.	A. Implement quarterly security tests for our databases by external consultants (cost $60 000 p.a.). B. Migrate client data to separate servers behind own firewall. (In hand, no additional cost.) C. HR department to review policy of employee handling of data and access to systems, and to make specific recommendations by 3/3/00.
3	Datacentre is shut down (e.g., by flood, fire or terrorism)	Low	Low for two hours, then medium for rest of day. Any longer than a day would be critical.	No action – existing disaster recovery and data backup systems are appropriate to level of probability and consequences.

Table 6.3   Rsk Review Exercise

1. Evaluate the risks your organization faces.	
Key questions:	■ What IT security problems have there been so far?
	■ What systems are covered right now by security measures? What measures are they?
	■ What are the main categories of risk that your organization faces? What is the probability of risk for each category? How severe would the consequences be in the event of an incident for each category (financially, reputationally)?
	■ What are the main information security issues in your industry?
Where to find answers:	■ IT dept. (asking everyone in the IT department to list what they see as the main risks is usually sufficient to flush out most potential answers.)
	■ Competitors.
	■ Trade association, industry reports.
	■ External IT consultants.

2. Determine what resources your organization has to manage information security risk.	
Key questions:	■ What do you spend on managing this risk?
	■ What is the average spend in your industry and the spend by best-practice firms? (The average spend on information security for a company with networked computers is between 5% and 8% of the IT budget.[8])
	■ What is the level of skill of the staff whose job it is to manage these risks?
	■ What policy is there on the security features required of new applications?
Where to find answers:	■ IT Department.
	■ Financial controllers.
	■ Competitors.
	■ External consultants.
	■ Results of security tests.

3. Policy on back-up for data.	
Key questions:	■ What are the options for back-up?
	■ How can you ensure that applications and data that should be backed up are backed up? Can it be done remotely by systems management? (End-user applications tend to have a poor provision for data back-up compared to other applications.)

Table 6.3 (cont.)

Where to find answers:	▪ Business management.
	▪ IT, CIO.
	▪ Key end-users.
Examples of possible answers:	▪ Network management runs a daily back-up of all data on network drives. Thus all end-user computing data that is stored on a network drive will be automatically backed up. We recommend that as policy all end-user computing should store data on network drives. If this is not feasible, users should be responsible for their own data back up and be made aware of the risks of not backing-up data. The IT department are investigating what options exist for using the corporate intranet to provide a back-up service for end-user applications carried on laptops.

4. Implement a threat-based strategy to managing information security.

Key questions:	▪ What are the main threats that are not currently managed well? – especially in the areas of data and systems availability, data integrity, access control, confidentiality and authentication.
	▪ Who should own the issue of information security? Should there be centralized ownership?
	▪ What changes should there be to policy for the security design of new applications?
	▪ What event driven security measures can be taken?
Where to find answers:	▪ Outputs of 1 & 2.
	▪ IT department.
	▪ External consultants.
Examples of possible answers:	▪ A main board director will take overall responsibility for data security, although for day-to-day management this will be delegated to an IT department manager through the CIO.
	▪ Implement an event-driven security measure to counter hacking:
	(1) Monitor Internet traffic volumes and on the basis that a surge in traffic is often associated with an attempted hack, have security procedures activated once traffic reaches a certain volume.
	(2) Shut-off network access at back-up time, on the basis that the risk to your data is increased during back-up time.

substantially reduce or eliminate high risks with serious consequences. For example, email filters are a low cost precaution against viruses born by email, and increasing employee awareness of the problem is almost free, but few organizations use either approach in their IT security.

One way to prioritize risk management efforts efficiently is to conduct a short risk review exercise. This can take the form of a half-day workshop for a small group of managers who collectively have good judgement of all the major IT risks faced by the organization. A common agenda for the workshop is to start with a brainstorm of all risks faced, then to categorize the risks, and finally to assess each category by probability and severity of consequences. Highly probable risks with severe consequences then get more attention than low probability risks with slight consequences. Whatever form the risk review takes, it should result in management having a clear understanding of the most significant IT risks faced by the organization. Sometimes an outside IT or management consultancy can help ensure that the risk review is kept honest and that no unpleasant risks are ignored. Table 6.2 shows an example of the output of a risk assessment.

Software asset management

What is software asset management?

Does your organization know how many copies of word processor software it has? At several hundred dollars per copy, the total word-processor software assets of a medium-sized organization are likely to be substantial, yet many organizations do not manage software assets as carefully as they manage their conventional assets. Fifteen years ago software did not form a financially significant asset of most organizations. Since then, there has been a massive change, and now software forms a significant asset for most organizations in financial terms. Assuming that an average desktop installation has $1000 of software and that 90% of staff have a desktop, then an organization of 2500 people will have desktop software assets of over $2m. This excludes the value of any specialized desktop software, any network management software, server software and mainframe or mid-range software. In information-intensive industries such as banking, finance, pharmaceuticals, aerospace or IT, the average desktop may have well in excess of $1000 of software. The point is that recently the management of software assets has become a significant issue in business. The need to manage stocks of raw materials, work-in-progress and finished inventory is well known, and management practice has evolved over more than a century to address these issues. Management practice is only just beginning to address the need to management software assets in a similar way.

The goal of software asset management is to know what software assets you have, in order to be able to use them more effectively and more efficiently. In the early days of computing, and especially of the networked PC, management emphasized the effectiveness of applications, getting an application that worked and delivered business results. Once this need was met, the focus started to shift towards efficiency, which means processes and record keeping. Right now, software asset management is at the beginning of the shift away from effectiveness and towards efficiency.

The good news is that as this need becomes recognised more widely, so more tools are becoming available to help manage software assets efficiently. For instance, the remote installation and management of software is much easier now than five years ago, because of automated tools. The latest automated software asset management tools can collect information about assets automatically, including serial numbers, software revision and location data, and frequency of asset utilization. These tools can also generate automatic reports showing different analyzes of such data.

Why have a software asset management strategy?

In short, because if you don't know what you have, you can't use it effectively or efficiently. A typical organization with 2500 PCs is estimated to spend about $20m on direct and hidden costs of end-user computing annually[9] – or, to put it another way, $8000 per PC. These costs can be halved with effective asset management strategy: 5% to 30% of total IT spend can be cut by good asset management.[10]

There are five main reasons why such significant cost reductions are achievable through asset management. These are shown below, and we recommend that they are considered in any IT strategy.

■ **Effectiveness**

1. Eliminating under-utilized assets

Developing or buying applications that support the business need is pointless if they cannot be deployed to people who can use them. Poor asset management can result in a potentially useful assets not being deployed to where they will be used.

2. Use of staff time

The most obvious cost of a poorly utilised software asset is the purchase cost. However, one of the largest costs, and frequently the least obvious, is the time spent by staff in installing applications, learning to use them, and then maintaining them. In organizations with poor software asset management strategies, the resultant ineffective use of staff time is very major hidden cost.

■ **Efficiency**

3. Headcount

Efficient software asset management will reduce the number of IT support staff required. It is also very likely to reduce the number of contractors and the hours charged by consultants.

4. Asset audit costs

An increasing proportion of projects require an inventory of IT. Most organizations will have conducted an audit of the IT equipment to create or update such an inventory, but this is expensive and typically costs about $40 per hour. Automated inventory management tools can eliminate the need for creating and recruiting software asset inventories manually.

5. Inventory management

Just as managing an inventory of traditional plant and equipment is about ensuring that sufficient but not excessive plant and equipment is available and obsolete equipment is replaced when beyond economic repair, so software asset management is about ensuring sufficient but not excessive software assets exist to support operations, and ensuring that when economically justified obsolete software is replaced by up-to-date software. In practice, the risk is often of replacing software assets too soon rather than too late. Many industry experts agree that more often existing systems should be upgraded rather than replaced, because this would reduce costs significantly while maintaining adequate functionality. Unfortunately, new technology has irresistible allure for many who make decisions about purchasing new software.

A recent development in inventory management is the free word processor and office applications provided by Sun; will corporations be able to reduce costs by giving up Microsoft Office and using Sun's free products instead?

Case study | **Examples of software asset management**

Blue Cross/Blue Shield of Minnesota

Blue Cross/Blue Shield of Minnesota is one of the largest health care providers in the northeastern USA. By 1993 this Blue Cross was maintaining more than 350 mainframe software licences. It had three systems staff to perform this maintenance function. This was an insufficient number for the job. Blue Shield was not managing its software assets well – according to one manager 'basically we were in chaos. When the bills came in, we didn't know who was using the software, or we often had two or three packages that were doing the same thing.' Blue Cross Minnesota took action and installed a software asset management package to identify what packages were being used and to monitor the extent of the usage. This was in 1994, and by 1999 this approach had been key in reducing the number of packages used to 200 and reducing software expenditure by $1.7 m annually. For example, two identical fourth-generation computer languages were in use. One of them was used by only five staff, who agreed to move on to the other language, which was used by many more staff. This meant that not only was money saved on a licence fee for the redundant language, but also there was a reduction in support and computer capacity required. Blue Cross was also able to negotiate major reductions in licence fees with software suppliers because for the first time they had an accurate list of exactly what assets were in place. Blue Cross had set out to reduce software spend by 10%, but achieved a 25% underspend against budget.

An East Coast transport company

An East Coast transport company with c. 13 000 PCs decided to install an anti-virus package at $15 per desk, but installation costs were $250 000 because there was no electronic distribution capability, and so everything had to be installed by hand. A senior executive at the company said that they were definitely overspending on IT because they didn't have electronic software distribution. The executive felt that the $250 000 cost could have been reduced first by negotiating a lower price than $15 per seat for the anti-virus software, and secondly by distributing this software automatically, which would have reduced the labour cost of installing the software by over 90%.

Barnett Bank

Barnett Bank plans to adopt a centralized asset management programme for its 20 000 desktop systems because of the massive potential for reducing costs while increasing performance of IT assets.

US Hospital

In a hospital an employee downloaded a font from the Internet and used it in a document instead of one of the hospital's standard fonts. Other employees who had been sent the document then started asking for the font, and their calls to the document's author asking for information about how to install and use the font overwhelmed him. IT support became involved, at an eventual cost of $3000.[11]

How to formulate IT strategy for software asset management

1. **Decide if software asset management is a key issue.**

   Would better asset management make more than a 10% difference to your IT costs? If not, then you probably shouldn't invest time in thinking about software asset management strategy.

2. **Identify any asset management systems already in place and evaluate their capabilities.**

   Any existing asset management systems are likely to be in either the IT department or the finance department. To determine their capabilities, see how these systems answer the following three questions:

   ◼ What dollar value of software assets are in place?

■ At what rates are new software assets being added and old software assets being retired?

■ How concentrated is the supply of software? Or, how many software suppliers do you have and how much of the annual spend on maintaining those software assets goes to your biggest suppliers? (For example, if you spend $10m annually, you have ten suppliers and of the $10m 50% goes to the top three suppliers, then you have a supply twice as concentrated as if the top three suppliers account for only 25% of your spend.)

If these kinds of questions are easy to answer, then your asset management system is doing a good job, and either your assets are well-managed or it is just a case of acting on the data. If these questions cannot be answered either because there is no software asset management system or because the existing system cannot answer the questions, then you should consider implementing an effective software asset management system.

3. Determine how software assets should be managed – create a plan.

The question of how your organization should manage its software assets is not a question in a vacuum to be answered on the basis of theory alone. The approaches you can take will be severely restricted by culture. An organization where the culture is for standard operating procedures to be followed precisely will have different possible approaches open to it for managing its software assets than an organization where procedures are regarded as being more optional and reports are filled with approximate data. So as well as determining an ideal asset management plan, you should also understand what is possible given your organization's culture. One way to do this quickly is to see what systems already exist for software asset management – they will typically be found either in the IT department or in the finance department, if they exist at all.

The right policy will also depend on what the assets are and how they are likely to evolve. For instance, databases accessed by most employees will have different management requirements that similar databases to be accessed by only one small team. Two key questions are:

■ What are the principal software assets of your organization now?

■ Which assets are likely to require further development in the next three years?

Your policy for software asset management should cover:

■ what software can be used

■ the approval process for new software

■ usage guidelines

■ management policy for software licences: should site licenses be negotiated instead of individual licences? should there be a process to identify and cancel unused licences?

The aim is to ensure that sufficient software assets are in place to support the firm's operations, and to avoid wasteful excess of systems.

To manage software assets effectively requires data on software assets, and this data needs to be managed. The two main approaches are either to create a central database containing all the necessary data, or to set up local databases in each region or department. Until recently, central databases were considered best in theory but were often considered impractical because the data was often inaccurate or out of date. However, recent use of Internet technology to encourage users to update their own data within the central database seems to be making a central database more feasible. One way to get a feel for the feasibility of a central database is to find out whether your organization has implemented any other centralized databases successfully. Many firms are trying to create centralized customer databases and HR databases, so these could be places to look.

Some organizations decide to outsource their asset management either entirely or in some areas. This may be appropriate if your organization is deficient in the people, systems or skills required for asset management. Typical fees range from $3 to $10 per asset per month.

4. Implement the plan for managing software assets.

The main issue in implementing the plan is how much time users should be given to change over applications and for management to eliminate surplus applications. Typically organizations allow between three months and a year for desktop applications, and longer for core business applications.

Intellectual capital management

What is intellectual capital management?

We use the terms 'intellectual capital', 'organizational knowledge', and 'corporate knowledge' synonymously. Consider something very simple and commonplace, such as an ordinary pencil. Compare today's pencil to one of 100 years ago. Today's pencil has a graphite core where the pencil of 100 years ago had a lead core. Today's pencil may be made from a composite of wood chippings that 100 years ago would have been discarded. Today's pencil may have an eraser at one end that is made of artificial rubber, whereas 100 years ago the rubber would have been natural rubber. One way of viewing the change in the pencil is to say that today's pencil embodies much more intellectual capital, or knowledge, than a pencil 100 years ago. Knowledge is as much an input to the value-creating processes of the business as are raw materials, labour, and management talent. Many corporations use the idea of an intellectual capital to improve their business performance.

There are many definitions of intellectual capital, but two suffice to give a representative understanding of the idea. Hugh MacDonald of ICL defined intellectual capital as 'knowledge that exists in an organization that can be used to create differential advantage'.[12] Klein and Prusak define intellectual capital as 'intellectual material that has been formalized, captured, and leveraged to produce a higher-valued asset.'[13] Two aspects of these definitions should be highlighted. First intellectual capital is a kind of data or knowledge. Secondly, intellectual capital must be usable in a way that creates a result. In particular, it should be capable of creating a competitive advantage.

Further, the notion of intellectual capital implies that it is something embedded in the organization, embedded in the experience or intellect or skill of employees. And yet the opportunity to create value from better management of intellectual property is about isolating this knowledge and storing it in a way that is not embedded in the minds of employees. Some of the authorities on intellectual capital distinguish between intellectual capital in employee's minds from other kinds of intellectual capital. (The intellectual capital in employees' minds is sometimes referred to as 'intellectual capital that goes home at night.') Intellectual capital that is not in employees' minds includes organizational and customer-derived intellectual capital. Organizational intellectual capital includes proprietary standards, operating procedures, databases, and according to some experts, even teamwork. Customer-derived intellectual capital includes information about changes in market conditions that flow from a customer and improved knowledge about products and suggestions for improvements to products that are derived from the customer.

Why have an intellectual capital management strategy?

Many businesses believe that intellectual capital management offers significant opportunities to improve business and create shareholder value. They believe this because the basic idea of intellectual capital management to leverage the knowledge of one employee across the capacity and the ability of many other employees: good intellectual capital management lets 10 000 people replicate the success of one individual. In terms of return on investment in well-known companies, Motorola has reported a 30:1 return on its intellectual capital management initiatives and Shell believes that a 25:1 return made be very easily achievable.[14] Organizations are showing their commitment to the idea of intellectual capital management by creating new posts. For instance, Dow Chemical has a director of intellectual asset management, Ernst & Young has a chief knowledge officer, and CIBC has a vice-president of learning and organizational development.

Intellectual capital management is also seen as a means of helping management to address the 80/20 problem. If only 20% of corporate knowledge creates 80% of corporate value, then the most efficient way to create increased value is to improve the management of that first 20% of corporate knowledge.

Examples of intellectual capital management

The management consulting industry has been the forefront of developing tools and techniques for improving intellectual capital management. A typical consulting engagement has three phases: data gathering, analysis, and the preparation and presentation of a final report. The management consulting market is competitive and often when undertaking a new kind of project for the first time a management consultancy does not expect to make an economic return. Rather, the profits come from winning repeat business in the same area. While the raw data vary from engagement to engagement, the analytical process remains the same, and usually there are no more than three or four possible recommendations to the client. Data-gathering is the least highly skilled part of the work and is undertaken by the lower-paid junior consultants predominantly. The analysis and writing of the recommendations requires the attention of the most expensive staff because the greatest experience and intellect is needed. The economics of the business are such that any re-use of analytical tools or even an entire final recommendation to clients is extremely attractive and profitable to the management consultants, and hence the incentive for the management consulting industry to develop intellectual capital management tools and techniques.

All management consultancies have large databases of previous work done, sanitized so that client names or other distinguishing words have been removed. In effect large amounts of boiler plate are available for immediate reuse with the new clients. Of course, management consultants bill by the hour but when billing for material thrown together from such an intellectual capital database, they bill by the hours of the original work, not the hour taken to cut and paste this time around. There is an example that illustrates some of the perversities of the approach that the management consulting industry has taken to intellectual capital management, but which also shows something of value in the idea of intellectual capital management. In the mid-1980s a new entrant to the management consulting industry had not then yet managed to organize its intellectual capital database effectively. Consequently, its consultants were forced to undertake completely original work on every engagement. What seemed highly inefficient by industry standards paradoxically had very good effects for reputation and winning new business. One client summed up the situation as follows: 'when I hire [here he named one of the most famous management consulting firms] I can see the Tippex with [he here named the bank's main competitor] underneath. But when I hire these guys it's always original work.' However, a few years later this firm had managed to sort out its intellectual capital database and stopped doing more original work than its competitors. However – and this is the whole point of intellectual capital management – the consulting firm thereby became very profitable and is now one of the largest in the world by revenue.

How to formulate IT strategy for intellectual capital management

Intellectual capital management is about more than just IT. However, it is fair to say that IT has enabled the modern approach to intellectual capital management. It would simply have been impractical to attempt modern intellectual capital management techniques with paper-based tools in an organization of any size. In other words, IT is a necessary but not sufficient requirement for good intellectual capital management. The aim of the intellectual capital element of the IT strategy should be to ensure that the IT infrastructure and skills are suitable for the intellectual capital management needs of the firm. For instance, if widely used, an intellectual capital management system typically means employees sending large volumes of data around company networks. If the networks have been designed with insufficient capacity then not only is the intellectual capital management impaired, but other business critical of functions of the network may also suffer. This example shows some of the practicalities in implementing an intellectual capital management strategy.

An intellectual capital management project typically starts with an analysis of the value chain as it flows through the organization to determine how much value each business process adds, which department owns the process, and what information inputs are required by each process. The aim is to find out where the knowledge is and how it flows. Is the secret formula for the wonder product kept only in the head of the part-time consultant, or is it documented and safeguarded in a secure corporate database? What knowledge repositories are currently supported by the IT infrastructure? Can it flow from where it's stored to where it's needed? What new knowledge stores are required? What management information about knowledge flows is created? How accessible is knowledge to those who need it? What databases are in use, what search tools are available? All these questions go beyond the remit of IT, yet IT is going to supply part of any answer. If your organization is going to invest significant resources in intellectual capital management, then the existing IT infrastructure should be reviewed again these kinds of questions, and any gaps for changes should be reflected in the IT strategy. Will this mean budgeting for greater IT spend? Yes, but the alternative will certainly cost even more.

So what does this mean in terms of formulating a intellectual capital management element of I T strategy? It means:

- communicating with whoever is leading the intellectual capital management project;
- understanding what IT will be the backbone of this initiative (for example, Lotus Notes, Microsoft Exchange, Netscape Navigator, a proprietary database, or an outsourced solution);
- determining what changes to laptop, networks and security arrangements are likely to be required.

Even if the details of the answers are not known, by planning for likely developments in your IT strategy now, you can reduce the risk of having to throw out newly purchased material within months of installation because it is inadequate for the needs of the intellectual capital management initiative.

An IT strategy

Today CIGNA is a leading US provider of healthcare, insurance, employee benefits and financial services, and also has worldwide operations. It now has shareholder's equity of over $8bn, and assets of over $100bn. CIGNA was created in 1982 by the merger of INA Corporation and Connecticut General Corporation, each of which had a history going back over 100 years. CIGNA's operating divisions provide group health and life insurance, managed care services, retirement savings and welfare services, and property and casualty insurance. Wilson Taylor has been chairman of CIGNA since 1989 and CEO since 1988.

Like all financial institutions, CIGNA must use IT in ever more effective ways in order to remain competitive. CIGNA has ten operating divisions. IT has been key to the success of each of these divisions, but three are regularly featured in the literature for representing best practice in IT strategy. They are: CIGNA Financial Services, Benefits Access Inc. and IntegratedCare. CIGNA Financial Services is a discount broker based in Hartford, Connecticut. Benefits Access Inc. provides employers with tools and services for managing all their employee benefits. IntegratedCare provides fully integrated workers' compensation, disability and healthcare products. This case will look at CIGNA's overall IT strategy, with specific examples drawn mainly from the IntegratedCare business.

In 1993 it did not look as though CIGNA was likely to become the success that it is today. In that year CIGNA lost more than $250 million. In the third quarter of 1995, it generated a pre-tax profit of $60 million. How did CIGNA transform itself from corporate basket case to one of the world's most successful insurance businesses? The management that turned CIGNA around had a clear vision of the business strategy for the new CIGNA. That strategic vision was to change the company from being a general commercial carrier to an insurance specialist. Equally importantly, they also had expertise in implementing the strategic vision. Three related aspects of that implementation were IT strategy, knowledge management and business process re-engineering (BPR).

Gerry Isom became the new CEO of CIGNA Property & Casualty Insurance Co., one of CIGNA's operating divisions, in March 1993, and is one of the executives credited with helping CIGNA to create value by using IT well. Within the broad business strategy of making the company a specialist insurer, there was room for managers to add details and interpret just how the strategy should be implemented. At the same time, there was also sufficient pain from recent losses to guarantee that change would be forced through, and to ensure that old corporate habits behind the decline in profitability could be killed off. This is significant because managers often say that it is easier to implement new ideas such as IT strategies when things have been going badly than when things are going well. Isom responded to CIGNA's problems by downsizing and restructuring. But he also devoted much effort to growth programmes from the beginning of his time at CIGNA. One such programme was to invest in technology. CIGNA spent several millions of dollars to build an intelligent desktop environment for all its insurance agents. This added value because it leveraged the knowledge of each insurance agent, underwriter and claims administrator across the whole CIGNA organization. But Isom was careful about how money was invested in IT, and he made sure that CIGNA had an IT strategy in order to ensure that CIGNA's IT investment and running costs supported the business strategy.

The business strategy was to become more specialist and cast off peripheral and marginally profitable activities. At the time, the insurance market was a mess from the consumer's point of view. The range of products on offer was highly fragmented, with little attention paid to the overall insurance needs of families, individuals and employers. For example, the insurance and pensions aspects of the insurance products overlapped and confused the customer. This confusion was made worse by complex channels, which included employers, financial advisers and affinity programmes. Consequently, the first insurer to offer the market a clear range of products aligned to modern needs would be very successful. CIGNA aimed to be one of the first to do this, and it succeeded. How? One of the ways in which CIGNA did this was with CIGNA IntegratedCare. As we saw above, IntegratedCare is about providing fully integrated workers' compensation, disability and healthcare products. IntegratedCare is an example of the synergy that exists if IT strategy is aligned to support business strategy. Insurers had been experimenting with integrated benefits for at least 20 years. CIGNA was one of the earliest to implement this new approach to the insurance market, and IT strategy was a critical factor in CIGNA's success here.

IT strategy

There are five aspects of CIGNA's IT strategy that are worth special attention:

- **business drivers of IT strategy:** the relationship between business strategy and IT strategy, and especially what business issues were considered drivers of IT strategy;
- **criteria for using IT:** the criteria that CIGNA applied before deciding to apply IT as a solution to a business problem;
- **approach to implementation:** CIGNA's approach to IT once it had decided to use a particular piece of IT;
- **organizational structure of the IT function:** this often determines what kinds of IT strategy are feasible;
- **consultants:** consultants often play a significant but sometimes invisible role in shaping and implementing IT strategy.

1. Business drivers of IT strategy

When CIGNA restructured, the insurance and benefits market was fragmented, inefficient and confused. The new business strategy aimed at creating value by bringing order to this confusion. This meant not just designing new products and services, but also creating new ways to deliver these products and services. This in turn meant not only new channels, which are often thought of as being external to the vendor, but also new ways of managing these products and their marketing and supply within CIGNA itself. It seemed that CIGNA already had much of the information that the new business model required but just couldn't locate it easily or fast enough to meet the requirements; the information existed in CIGNA's corporate subconscious, as it were, but the act of recalling the information in time to use it was a problem for CIGNA. This problem called for better knowledge management.

CIGNA also had some effective business processes that were inefficient, and would need other entirely new processes for the new business model, which suggested that business process re-engineering was likely to be part of any solution. For example, its new policy processes were sometimes inefficient, and new legislative demands required some new processes. New policy processes were inefficient in that new customers had to wait sometimes for several weeks before the purchase of their policy was complete, when in fact no more than two days of actual work had gone into the business processes necessary to complete their policies. The two principle business drivers of the IT strategy that supported this business strategy at CIGNA were knowledge management and business process re-engineering.

Knowledge management

Besides researching the problem of how to get the right information to the right part of its organization at the right time, CIGNA also believed that in its new business model, knowledge management was a way to discover and maintain profitable niches. The skills and experience of its people in underwriting and claims could be used much more directly to determine which niches to enter and how much capital should be allocated to each niche. Previously, like in many other large companies, research and decision-making on new product development was of necessity somewhat removed from the front line, away from the staff who were facing the customers. In the new CIGNA, the idea was that new product development should be driven more by the front-line business as part of their routine processes. Using new IT, especially laptop PCs and distributed databases, a feedback loop could be built to ensure that marketing and capital allocation decisions were a natural extension of feedback from CIGNA's market. At the same time, technology also allowed CIGNA to make much better use of its own people and what they knew. For instance, customer service staff would be able to access information from both mainframe systems and new desktop tools, such as fax, imaging and word processing, to get proposals for higher-quality insurance and savings solutions to customers faster than before. Previously many different manual processes would have been required to bring all the necessary information together at a single point in front of the customer, with the result that either it took a long time – weeks perhaps – or it was simply too expensive to collate and format the information that already existed in CIGNA.

An example of how CIGNA applied the concept of knowledge management is the performance model for underwriters. A performance model identifies the kinds and sources of knowledge required for completion of each step in a business process. In the CIGNA performance model, key steps in the process of reviewing an application for insurance were identified rigorously and analyzed in detail. CIGNA identified 29 steps in the underwriting process, and linked each one to specific databases. For instance, the step of collecting accident history for a prospective customer's industry segment was linked to a database of government records about injuries at work. Before this step was formalized, there were at least four different possible ways that this business requirement was approached when a new policy was sold. The search for the data might have been skipped entirely; there may have been a search for the data, but in the wrong place; there may have been a search in the right place but at a greater cost than necessary, or the optimum search may have been made. A formal approach to knowledge management ensured that CIGNA collects accident history data in a consistent, effective and economical way.

For CIGNA the idea of a learning loop is an important feature of knowledge management. A learning loop can be thought of as a special case of a business process, and it should be a feedback loop where the feedback helps CIGNA to learn something that adds value to the company. An example of a learning loop is the flow of information through underwriters. Most CIGNA employees who collect and disseminate information from outside CIGNA are underwriters. Underwriters know the industry and have the time and IT and management tools to analyze and collate that information. Underwriters process information submitted by claims and sales agents and others in the organization, and then send the processed information to where it is needed in the company, such as the actuarial office, marketing, and operations. This stimulates a response or feedback from the other parts of the company.

In the old structure, information tended to flow more in just one direction, and much of the decision-making about what to collate and how to interpret the data was located away from the customer-facing part of the business. For example, there was less involvement of the underwriters in new product design. This was not because CIGNA senior management didn't want input from the front. Not at all! The problem was getting it from the large number of underwriters in an efficient manner. Now such information requirements are part of routine processes, and are not confined to one-off new product development projects. The learning loop is about putting more of the new product development and other strategic information processing at the front line of the business; it is about having a two-way information flow rather than a predominantly one way flow; and it is about making all this part of routine, everyday work.

One of the most significant contributions that the IT strategy made to CIGNA's amazing financial recovery was the role that CIGNA's IT department should play in knowledge management. However, it was in fact only after knowledge management had begun to be implemented that people realized that this had been a major issue. As so often, the hardest issues are the ones that can't be clearly seen or easily labelled until afterwards. Although this issue wasn't clear right at the outset of the restructuring, CIGNA did realize early on in the restructuring that the IT department could not and should not control the knowledge infrastructure of the organization, and this early realization probably saved several million dollars. The main reason why the IT department should not control the knowledge infrastructure was that information users had a better understanding of their own needs and working practices than the IT department. Of course the IT department would have useful advice, experience and insights to offer, but these should be options for consideration, not impositions from a heavy-handed IT organization. Another reason was that the idea of controlling information, which implies a highly centralized bureaucracy, was not what CIGNA's management had in mind for the new organization. The idea all along was to empower the underwriters, not to impose more bureaucracy on them.

CIGNA's vision was that its IT department should become a partner in the knowledge management process, and its rich IT management experience and specialist technical insight into knowledge management should be delivered to the rest of the organization through the partnership model. As a result of this approach, CIGNA's IT organization is now deeply involved in knowledge management at a strategic level rather than merely at a supporting level. CIGNA's IT function is involved in building the knowledge infrastructure and in developing the interfaces that support the efficient knowledge flow through the whole organization. The IT department could have been marginalized into a purely supporting role in the company, responding to tasks defined in detail by other parts of the business, but instead it is part of the team that decides what CIGNA should do and how it should do it.

Business process re-engineering

When CIGNA re-engineered its business process, it used the knowledge of its best underwriters to capture all the relevant information about risk, and then put this at the centre of the new processes. An example of what this means is that a nurse can enter details of an illness or accident, even incomplete or vague details, and this then initiates the claims process. Early on the new process links to legacy databases to verify the customer's status and eligibility for treatment, and any suspicious record of claims is identified automatically. The result is that fewer people can handle more claims, with a lower risk of fraud, than under the previous processes.

IT made it possible for the re-engineered processes to create much value by looking at the whole of CIGNA's information in its wider business context and making explicit the value to business units that sharing this information across the company would have. For instance, under the old business processes, customers were typically administered by customer number, and so it was hard to identify opportunities for cross-selling products. It also made it hard to obtain the raw data for planning new products that would benefit both the customer by reducing prices, and CIGNA by reducing costs and increasing revenue and market share. IT was pivotal in enabling new business processes to reduce these kinds of problems. In the context of business process re-engineering, CIGNA's IT strategy was about remembering that employees' minds contain much knowledge that will create tremendous value if used in the right way. The challenge was to find the right way to extract that knowledge and to find better ways to move it around the CIGNA organization.

2. Criteria for using IT

Three clear principles stand out in the way that CIGNA decides whether to use IT in solving a particular business problem. These principles shape management thinking throughout the organization, not just in the IT department but in the business units and support departments also. These three principles can be formulated as questions:

- What will IT do for CIGNA's customers? If it seems it will add value, then –
- Does the customer agree with CIGNA's analysis? and
- What is the risk-adjusted return expected from an IT investment (financial analysis)?

The third principle might surprise some people. Many IT and operations managers, even in the financial services industry, claim that the uncertainties of new IT mean that there is no point in making a financial analysis of potential IT investments. This view does not take account of the power and capability of professional financial analysis, particularly the tremendous advances in the handling of risk and uncertainty in applied modern finance theory. Companies like CIGNA show that it is feasible to do a financial analysis of all proposed IT projects. At the minimum this means estimating the investment required for the project, its financial return, and the riskiness of that return.

What will IT do for CIGNA's customers?

CIGNA asks whether an application will help its customers to reduce their costs. The IntegratedCare business model is an example. One of CIGNA's largest customer groups consists of managers at the major healthcare organizations, and CIGNA's analysis suggested that IntegratedCare could help this group to reduce their costs.

Does the customer approve?

What CIGNA thinks its customers need might not necessarily be what its customers really want. Validating its plans with customers minimizes the risk that an IT project will turn into a lemon project. By asking whether the customers approve the use of technology, CIGNA avoids investment in technology for technology's sake. This practice of CIGNA's sounds obvious, but many organizations do not check that their customers will benefit from new proposed IT investment. For examples of technology investments for technology's sake, just have a look at many UK and European World Wide Web sites today. Some are slick, but many cost a significant amount in design effort and supporting technology and still failed to help potential customers spend money with the owners of the website. CIGNA takes the view that it must convince its customers that CIGNA cares more about its customers' issues than about having the latest fashion in technology. This seemingly simple part of its IT strategy probably adds as much value to CIGNA as any major new application or major business process re-engineering project.

Financial analysis

The issue in financial analysis of potential IT projects is the risk-adjusted return of a project. CIGNA, like all commercial organizations, aims to invest its resources in projects with large returns and low risk; that is, higher than average risk-adjusted returns. CIGNA is different from some commercial organizations in that it extends this principle to its customers as well, so that it prioritizes on technology that will provide large risk-adjusted returns for its customers as well as itself. CIGNA is thus taking a view over the whole value chain, rather than just its own part of the value chain, in making a financial analysis of potential technology investments.

3. Approach to IT implementation

The implementation phase comes after making the investment decision for an IT project. Implementation includes developing the application or selecting it and obtaining it if it is not developed in-house, rolling out the application to the users, training and supporting users and generally making the system work to deliver the planned business benefits. This can include quick fixes to problems discovered during the roll-out. An analysis of CIGNA's IT strategy shows that three principles apply in the implementation phase: leverage, centralization and standardization.

Leverage

Leverage means making the most use of an asset. CIGNA emphasizes that legacy systems should be leveraged as much as possible. To see the value in this, we should ignore the marketing spin put on the term 'legacy system' by those paid to push client-server technology. Indeed, the value of leveraging legacy systems applies whether the legacy system in question is a mainframe, a client server, or some sort of distributed computing. (At the time of the CIGNA turnaround, most legacy systems there were in fact mainframes.) The two key points about a legacy system when considering leverage are that legacy systems have been in use in the organization for some time, and that as financial assets they represent substantial sunk cost. Provided that management avoids the sunk cost fallacy,[15] extracting further value from a substantial sunk cost is good business sense, and if the sunk cost in an investment or project has paid for itself in full, then extracting further value from it is even better business sense.

What did this mean for CIGNA? CIGNA needed databases to support each step of its re-engineered business processes, and so it meant that CIGNA faced a particular choice a number of times. The choice was how to provide a database that was required by new business processes: CIGNA could either create a new database on new technology, or it could adapt an existing or legacy system.

In CIGNA, as in all large organizations, there is never a shortage of people to recommend technology newer than that currently installed in the organization. Some people like technology for its own sake. Some of the more aggressive managers think they see a new technology as a shortcut to enhancing their own careers, for instance by creating an organization to manage the new technology. These managers are making a bet, in effect, that they can own the new technology and its staff if the new technology works, or that if it doesn't work they can offload it to the IT department. (There is no evidence or any suggestion, by the way, that this more aggressive kind of manager existed at CIGNA, but there were the ordinary technology champions.) Moreover, technophiles argue that new technology is a better solution to business problems than old technology. However, for any large IT-intensive project new technology tends to be riskier than old technology, and is often more expensive than using spare capacity in technology that is already installed.

In short, CIGNA uses the idea of leverage when implementing technology by ensuring that where legacy systems exist they are kept if they can still serve a valuable purpose. Legacy systems are utilized to the full instead of being replaced by unproven but newer technology, unless there is an overwhelming justification for the new technology. CIGNA insists on real business justification for new IT systems. This sounds basic, but in many organizations much money is wasted on IT when there simply is no business justification. As one expert puts it, 'largely on the say so of the [IT] suppliers, boards of directors throughout the world authorized the purchase of computers.'[16] CIGNA does everything possible to avoid this expensive mistake. New technology is generally riskier than old because when deployed on any scale new technology has more problems than older technology.[17] When all costs are considered, new technology is often more expensive then older technology because the total cost of the new project will have to be recovered from its returns, whereas an existing system is a sunk cost – a cost that exists whether or not the new system comes in. This is a basic axiom of technology management, and together the tendency of risk and cost to reduce as a technological system matures is known as the learning curve effect.[18] CIGNA substantially reduces its overall IT costs and risks by maximizing its re-use of legacy systems. Of course there are problems with legacy systems, particularly in their user-friendliness. However, user-friendliness or interfacing problems can be solved by implementing new interfaces without replacing the whole legacy system. CIGNA built Windows NT interfaces for many of its legacy systems in order to solve just this problem.

Centralization

CIGNA's approach favours the centralization of IT. Centralization reduces costs and improves quality of IT service for two reasons. First, it gives economies of scale, and secondly it helps IT plant and resources to be managed uniformly. For instance, claims processing is a significant business process in the insurance sector. CIGNA centralized claims processing into one location. Experts from nurses to claims administrators work alongside each other to find ways to eliminate fraud, to return employees to work sooner, and to co-ordinate care between many healthcare providers. Having such staff in one organization and in one location meant that CIGNA could easily apply common standards to working practices, encourage the sharing of ideas, and cross-fertilize among employees with different skills.

While centralization sounds good, especially in the abstract, in reality it is often very hard to implement. Just imagine what it's actually like in a large organization: the consultant's flipcharts with their frequent use of the word 'centralize' look very slick and are persuasive, the business models put together so laboriously by the finance and planning department show a fantastic payback, and conceptually centralization is the obvious thing to do. Consider an organization the size of CIGNA and what it's like even thinking of implementing such a change. There are many people who will be affected – hundreds and perhaps thousands who will be working in offices, datacentres and customer service teams. Centralizing means looking these people in the eye, and telling them that their work teams will change, their managers may change and even that some of them might have no future. And for what? For a grand plan, probably the ninth or tenth grand plan these people have survived in the past several years. From the employees' point of view, centralizing often means replacing many offices with just one office. See any Dilbert cartoon[19] for the sort of fear and suspicion that centralization can instil in many employees who hear that their company is considering it. The point is that there is a great difference between proposing centralization of IT as a good management practice in theory and actually doing it. That CIGNA managed to centralize much of its IT is a great achievement, and its IT strategy helped it to do that by helping managers to understand why the sometimes unpleasant task they had to do would work in the end. CIGNA's approach to centralization was to start small, with a pilot scheme at Irving, Texas. It took lessons learned from the Irving experience and applied them as it centralized further IT functions incrementally over several years. One of the hardest parts was the human resources aspect.

Standardization

Very close in terms of rationale to the principle of centralization in IT strategy is the principle of standardization. CIGNA has exploited the principle of rationalization to the full, and one aspect of standardization comes through in a CIGNA IT department motto: 'Collaborate, don't replicate.' CIGNA doesn't want several different applications each written in a different language. For this reason it decided to adopt one advanced desktop platform throughout the organization. This achieves standardization, and eliminates one of the main reasons for developing similar but different business applications, which is differing user equipment specifications. If all customer facing users have standard equipment – a standard desktop – then none can argue that he or she has unique requirements for interfacing from the desktop systems to shared corporate systems when it comes to specifying new applications.

4. Organizational structure of the IT function

The structure of the IT department at CIGNA was in part determined by – and also in part determined – its role and responsibilities, and those of the IT staff in it. Like many large organizations, CIGNA's IT function is a matrix organization. There is a CIO for the corporate entity, and in addition each division has a DISO, (divisional information systems officer). The corporate level CIO provides IT input to the corporate strategy and leads the development of the IT strategy that supports the corporate strategy. The DISOs sponsor technology for CIGNA's three major initiatives: producer relations, underwriting and claims management. The CIO also reviews the ways in which technology is used in each of these three areas.

5. Consultants

For CIGNA the most important reason for using consultants is to get validation for its technology strategies. For instance, CIGNA asked Gartner consultants for their opinions on the plan to provide agents with new desktop environments and tools, on application development tools and on executive information systems. CIGNA valued the insights Gartner had gained from working with other customers both in the insurance sector and elsewhere, and their knowledge of the insurance industry. In particular, it brought externally validated credibility and strategic perspective to the product selection process. CIGNA spends significant sums on IT consultants each year, and one of the ways in which it manages consultants is by having a senior executive who evaluates consultants against the needs of CIGNA and consulting best practice.

Business approach to individual projects

Just as there are certain critical factors in how CIGNA approaches the implementation of major IT projects from the IT side, so there are also critical success factors in how the business management side make their approach. The two key issues for business management to grasp in making a success of CIGNA's IT strategy are buy-in and vision. Without these, CIGNA knows that it is likely that a project will fail. Senior managers need to recognize the value of IT, which means believing in it themselves, and not just approving passively someone else's thinking. They need to map out and communicate a vision of corporate success and the part IT plays in it. Vision includes understanding the big picture. The big picture allows big vision. Big vision makes big value creation possible. Limited vision means small, piecemeal gains of marginal value.

Only after individual managers have a vision of the role IT should play in CIGNA, and managers collectively buy in to that vision and what it will mean in practice, can CIGNA be sure that its management will provide sufficient leadership. And only then is it safe to release funding for IT-intensive projects. An example of a vision of the business management side of CIGNA that helped to ensure the success of what became one of the largest projects in the new CIGNA is CIGNA's 24-hour coverage. This means that a client's employees are covered by their employer's CIGNA insurance policy all the time, not just when they are at work. The original motivation was to reduce double-dipping. This is when a policyholder collects benefits from both a group health plan and a workers' compensation insurer for the same injury or illness. As CIGNA explored further into what its customers wanted, it found that employers who bought 24-hour coverage insurance for their workers also wanted disability and other coverage included. In this way CIGNA senior management developed a powerful vision of strategic needs it could fill with an integrated offering.

Changes in business-to-IT relationship

CIGNA's new IT strategy brought about significant changes in the relationship between the IT function and the business units. Business managers started focusing more on IT costs and returns. As IT spending became more visible and new projects were managed jointly as projects, the amount of money spent on IT was no longer someone else's problem but concerned business managers at CIGNA. The role and responsibilities of CIGNA's IT function changed too. Like many other large organizations, CIGNA's old IT department had evolved from the 1960s data-processing department. This model was gradually replaced under the new IT strategy by business development teams on which IT leaders serve alongside corporate lawyers, marketing executives, operations managers and even customers. These cross-functional teams mean that the IT vision and key IT decisions are no longer dominated by the IT department, but are made jointly by all affected parts of the business. The IT function provides technical expertise and mentoring to the decision-making group, and in the same way, IT's input to non-IT areas such as marketing, human resouces and finance is more significant than before. The overall effect was that control over IT, especially IT spending, shifted somewhat from the IT function to end-users.

IntegratedCare

CIGNA's IntegratedCare business shows how having an IT strategy can benefit an organization. The IntegratedCare business model is about changing the basis on which employers provide their staff with healthcare, disability coverage and other insurance benefits. Traditionally CIGNA and the industry had managed the administration and paperwork for each kind of employee benefit separately, which meant shunting a beneficiary's paperwork among different benefit providers. The business strategy behind IntegratedCare was that CIGNA should manage all such work itself, which would give significant benefits. To make the IntegratedCare model work in practice, CIGNA was going to have to make sure that information from many different sources was available in one place. The quantity of information was not the key issue here, and never has been for profitable underwriting; much more important was the quality of the information, and how to determine which information is relevant to particular business processes.

Benefits of the IntegratedCare project

CIGNA believed that the IntegratedCare project would boost future earnings by yielding three main kinds of benefits. There would be benefits to CIGNA itself, benefits to CIGNA's corporate customers, the employers, and benefits to the end-users of insurance, the employees of CIGNA's corporate customers.

Benefits to CIGNA

The new approach was expected to lead to substantial reductions in the cost of major IT projects. It did. For instance, a web and application server connectivity software was rolled out for less than $50 000. Other IT applications that would have been expensive to achieve under CIGNA's previous approach to IT were produced at lower cost. Another internal benefit was that the new IT infrastructure maintained the accuracy of the data extracted from CIGNA's production databases. This meant that the amount of staff and management time spent checking data or resolving conflicting data was greatly reduced, thereby lowering administrative and sales expenses. A third benefit to CIGNA was that it was able to reduce the time to market for new products, because the new IT strategy introduced advanced software tools that allowed faster development of in-house applications. This gave CIGNA an increased competitive edge. This in turn helped to increase the company's market share. A further internal benefit was that the new IT strategy enabled a better understanding to develop between business and IT leadership, which was necessary if projects like IntegratedCare were to become successful products.

Benefits to employers

At least as important as the internal benefits were the benefits to CIGNA's customers. These were significant. CIGNA estimated that the IntegratedCare project, if successful, would enable a 10% reduction in payroll costs, lost wages and medical expenses. This is exactly what happened. Workers' compensation and disability costs dropped 10%, absences due to short-term disability dropped 10% and attorneys were called in half as often. AlliedSignal, Inc., a CIGNA corporate customer, estimated that such an approach could shave 8% to 12% off its total payroll costs. This range included direct savings, such as the actual cost for benefits, and indirect costs, such as reduced absenteeism and higher productivity.

End-customer benefits

Finally, the end-customer would also receive substantial benefits from IntegratedCare. The 24-hour coverage meant a policyholder would be covered for injuries whether or not they were suffered on the job, at lower cost and with less effort than if they had two separate insurance policies.

Implementation issues

CIGNA found three main issues at the firm-wide level when implementing its new IT strategy. There were the inevitable cultural issues, not too different from those stirred up by any change project in a large organization. Secondly, there were organizational issues that needed to be resolved. And thirdly there were some big issues around implementing knowledge management. The benefits to the end-user helped CIGNA's corporate customers, who were seen by their employees as improving the benefits of employment, which in turn benefited CIGNA.

Cultural issues: empires fear loss of control

Linking different forms of insurance required CIGNA not only to bridge gaps within itself, but also between itself and some of its customer's organizations. These gaps existed because it had simply not been necessary for the various business units and support functions to communicate so closely under the old business model. Within a large customer company, different benefits might be handled by risk management, human resources or payroll departments, each of which might fear it would lose influence under integration. These fears had to be addressed and managed.

Organizational issues

CIGNA's new IT strategy and its change programme in general created significant organizational and political issues. If three datacentres are centralized, then two managers at best lose status and at worst lose their jobs; and similarly where projects are rationalized, in-house software development in contracted out or hardware procurement is standardized. CIGNA could have tackled these political issues head-on as they arose, but instead like many of its competitors it formed new subsidiaries specifically to focus on the integrated coverage market. The new IT strategy could be implemented easily in a new corporate entity and contribute to business growth, leaving the old corporate entity to wither on the vine. As well as side-stepping the politics of the large parent organization, this approach avoids having to spend excessive effort integrating the new businesses' IT infrastructure into all of the existing company. (The UK's biggest mutual life assurers Standard Life, Equitable Life and Prudential took exactly the same approach when setting up new businesses that exploited the opportunities offered by effective use of modern IT.)

Difficult aspects of knowledge management

Knowledge management is about getting people to share information willingly. But as everyone knows, knowledge is power, and therefore persuading staff to share knowledge effectively was one of the most difficult tasks facing CIGNA in making a success of its new IT strategy. One of the ways CIGNA did this was to envisage successful knowledge sharing as an upward spiral. In an upward spiral, knowledge and information contributed by employees is processed by 'knowledge editors,' for instance experienced underwriters, who then distribute it across the organization. For example, such underwriters might obtain data from the front line offices and then broadcast relevant information to associates and superiors over CIGNA's internal network. Relevant information could be a sales approach that was successful in one part of the country and might be worth trying in another, or a new kind of information requested by a state insurance commissioner that could be expected to surface in other states soon.

Conclusion

CIGNA provides a good example of how an IT strategy can be used to create enormous value. CIGNA did not operate in a glamorous high technology industry, but this didn't mean that it couldn't capture the massive benefits of IT. It did this by adopting a carefully planned IT strategy that was aligned to and supported an innovative business strategy. This was not a simple task, and significant implementation issues both within CIGNA's IT department and in the business units had to be worked through. The IT function relinquished some of its power over IT but learned more about the business; likewise, business management shared strategic decision making more with IT and assumed responsibility for managing more IT costs. But the end result benefited CIGNA, benefited CIGNA's customers, and benefited CIGNA's customers' employees.

Endnotes

1   Among the many publications in this field are: Hochstrasser (1992), Silk (1991) and Brown.
2   Research conducted by the author in London and New York, January to April 1999.
3   Personal research. This figure is the one most frequently quoted by CIOs when asked to estimate how many IT security breaches are reported in the press, to the nearest 5%.
4   Koenig (1998).
5   Dolinar (1998).
6   Campbell (1999).
7   Cribb (1999).
8   Source – Gartner, quoted in Cribb (1999).
9   Source – Gartner, quoted in Cafasso (1996).
10 Source – Comdisco, Inc., quoted in *ibid*.
11 Cafasso (1996).

12 Stewart (1997), p.67.

13 *Ibid.*

14 The Shell and Dow numbers are from Fulmer (1998). (However, if these figures are accurate, one is tempted to wonder why neither company has not made well-publicized moves into the intellectual capital management business itself.)

15 That is, making sure you are getting a net return from your legacy system rather than continuing to make net investment. Put another way, make sure you are not throwing good money after bad. Also see the Glossary.

16 Grindley (1995) p.27.

17 This is also known as the 'Pandora's Box Rule' – see p.142 of Weinberg (1985).

18 One of the classic studies of this is the learning curve for B-29 bombers at Boeing's Wichita plant in Ross (19??) – see especially Fig. 4.1 therein.

19 For example, Adams (1996).

Appendix A Review of accounting

Rationale, terms and tools

Why is accounting important in managing IT costs?
A brief historical perspective

In 3500 BC Babylonian man was busy composing sets of management accounts in and around Ur of the Chaldees, in modern-day Iraq. Babylonian man recorded goods stored and shipped in marks on clay tablets, and we now record items stored and shipped, and make other accounting entries, on paper or even on computers. More important than advances in the materials on which we record accounts are the accounting concepts themselves, and these too have evolved, but the evolution of concepts used in accounting has been even more extensive than the change from clay to paper or computer systems. Accounting evolved in response to the needs and pressures of the businesses which it served.

It is entirely possible, and we think likely, that accounting has not yet adapted to the changes in management requirements of it induced by the great IT revolution, and that it is largely for this reason that it is often hard for competent, well-trained and intelligent management to exercise good control over IT costs and, more generally, IT investment. This argument is supported throughout this book in various ways. This claim may seem sweeping, but in our defence we would point out the state of accounting just before the last great upheaval and surge of evolution in accounting methods brought on by the industrial revolution.

Before the industrial revolution there were at least three different approaches to management accounting in England.[1] In the stewardship system accounting had evolved in the management of landed estates, and a primary evolutionary driver had been the need to prevent the stewards of the estate defrauding the estate owners. In the mercantile system, accounting had evolved to help merchants analyze the problems of complexity and size in large scale organizations. Thirdly, accounting in the putting-out system had evolved under pressure from the twin requirements of measuring the production of each out-worker and preventing pilferage of raw materials by the out-workers. Accounting in the stewardship system did not focus on the efficiency of the different parts of the estate, because the estate owners were primarily interested in simply owning and enjoying the estate; likewise accounting in the mercantile systems did not focus on fixed assets; and accounting in the putting out system did not focus on fixed capital, as this was the responsibility of the out-worker. Thus we feel that there is at least historical precedent for our claim that accounting techniques are driven by the needs of the enterprise being managed, and it would not surprise the history of accounting if current accounting methods prove insufficient for the needs of the modern, IT-intensive firm.

Aim

This chapter is intended to serve as a refresher of key terms that will be used in analysing the problems and proposing solutions to managing IT costs in the modern firm, and to set out some of the major accounting issues that affect IT spend in IT-intensive organizations. It is not intended that the chapter should be any substitute for a proper training in management accounting.[2]

Familiarity with the accounting terms and techniques reviewed in this chapter will enable the reader to understand the issues in identifying and managing IT costs, and why these issues sometimes differ significantly from those foremost in identifying and managing non-IT-related costs.

The reader who currently uses or creates management accounts as part of his role can skip this Appendix.

Rationale

Accounting is sometimes perceived to be a very boring subject, unless your job is to manage a business, when even the most dynamic, seat-of-the-pants entrepreneur finds at least some parts of accounting interesting. There needs to be an efficient understanding of IT-related accounting issues in two dimensions if IT is to be managed properly, so that costs are controlled and the greatest innovation and economic benefit to the firm can derive from IT. First, business managers need to know enough about IT to be able to relate various items of IT cost to the familiar accounting categories. Secondly, IT developers, researchers and IT management need to know enough about accounting conventions to understand why certain information is important, and the effects on overall management of the enterprise of decisions about how IT is managed.

The importance of this can be shown by an example. Suppose that you run Zeno Enterprises, and the tax regime in which your company operates treats capital equipment and intellectual property differently. Suppose capital equipment attracts a capital allowance of 10%, and is subject to a 5% import duty, while on the other hand, all research attracts a 20% tax relief. Suppose also that in order to meet the demand from one of your key markets, Zeno Enterprises must develop a new way of managing customer data. There are in fact two solutions, each offered at the same cost. One solution entails purchasing 'switches' – a kind of specialized hardware – from overseas, and the other involves using your own staff to develop and write a few million lines of computer code to run on standard hardware. The list price may be the same, but the cost to Zeno Enterprises will be different as there is a net tax relief of less than 10% on the hardware based approach, but a 20% relief on the software based approach.[3] The problem is not that the firm's management would have difficulty analysing the alternatives and identifying which is best; this is management's job, and in an organization of any size teams of people make such analyses and recommendations daily. The problem is that when IT and firm management understand too little of the key concepts and options used in the other's work, it may be that management never knows of a significant alternative approach, and IT is not sufficiently aware of the major business forces, such as tax differentials, that can make major differences to the business case for different technological approaches.

The purpose of accounting in managing IT costs and efficiency

Why dost thou strive against him? for he giveth not account of any of his matters.

Job 33:13

No money shall be drawn from the treasury, but in consequence of appropriations made by law; and a regular statement and account of receipts and expenditures of all public money shall be published from time to time.

Constitution of the United States of America

Of life, of crown, of queen, at once dispatched,
Cut off even in the blossoms of my sin,
Unhouseled, disappointed, unaneled,
No reck'ning made, but sent to my account

Shakespeare, Hamlet, Act 1, Scene V

Many years ago a British bank chairman observed that not only did the bank's accounts show the true position but the actual situation was a little better still.[4]

In the brief historical perspective at the start of this Appendix we made the claim that the purpose of accounting depended on the particular needs of the organization in which accounting was used. In this section we will start by outlining in very general terms the main potential reasons for a firm to use accounting, and it is inevitable that such a general description will be abstract in places. Then we will look at some concrete examples showing potential reasons for using accounting in a business where IT is used extensively, and relate these reasons to the general needs we started with.

It is possible to find many books about accounting which contain no definition of the subject, and some which even omit the term from the index. If accountants are less than ready to give a precise definition of what accounting is supposed to mean, then the ambiguity in parts of the accounting endeavour should not be too surprising. In fact if one ever needs to dampen the enthusiasm of an accountant in a meeting, ask him to define the term 'accounting'. In general, however, the ordinary English definition of the term is exactly what we need, especially for the purposes of managing IT costs. 'To account' means to judge or to value, and in its intransitive form, 'to account for' means to give a reason. Let us therefore define management accounting as (1) recording, and (2) providing evidence for evaluating, the procurement, creation and use of resources in the firm to further the purposes of the firm. In a commercial firm, the primary purpose will always be to increase shareholder value, but non-commercial organizations may have various other purposes.

The purpose of accounting is to show where money has come from, where it has gone, and how much, if any, is left over (or is owed), and to explain all this. This is at any rate the ideal. Many accounting systems do a poor job in some of these things. In 1996 one of the UK's largest banks faced a major problem in a key revenue generating department. Bitter animosity had developed between a group of business managers and the IT department over proposed new technology. The argument was complex, but to give a flavour of the disagreement, one of many issues was whether there should be floppy disk drives in the new desktop computers. The IT department wanted no-one except IT to have floppy disk drives, because the head of IT believed that floppy disk drives spread computer viruses. The business managers needed to be able to use floppy disks. The argument had become acrimonious and personal.

To defuse the situation, which was beginning to get out of hand and limit the amount of work done in the bank's department, the chief executive ordered an investigation into IT costs to date, to try to identify the major cost drivers, and establish, among many other things, to what extent viruses were a major source of costs – i.e., should they be a material consideration in the design of a new IT infrastructure for the bank? This investigation was planned to last four weeks. It extended to three months, at great cost itself, because there was no useful accounting data on IT costs. The internal accounting processes were in disarray, and it was practically impossible to tell how much had been spent on what, with what economic result. In the case of hardware, one of the investigation's findings was that it appeared that the department had bought no hardware for two years. The line in the accounts for PC hardware purchases showed zero. This was at odds with numerous brand new PCs being used in the department.

After six weeks of investigation, involving chartered accountants on contracts at high hourly rates, it was found that most of the hardware was being expensed as sandwiches. Not only did this cause management to have no reliable data about PC costs, it had also, by the time of the enquiry, led to management making two catering staff redundant in a misguided effort to control catering costs. What happened? In the short-term, the project finished without identifying anything useful about what really drove IT costs in the bank. However, within months the bank was sold off to a foreign competitor, whose first move was to install proper accounting controls.

The case of PC hardware being expensed as sandwiches typifies the level of understanding of IT costs in many firms, and makes the point that accounting is important because management needs to know how much is being spent, on what, and with what results. If your firm fires innocent caterers as a misguided reaction to excessive PC costs, you will go out of business, and you will be lucky to find a buyer for your business.

But how much does the non-finance specialist need to know about accounting to do an effective job in managing the firm's IT costs and maximizing the efficiency of investment in IT? Not too much, we believe. The focus is on business decision making; specialized details for auditing, financing decisions and tax optimizations are best left to the relevant specialist. Interestingly, some recent research claims that too extensive a knowledge of accounting can actually cause worse decision-making than an elementary understanding, because it seems that 'people with a good deal of formal accounting training are more likely to ignore opportunity costs than those people with less accounting training.'[5] If true, this would be surprising.

The three aspects of accounting

The three aspects of accounting are the balance sheet, the cashflow, and the profit and loss statement. We call these three aspects because they are each different views of the same thing, the firm, and are therefore interrelated. The balance sheet is a statement of the net worth of the firm, or other entity for which accounts have been prepared. The cashflow shows what cash (or certain other non-cash items) have flowed into and out of the firm. The profit and loss statement sets out how profitable the accountant thinks the firm is. All aspects of accounting are to some extent subjective. This claim can surprise some people, but fundamentally the reason lies in the very nature of business itself, and business is by nature largely subjective. We are not denying that there are objective rules that govern accounting, and it is the aim of accounting to minimize subjectivity wherever feasible; our point is more modest, and is simply that there are limits to this feasibility.

Balance sheet

The balance sheet of a firm is a list of all the firm's assets and liabilities, showing their value – in many cases historic. The balance sheet is a snapshot, that is it records the assets and liabilities, and their values at a certain time. Before that time and afterwards the composition of the firm's assets may differ.

An example of a firm's balance sheet is shown in Fig. A.1, in this case the fictional company Complexity International. This balance sheet has three main parts, assets,

Complexity International balance sheet

Assets	
Fixed assets	
Tangible assets	200
Investments	5
Current assets	
Stocks	5
Debtors	1200
Cash	400
Total assets	**1810**
Liabilities	
Current liabilities	
Creditors < 1yr	(505)
Long-term liabilities	
Creditors > 1yr	(10)
Total liabilities	**(515)**
Net assets	**1295**

Fig. A.1   Balance sheet: presentation 1

liabilities, and net worth or net assets. The assets are subdivided into fixed assets and current assets. Fixed assets are those of which the firm intends to make continuing use, in contrast to current assets, which the firm intends to use up within a year. Buildings, plant, office furniture, patents and long-term intellectual property rights are generally examples of fixed assets. We say, generally, because there are exceptions; property development firms may own buildings or land as part of their business in dealing in property investment, and similarly, an office furniture supplier might treat its stock of desks as short-term assets but its desks used by its managers as fixed assets.

Figure A.2 is a more conventional presentation of the same information contained in Fig. A.1. There are two slight differences. First, in Fig. A.1 the main headings are different. In Fig. A.2, the assets and liabilities are shown together under the heading 'net assets'. Secondly, a breakdown of net assets has been added, which is called 'capital and reserve', which in turn is broken down into 'shareholders' funds and minority interests'. The point of showing 'capital and reserves' is to show how the assets are owned, so it is no accident that 'capital and reserves' must equal 'net assets'.

Complexity International balance sheet

Net assets		
Fixed assets		
Tangible assets	200	
Investments	5	
		205
Current assets		
Stocks	5	
Debtors	1200	
Cash	400	
		1605
Current liabilities		
Creditors < 1yr		(505)
Net current assets		1100
Total assets less current liabilities		1305
Creditors > 1yr		(10)
Net assets		**1295**
Capital & reserves		
Shareholders' funds		
Share capital	125	
Share premium a/c	1000	
P&L reserve	75	
		1200
Minority interests		95
Capital & reserves		**1295**

Fig. A.2   Balance sheet: presentation 2

Share capital

Share capital is the *nominal value* of the shares issued by a company, in those countries (such as the UK) where shares must have some nominal value.

Nominal value/par value

The *nominal value/par value* of shares is their face value, and is set when the shares are first issued. Shares in Amazon.com had a nominal value of $0.01. This does not mean that they are sold for $0.01, or even that they ever were sold for $0.01. If anything, it means that at the precise moment that Amazon.com became incorporated, each share could not have been worth less than $0.01 on the basis of what had been invested into it. Nothing in understanding and managing IT costs depends on knowing anything more about the nominal value of shares.

Share premium reserve

The *share premium reserve* records the difference between the *nominal value* of shares issued and the actual issue price. If Amazon.com decided to sell some of its $0.01 shares which had been issued but not sold, i.e. they had been retained in Amazon's treasury, and if Amazon.com issued them each for $100, then for each share sold $99.99 would be added to the sum in the share premium reserve. (Both the values under the headings 'fixed assets' and 'shareholders' funds & reserves' would increase by the same amount.)

In most jurisdictions the share premium reserve is an undistributable reserve, i.e., it cannot be paid out as a dividend to shareholders, it is part of share capital.

Minority interests

In the context of accounts, *minority interests* are outside shareholders of subsidiaries of the firm, and they are a source of funding just as the parent firm's shareholders are. The amount attributed to them in the accounts is the minority shareholders' share of the net assets of the subsidiary enterprise in which they have invested.

Profit and Loss reserve

The *profit and loss reserve* is the accumulation of all the undistributed profits.

Tangible assets

A *tangible asset* is an asset that can be touched, or has physical existence.

Intangible assets

An *intangible asset* is one that has no physical existence, such as a patent or other intellectual property right.

Cashflow statement

The main purpose of the cashflow statement is to show the sources and outflows of cash. The main categories within the cashflow statement are:

- operating activities, adjusted for non-cash items such as depreciation charges
- returns on investment and servicing of finance
- tax
- investing
- financing.

There is no necessary immediate linkage between cashflow and profit. There are three principle differences between cash and profit: movements in working capital, capital expenditure, and the financing of cashflows. Cashflow and profit tell you different things about a business, and many people place greater emphasis on cashflow than on profit. This is not necessarily always a good idea, but is probably because cashflow is often easier to identify and understand than profit. Does this matter in controlling IT costs? Certainly: many people believe that in many organizations IT is inefficient, and therefore unnecessarily expensive, because of a history of underinvestment in IT. A possible explanation is that in areas of the firm less well-understood by senior management, such as IT, managers revert to instinct in making investment decisions, which is when cash flow is favoured over profit or its internal analogue, IT efficiency.

It is necessary to adopt some method of allocating cash flows over time periods, because some cash flow items such as a depreciation charge on an asset, may not extend neatly over precisely the same period of time as is covered by the accounts and cashflow statement. A different kind of allocation issue arises when a sum of IT cost is potentially categorizable in different ways. For example, suppose a company starts to set up a complex database, perhaps to improve its understanding of a target group of customers. Building this database may to some extent become a part of routine business operations. The company may decide to sell off or swap for some other asset part or all of the database, but to continue using or even developing part of the database. This could create a situation where the costs, and benefits, incurred and derived from developing the database must be allocated between operating activities and investing activities. This is the sort of area where decisions are subjective, and there may be scope to align the principle used for such allocations to the interest of the firm.

Cash equivalent

A *cash equivalent* is a short-term highly liquid investment which is within three months of maturity on acquisition, easily convertible into a known quantity of cash.

Investment activity

An investment activity is activity which is related to the acquisition or sale of fixed or current non-cash asset investments.

Financing

In the context of the cashflow statement, the *financing* category includes payment to (and payment from) providers of finance, for principal only. This category includes cash raised or paid out by issuing or redeeming securities and loans and associated commissions and expenses, and the payment of the capital element of finance leases.

Taxation

In the context of the cashflow statement, only the payment of taxes on profits is recorded. Sales tax (such as value added tax) is not recorded in this category of the cashflow statement.

Returns on investment and servicing of finance

This category includes all payments and receipts arising from (a) owning investments, and (b) payments to the providers of finance. This category includes the cash raised or paid out in association with these activities, such as: interest paid or received, dividends received from related undertakings, and the interest element of finance leases. Not included are unrealized gains and losses.

The profit and loss account

The profit and loss (P&L) account is a statement summarizing the activities of the firm over a set period, and focuses on showing the profit (or loss) made.

The intuitive meaning of profit is the money left over after all the costs have been met, and is what the entrepreneur creates if he succeeds. Company accounts are more precise in their definition: it is the sum of the sales revenue less all the costs of generating those sales. Costs include pay and other staff benefits, licensing fees, property costs, the cost of any borrowing, and depreciation.

The profit and loss account normally starts with the turnover of the firm, and proceeds through every kind of deduction or addition until the profit owed to the shareholders is left. Two things can happen to this profit. It can be distributed to the shareholders, or it can be kept within the firm to be used in making investments. We see that Complexity International has decided to distribute two-fifths of its profits to shareholders and keep the rest.

Earlier we said that the balance sheet, the P&L and the cashflow are three aspects of the same thing, i.e., the firm. We have just seen one of the links between these aspects in the P&L reserve. The sum in 'Profits to be transferred to reserves' will be added to the previous period's balance, to give the sum in this year's balance sheet under 'P&L reserve.'

Subjectivity in accounting for IT

Many people who have little or no experience of accounting tend to assume that accounting is characterized by precision and objectivity. While this is the ideal, and can be achieved in some parts of a set of accounts, in the private sector especially accounting also relies to a significant extent on subjective judgement. This is not because the private sector adopts a more cavalier approach to accounting than government; indeed there are notorious cases where governments of leading western nations have knowingly and wilfully committed misrepresentations in accounts that would horrify any major private sector firm.[6]

We saw that the balance sheet is a statement of the assets and liabilities of the firm. One of the problems in understanding and managing IT costs is 'what is an asset?' So much of the cost of IT is tied up in intangible assets: software licences, operating system licences, contracts with consultants and outsourcers.

Accounting exhibits a significant degree of subjectivity in many respects, even when the subject of the accountant's judgement is something that has been common in the business world for many years, perhaps thousands of years.

Endnotes

1 Jones (1995), p.25, on which the analysis in the remainder of the paragraph is based.
2 For a detailed account of company accounts see Pendlebury (1994).
3 In real life the level of risk, timescales and management resources for each solution would also be material considerations, but in this example are ignored.
4 Speech by the chairman of the London and County Bank at its annual meeting, February 1901. Reported in *The Economist*, 1901, p.204, and cited in Brealey (1996), p.776.
5 Kroll (1998).
6 For example, the UK government's pretence, for many years that National Insurance contributions were insurance contributions rather than a tax. Even worse was the UK government's exceptionally creative devaluation of War Loan stock, of which the *Daily Telegraph* Trefgarne (1999) said 'the treatment of War Loan holders helped reduce British government stock from being the world's safest investment in the 19th century to a notoriously risky one after the war' and 'Millions of patriotic citizens, schools and clubs subscribed – only to find the rules changed and the value of their investments destroyed'. The UK government issued the bond between 1915 and 1917 during the Great War, and marketed it as a patriotic investment. The UK government promised to pay a 5% coupon with a redemption not before 1952. However, in 1932 the government reneged and cut the coupon to 3.5% for all bondholders who refused to accept immediate redemption and paid attractive commisions to intermediaries who went along in persuading the bondholders to accept immediate redemption.

A structure of the typical principle IT costs

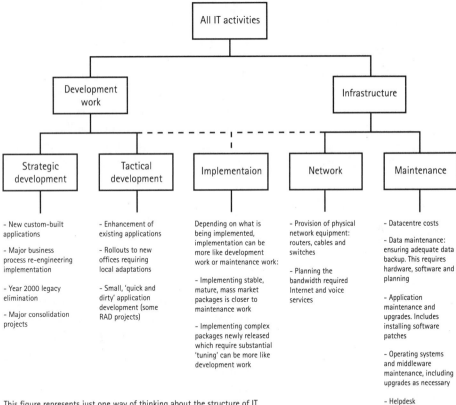

This figure represents just one way of thinking about the structure of IT functions within an organization. There are many other ways. The point is that however your IT function is structured, IT cost allocations tend to follow structure. That is, each subdivision of IT may have its costs allocated on different principles.

Glossary

AWAC

Airborn Warning and Control. AWACs aircraft are among the most expensive and complex types of aircraft in a modern air force, largely because they have a large amount of leading edge, complex IT on board. The UK's Nimrod AWACs project was one of the most expensive IT failures ever, but the UK government at least did not succumb to the *sunk cost fallacy*.

Client/server

A way of organizing computing. Users each have a 'client' computer, typically a PC or a workstation, and these are connected by network to a 'server' computer. The server is so called because it 'serves up' applications and data to its clients on demand, which means that the client computers are relieved of the work load of managing files, networks and much security.

EPS

Earnings per share.

IRR

Internal rate of return. The discount rate at which a project's NPV is zero.

Learning curve

A learning curve is said to exist where the cost of providing a certain level of service or of producing a certain quantity of goods falls with experience. This is typically because staff get used to the set of tasks involved, the tasks themselves become simplified as the design of the tools and equipment used evolves, and managers schedule work more effectively. Learning curve effects are major factors in IT costs. For instance, the average worker in the West takes far less time to become productive on a word processor now than their predecessors did in the early 1980s. This is because the IT skill level of the average employee is much greater now than in the 1980s, and also because the design of word processors makes them much easier to use.

Legacy system	Generally used to mean an old IT system that does not use the latest technology. The term tends either to be used by people with an interest in either replacing the legacy system with something newer, for which they will be paid commission, or given a larger staff or more organizational power, or to be used by people with a similar interest in selling something to be added to the legacy system to make it more usable. Some client-server enthusiasts use the term as a synonym for mainframe.
Minimum efficiency scale	The scale of a project or of an operation at which the unit cost is minimized. Traditionally this idea has been applied to manufacturing projects; for instance, producing more cars, thus reducing the management cost component of the cost of each car, and similarly economies of scale will be achieved for many other costs. In practice there is a point at which diseconomies of scale start to appear, and the minimum efficiency scale lies just before this point. The idea of minimum efficiency scales is now being applied to service and knowledge industries. In software development the training of programmers and testers and the structuring of the project teams may have minimum efficiency scales.
MIS	Management information system. A loose term that can mean different things in different organizations; for instance sometimes the term includes the general ledger, but elsewhere it applies only to a system or systems that analyse the data in the general ledger (or other books and records of a firm) to produce management reports – reports such as sales, inventory turnover, cost trends or reports analysing the success of marketing campaigns. Some organizations include email as an MIS.
Nimrod	See AWAC and Legacy system.
NPV	Net present value. The NPV of a project is an estimate of its value in terms of today's money. To obtain NPV all projected cashflows (investments and returns) for the project are discounted at a rate for that particular project. The discount rate depends on the anticipated interest rates and the risk of the project. Riskier projects have higher discount rates. In practice many organizations use just one discount rate for all projects,

partly because of the difficulty of quantifying the level of risk in different individual projects.

PC   Personal computer.

ROCE   Return on capital employed. It is calculated thus:

$$\frac{\text{Earnings before Interest Payments and Tax}}{\text{Capital Employed}}$$

Sunk cost fallacy   The financial term for throwing good money after bad. Once a cost is sunk, that is, spent, on an idea or project that is fundamentally uneconomic, no amount of extra investment will make the change to the fundamentals to make the project economic. Sunk costs are in the past and cannot be changed subsequently.

This basic fact of life and financial management is often ignored or forgotten, as when a manager argues that if several million dollars have been spent on a project that has failed so far, then the project can't just be abandoned – surely it is worth some further investment to try to recoup the previous investment. No, the only sure thing here is that the money spent on the project has produced no return, and any further spending should be evaluated against other investment opportunities.

References

Adams, S. (1996) *The Dilbert Principle*. New York: HarperCollins.

Airline Industry Information (1998) 'In the Industry' (News Roundup), 13 October.

Alford, B.L. (1996) 'Welcome to the Nighmare Zone: in Search of Compatible Global Communications', *Enterprise Systems Journal*, October.

Arlington Morning News (1998) 'Six-Hour Sabre Outrage Cripples Airline', 7 February.

Bacon, K., Defense Department spokesman holds regular news briefing. Washington Transcript Service, 11 August 1998.

Bates, J.J. (1999) 'Cross border corporate governance at BP Amoco', Issue Alert, Institutional Investor Services, September.

Bezos, J. (1999) Letter to Amazon's customers, May 1999.

Brealey, R.A. and Myers, S.C. (1996) *Principles of Corporate Finance*. New York: McGraw Hill.

Brown, A.E. (Editor) *Creating a Business-Based IT Strategy*. Unicom Applied Information Technology Serries No. 14.

Business Wire (1977) 'Comshare Delivers Performance Measurement Application to PolyGram International; Commander Sales Analysis Focuses on Improved Use of Market Research', 21 November.

Cafasso, R. (1996) 'Seize Control', *Computerworld Client/Server Journal*, 1 February.

Campbell, M. (1999) 'Russian Hackers Steal US Weapons Secrets', *Sunday Times*, 25 July.

Chandler, A.D., Jr. (1990) *Scale and Scope: the Dynamics of Industrial Captialism*. Cambridge, Mass: Harvard/Bellknap.

Chapman, C. and Ward, S. (1997) *Project Risk Management*. Chichester: John Wiley & Sons.

Crainer, S.E. (1995) *The Financial Times Handbook of Management*. London: Pitman.

Cribb, R. (1999) 'Air Miles Breach Not Unique', *Toronto Star*, 23 January.

Davenport, T.H. and Prusak, L. (1997) *Information Ecology*: Mastering the Information and Knowledge Environment. New York: Oxford University Press.

Diromualdo, R.F. (1997) SEC form 10K. Washington DC: Securities and Exchange Commission.

Dolinar, L. (1998) 'Hackers Hit Pentagon Systems', *Newsday*, 26 February.

Drucker, P.F. (1995) 'The Information Executives Truly Need', *Harvard Business Review*, January–February.

Ellis, C.D. (1975) 'The Loser's Game', *Financial Analysts Journal*.

Ellis, C.D. (1998) *Winning the Loser's Game: Timeless Strategies for Successful Investing*. New York: McGraw-Hill.

Financial Times (1999) 'Bad News on a Colossal Scale', London, 19 March.

Formeski, T. (1997) 'Oursourcing Can be a Strategic Move', *Financial Times*, 3 September.

Foster, R.N. (1986) *Innovation: the Attacker's Advantage*. London, Summit Books.

Frank, F. (1998) 'The IRS's Doomed Cure-All', *Computerworld*, 6 April.

Fulmer, R.M., Gibbs, P. and Keys, J.B. (1998) 'The Second Generation Learning Organizations', *Organizational Dynamics/American Management Association* (Vol. 27).

Grindley, K. (1995) *Managing IT at Board level – the Hidden Agenda Exposed*. London: Pitman.

Grove, A.S. (1995) *High Output Management*. New York: Vintage Books.

Harrison, M. (1994) 'Dogfight Begins over RAF Fleet', *Independent*, 25 January.

Hess, P. (1999) 'Pentagon Budget for Year 2000 Creeps Higher' *United Press International*, 1 March.

Hochstrasser, B. and Griffiths, C. (1992) *Controlling IT Investment Strategy and Management*. London: Chapman & Hall.

Hollinger, P. (1997) 'IBM Wins Contract for Asda Work', *Financial Times*, 8 May.

Horwitt, E. (1997) 'When Things Go Wrong ...', *Computerworld*, 15 December.

Infoworld (1966) 'Outsource Sense', 9 September.

Johnston, S.J. (1996) 'Chevron takes Control', *Information Week*, 4 November.

Jones, T.C. (1995) *Accounting and the Enterprise*. London: Routledge.

Kahn, D. (1996) *The Codebreakers*. New York: Scribner.

Karolefski, J. (1997) 'P&G Streamlining Boosts its Volume, Brand Share', *Supermarket News*, Brand Marketing Supplement.

Kay, J. (1993) *Foundations of Corporate Success*. Oxford: OUP.

Kelly, K. (1994) *Out of Control*. London: Fourth Estate.

Koening, P. (1998) 'Cyberbusting Comes of Age', *Independent on Sunday*, 18 October.

Kroll, K. (1998) 'Costly Omission', *Industry Week*, 7 June.

Landes, D.S. (1998) *The Wealth and Poverty of Nations*. New York: W.W. Norton.

Lock, D. (1992) *Project Management*. Aldershot: Gower.

Maister, D.H. (1993) *Managing the Professional Services Firm*. New York: The Free Press.

Morris, P.W. (1994) *The Management of Projects*. American Society of Civil Engineers.

National Institute of Standards & Technology. Malcolm Baldrige National Quality Award, http://www.quality.nist.gov/

Nozick, R. (1981) *Philosophical Explanations*. Oxford: Clarendon.

O'Brien, T. (1997) 'Rethinking IT Budgets – Redfining IT Values: Novel approaches help determine the right spending levels', *Information Week*, 7 April.

Pendlebury, M.G.R. (1994) Company Accounts. New York and London: Routledge.

Plato (360BC) *Phaedrus*.

Pontin, J. (1995) 'Top of the News: Tech Analysis', *Infoworld*, 24 April.

Potter, K. (1998) *The Dirty Little Secrets of IT Spending Statistics*. Stamford, CT: The Gartner Group Inc.

Prokesh, S.E. (1995) 'Competing on Customer Service: an Interview with British Airways' Sir Colin Marshall', *Harvard Business Review*, 1 November.

Romney, M. (1995) 'Business Process Re-Engineering', *Internal Auditor*, June.

Rowling, R. (1999) 'Working out Kinks – Motorola's Iridium Project Wrestles with Marketing', *The Arizona Republic*, 7 March.

Rubin, D.H.A. (1999) *The 1999 Worldwide Benchmark Report: Software Engineering and Information Technology Findings for 1998 and Projections for 1999*. Pound Ridge, NY: Dept. of Computer Science, Hunter College.

Salisbury, H.E. (1992) *The New Emperors: Mao and Deng: a Dual Biography*. London: HarperCollins.

Schellendorff, V. (1893) *Der Dienst des Generalstabes*. Berlin.

Scherer, F.M. and Ross, S. (1990) Industrial Market Structure and Economic Performance. Boston: Houghton Miflin.

Schuck, P. (1999) *Know which Way the Wind Blows/Market Research Is Not Cheap, but It's Less Costly than Launching a Product the Consumer Doesn't Want*. London: London Free Press.

Schulmeyer, G.G. (1990) *Zero Defect Software*. New York: McGraw Hill.

Shapiro, C. and Varian, Hal R. (1999) *Information Rules*. Boston, MA: Harvard Business School Press.

Sichel, D.E. (1997) *The Computer Revolution – an Economic Perspective*. Washington DC: The Brookings Institution.

Silk, D.J. (1991) Planning IT: Creating an Information Management Strategy. City?: Butterworth-Heinemann.

Stewart, R. (1994) 'Over Budget, Behind Schedule. Why?' (Book Review), *Independent*, 27 April.

Stewart, T.A. (1997) *Intellectual Capital – the New Wealth of Organizations*. New York: Doubleday/Currency.

Strassmann, P.A. (1995) *The Politics of Information Management*. New Canaan: Information Economic Press.

Strassmann, P.A. (1997) *The Squandered Computer*. New Canaan: Information Economic Press.

Timmins, N.B.R. (1999) 'Treasury to Probe PFI's Poor Record in IT Projects', *Financial Times*, 14 April.

Trefgarne, G. (1999) 'End to War Loan Scandal nears Long-Running Saga over First World War Stock Could Be at an End as redemption Looks more Attractive', *Daily Telegraph*, 1 November.

Tregeorgis, L. (1996) *Real Options: Managerial Flexibility and Strategy in Resource Allocation*. Cambridge, MA: MIT.

Tse-Tung, Mao (1954) *Selected Works of Mao Tse-Tung*. London: Lawrence & Wishart.

Turner, J.R. (1992) *The Handbook of Project Based Management*. New York: McGraw Hill.

Vartabedian, R. (1998) 'Astronimical Budget', *Minneapolis Star Tribune*. 16 February.

Weinberg, G.M. (1985) *The Secrets of Consulting*. New York: Dorset House.

Index